Charting the landscape of European youth voluntary activities

Edited by

Howard Williamson and Bryony Hoskins

with Philipp Boetzelen

This edited collection is the outcome of the Research Seminar on Voluntary Activities under the Partnership Programme on Youth Research 2003-05 between the European Commission and the Council of Europe held in Budapest in July 2004.

Council of Europe Publishing

Cover: Graphic Design Workshop
of the Council of Europe

Council of Europe
F-67075 Strasbourg Cedex

ISBN-10: 92-871-5826-6
ISBN-13: 978-92-871-5826-0
© Council of Europe, December 2005,
Reprinted May 2006
Printed at the Council of Europe

Contents

Foreword

I was very pleased to co-operate in the organisation of another research seminar on behalf of the European Commission in co-operation with the Council of Europe in the framework of the youth research partnership between these two institutions. The first seminar which took place in July 2003 dealt with the promotion of diversity and this second seminar that took place in July 2004 tackled voluntary activities of young people.

The seminar took place at a crucial moment in the political development of volunteering by young people at European level. On 30 April 2004 the European Commission had adopted a proposal for common objectives for voluntary activities of young people in the European Union. This proposal was based on a synthesis of member state replies to a Commission questionnaire on this topic and on consultations by young people. The Commission proposal itself was the basis for a resolution of the Council of Youth Ministers of the European Union of 15 November 2004 in which the Youth Ministers agreed on common objectives for voluntary activities of young people.

In between the Commission proposal and the council resolution the seminar gave researchers and practitioners the opportunity to share their research and experiences in this field and to make a contribution to the political process. The seminar had an ambitious goal: it aimed to bring together experts from such different fields as academia, administrations and voluntary organisations in order to discuss voluntary activities of young people and to elaborate recommendations. It was therefore not a research seminar in the strict sense, more of an experiment in bringing together representatives from different professional backgrounds who do not necessarily speak the same "language". Thus the dialogue provided a challenging setting. However, the participants did a fabulous job and found a "common language" which resulted in a series of recommendations on voluntary activities of young people. These recommendations were fed into the political process in the framework of the Youth Council working group and the Committee of the Regions.

The success of the seminar is due to the constructive and focused contributions of the participants and the excellent work of the chairpersons. It is also due to our kind host, Antje Rothemund (director of the European Youth Centre, Budapest), who not only offered us the inspiring European Youth Centre on Rozsadomb, the "Rose Hill", overlooking the city of Budapest, but also addressed the participants on the first day of the seminar. Peter Lauritzen of the Council of Europe Directorate of Youth and Sport was very supportive throughout the seminar and enriched the event by his contributions based on many years experience in the international youth field. I would like to thank in particular Bryony Hoskins from the Council of

Europe for her excellent, professional and pleasant co-operation in the preparation and running of the seminar. Last but not least, Bryony's colleague Philipp Boetzelen who helped to make this event a success through his efficient and friendly support.

I am sure that the seminar helped boost voluntary activities of young people in Europe and I am already looking forward to the next seminar in co-operation with the Council of Europe!

Karin Lopatta-Loibl

Youth Policy Unit
European Commission

Young people and voluntary activities in Europe

Howard Williamson

Introduction

For a host of sometimes less than clear reasons, the subject of "voluntary activities" or "voluntary service", especially on the part of young people, has become an increasing focus of political, professional and, indeed, academic attention. There are, of course, certainly in some parts of Europe, long traditions of such commitment; conversely, in other places, it is a relatively new phenomenon and certainly there is widespread evidence of new forms of such "participation". It is, however, complex territory, with many questions not yet even asked, let alone resolved. It is territory which is essentially about a relationship between the individual and the wider society, with a range of mediating factors and forces in between. "Voluntary activities" by young people lie within a framework which comprises a complex mosaic of conflated, often confusing and sometimes contradictory concepts and terminology: civilian service, community service, the non-profit sector of the economy, and NGO activity. These ideas and debates are often connected but are rarely co-terminus. The language informing these debates are what Kate Stanley refers to as "expressions fraught with difficulty", and the landscape of discussion is what Maria Laura Sudulich depicts as a "variegated universe". Defining in any precise way what exactly is meant by "voluntary activities", "volunteering", "volunteerism" or "voluntaryism" is, as Regine Schröer reminds us, a major challenge. Is the whole momentum behind promoting and encouraging youth involvement in voluntary activities in fact what Lind (reported by Stanley) suggests may be a "solution in search of a problem"? Or are new and renewed commitments to supporting such initiatives premised soundly on their value and contribution to "personal development", the securing of a more vibrant "civil society", questions of "employability", or something else?

The chapters in this book are drawn from a Council of Europe and European Commission partnership seminar held in Budapest in the summer of 2004 which sought to interrogate the myriad of issues which surround and permeate the theme of "voluntary activities" by young people, in particular whether or not, and the ways in which voluntary engagement contributes, as Gerd Mutz and Eva Schwimmbeck suggest, to the development of civil society and citizenship.

Introduction

First, of course, there are some elementary questions, though these inevitably generate not only partial answers but also more complex questions. It is important to try to understand what is already going on. On the one hand, we hear constantly concerns about the declining levels of engagement in voluntary activities by young people; on the other, we celebrate the sustaining levels of such engagement, though their character may have changed. Sudulich, Schröer, and Agnieszka Moswiak in particular, as well as other contributors, endeavour to unravel the scale of volunteering, across diverse national contexts, from Italy to Poland, and from the Czech Republic to Spain.

A second, related question is where does such voluntary activity take place – in the private realm of domestic and family life, within NGOs and the non-profit sector, in the social welfare arena or on more "political" platforms, though not necessarily in relation to traditional political structures? Almudena Moreno Mínguez explores such questions in the context of Spain.

The third question is how is voluntary activity supported, if at all. What is the political commitment to such endeavour? Is there a legislative and administrative infrastructure? What kinds of resources are available? How do young people learn of the opportunities to participate in voluntary activities? Many contributors, including Schröer and Moskwiak, point to the need for improved support for volunteering initiatives and better information to widen and deepen participation.

This leads to a fourth key question: who is engaged in such participation? The evidence is mixed. Some commentators, such as Anna Musiala, maintain that it is the more educated and privileged (who have the knowledge, motivation and resources to do so), whereas others, such as Diane Machin, suggest that such groups may in fact be already "too busy", leaving voluntary commitment to less educated young people, though usually not to the most socially excluded, despite some initiatives being directed quite explicitly towards this group. Young women tend to be more involved than young men, and there seems to be relatively little evidence about the prevalence of engagement by young people from ethnic minorities. Machin, through the extensive "Being Young in Scotland" surveys, is one contributor who provides a focus on this question.

A fifth question is when are young people most likely to make such a contribution: at what age, for how long, and in what circumstances? Do they combine it with study and employment, or are they more likely to do so during times of relative inactivity or unemployment? Moskwiak, for example, notes the trends towards participation at a younger age in Poland, though currently Polish young people are involved in voluntary activities at a considerably older average age than their counterparts elsewhere in Europe.

The final, perhaps all-important question is why: why should individuals or societies take an interest in such activity? The overarching purpose of voluntary activity, as Stanley suggests, needs to be resolved if a broader public policy is to be constructed to support it – though it may, of course, have a number of purposes, ranging across what she calls personal, community and instrumental objectives.

Assumptions

There are a number of (often largely untested) assumptions about the value of voluntary activities, to the individual, to civil society, to their "beneficiaries", to the state and, indeed, to the wider "community" of Europe. Beyond the essential "altruism" that is often assumed to epitomise voluntary commitment, the case is routinely made, at least rhetorically, for the place of voluntary activities in non-formal learning and personal development, in cementing a sense of active citizenship, and in contributing to wider social and economic needs. At times it is argued to be an important supplement to formal education and employment, at others an alternative to unemployment – a means of combating inactivity and engaging in "purposeful" activity, a strategy for "social inclusion". Stanley asks whether it should be considered as an "intrinsic good" (worth supporting and encouraging for its own sake), while others point to its essential place in third sector activities, bolstering up a less than adequate, and often diminishing, welfare state.

There are both "objective" perceptions (top-down commentary) that there is a prima facie case for supporting voluntary activities (see chapters by Mutz and Schwimmbeck, and Schröer), and more "subjective" perspectives, reporting – from the experiences of young people themselves (see chapters by Moswiak and Kateryna Shalayeva) – the "bottom-up" value of such engagement. The fact is that these remain perceptions, perspectives and assumptions that demand more measured exploration. This book is a step in that direction.

Concepts and definitions

The flexibility of the concept of "voluntary activities" assists greatly in wide-ranging debate about the vast territory of activity in which young people are involved beyond the formal parameters of schooling and the labour market. This is, *de facto*, "voluntary" activity, but is it all "voluntary activities"? Indeed, while the latter may not (almost certainly does not) encapsulate all of the former, the idea of "voluntary activities" has now intruded into the realms of less "voluntary" activity, such as alternatives to compulsory military service and elements of measures to combat youth unemployment. Thus the concept is increasingly contested from a number of different angles, not least when its infrastructure is becoming more professionalised and regulated, and when the question of payment for "volunteering" is increasingly mooted. Both Machin and Stanley (drawing on Gaskin 1998) invoke the strange acronym "FLEXIVOL" in an attempt to capture the essential characteristics of volunteering. For "voluntary activities" to be attractive and sustained, there needs to be:

- Flexibility
- Legitimacy
- Ease of access
- Experience
- Incentives
- Variety
- Organisation
- Laughs

These are all key issues within the concept of "voluntary activities" which frame the debates within this book, and to which some further attention will be given in this introduction. Stanley also elides the concept of "voluntary activity" and that of "youth action" to advance a working definition to guide and govern the overarching debate. She suggests these are umbrella terms to describe "all kinds of voluntary engagement characterised by being open to all, unpaid, undertaken of a person"s own free will, educational (in the sense of providing non-formal learning) and of social value". This follows the definitions adopted by both the Council of Europe and the European Commission.

However, both the principle of being "open to all" and that voluntary activity should be "unpaid" are currently subject to some strain and tension, and are potentially in conflict. Some maintain that to promote full access, some form of financial incentive may be necessary for some groups of potential participants, though whether this counts as "payment" is another matter (see chapters by Stanley and Moskwiak). If it is, however, it throws the concept of "volunteering" into further conceptual and definitional confusion. As a result, it has produced demands in some quarters that there should be some re-branding of the idea as "community service", despite concerns that such a revised concept might too easily be associated in some places with criminal penalties or alternatives to national (military) service. I make this point simply to illustrate some of the complexities within the debate that have hitherto largely remained unaddressed and to which the contributions to this book pay timely attention.

Change and development

One of the central reasons for such confusion is that "voluntary activities" lie within a body of both diverse antecedents and contemporary developments. This is not quite the "lost continent" to which Mínguez alludes, but there have been a number of pathways leading to the current position and many prospective pathways leading from it. Moreover, these have played out in very different ways in different parts of Europe. A number of contributors discuss the absence (indeed, discouragement) of authentic civic engagement under former Soviet regimes, while others point to a range of political and economic issues that have either required or created space for the emergence of voluntary activities. Civic renewal, combating the democratic deficit, and the resurgence of civil society are all cited as rationales or opportunities for more widespread voluntary involvement, as indeed is the decline of compulsory military service and its replacement by national civic programmes.

When it comes to the contemporary landscape of voluntary activities, different contributors paint very different pictures. Some draw attention to young people's growing involvement in new social movements (such as environmental protection or animal rights), often mirroring their declining participation in "old" political and NGO structures. Others identify young people's role in "bolstering" the welfare state, noting that their two dominant areas of voluntary activity are in recreational pursuits and in social services. Flanking such engagement in community and social practices are more "private" voluntary activities (within the orbit of the family) and those on an international or transnational level, where wider intercultural and linguistic benefits are argued to "top up" the generally assumed benefits of voluntary activity. Indeed, Sudulich maintains that it is the dramatically changed international context since 1989 that has opened the doors of possibility for voluntary activities, both at domestic and transnational levels.

At an international level, in relation to young people, the Council of Europe has been promoting the importance of voluntary activities for many years, and in recent years has developed a recommendation and a convention on transnational and long-term volunteering (Council of Europe 1997, 2003). The European Commission has clearly also played a pivotal part on this front, through both its 1995 teaching and learning White Paper (European Commission 1995) and its White Paper on youth (European Commission 2001). The former, as part of its objective to combat social exclusion, introduced the European Voluntary Service (EVS) programme, which was first piloted in 1996 and fully established in 1998. The latter identified "voluntary activities" as one of four key planks for the development of youth policy in Europe, and has since embarked on a process of "open method of co-ordination" to establish the current state of play on this front across the member states (see Part 5 of this book, and Conclusion). While none of these initiatives, in and of them-selves, has to date had the necessary resources or "clout" to engineer a sea change in approaches to "voluntary activities" by young people, they have been significant catalysts to positioning these issues more firmly on the agenda. And the fact that "voluntary activities" merits a brief mention in the draft European Constitution must surely strengthen that position. Different countries are, of course, at different stages of development and implementation.

Catalysts and obstacles

There is now general acceptance of the assumptions that the involvement by young people in "voluntary activities" contributes to personal development, their inser-tion in social networks and the broader renewal of civil society. That does not mean, however, that the necessary catalysts for broadening and sustaining participation have been put in place, nor that serious barriers to engagement do not remain. Many contributors to this book, such as Brian Gran and Musiala, pay attention to the (in)equality of access to information and opportunity. They note the risks con-cerning displacement and substitution in the labour market, and of "voluntary activities" perhaps becoming too close to, and controlled by, government policy and needs. Conversely, however, they also discuss the need for "quality stan-dards" (to ensure that volunteering opportunities are appropriately governed), for suitable legal and administrative frameworks for volunteering to take place, for suf-ficient financial support, and for proper recognition of engagement through accred-itation and certification. For more disadvantaged groups of young people, they draw attention to significant barriers (concerning, for example, information, resources, perception, and motivation) which still need to be overcome. Gran, Musiala, Machin, and Alan Southern and Terry Potter, in particular, though in very different ways, explore these obstacles and makes proposals as to how they might be addressed.

Key issues

Youth sociologists have drawn attention to the greater "individualisation" of the life-worlds of young people and political scientists to the processes of "ideological liberalisation" since the collapse of communism. All this points to a divergence of possibility and opportunity across the lifecourse. Conversely, however, there is the matter of convergence, as different parts of the wider Europe endeavour to create a more "level playing field" for its young people. It is on this playing field that the issue of "voluntary activities" sits. Alongside formal education and progression to the labour market, there is now a pathway of civic engagement which is no longer necessarily restricted to the private worlds of motivated individuals. It is something to be encouraged at a more collective and social level, for both the social and individual benefits it is believed to confer.

There are, however, many new ways of "doing" voluntary activities – across sectors, within and over time, at different levels. It is now possible to engage in voluntary activity across a spectrum from almost invisible, low-scale, unpaid, local, unorganised and uncertificated commitment to the full-time, "paid", European Union financed, transnational, carefully planned and recognised EVS programme. There is nothing wrong with such a diversity of possibility; indeed, it beds in with the "individualisation" of the life course. There are, nonetheless, critical issues to be considered if the vision and aspiration for "voluntary activities" are to be realised. These relate, amongst other things, to infrastructure, content and process.

In terms of infrastructure, who is responsible for supporting the sector and providing the necessary resources? Currently, "voluntary activities" are supported, *inter alia,* through personal payments, government grants, private sponsorship, and donations. To what extent should a more common "programme management" framework be developed? Beyond legal and regulatory issues, there are very practical questions of pensions and insurance – which sometimes preclude or deter participation.

There are then issues to do with the "pedagogical" framework, if voluntary activities are to offer a genuine context for non-formal education. To what extent should personal and learning support be proactive or reactive? Some young people will need this far more than others. This then raises issues to do with "access for all" – the production, promotion and provision of information (to ensure awareness of opportunities), and the possibilities of payments (a stipend for living costs, if not a modest "wage"). Should such strategies be universalist in their approach, or specifically targeted at young people least motivated or least likely to participate? Indeed, should programmes have "quotas" for the more disadvantaged, with more robust support structures to enable and ensure their participation? Within the programmes themselves (the content), there are issues about the quality of the experience on offer, and the recognition and accreditation of the activities undertaken (something addressed by Moskwiak and Lauri Savisaari).

The European Voluntary Service programme, with its attention to the sending and hosting organisations which "frame" the experience of young people, already provides a useful model. In terms of the process, there is clearly a balance to be struck between the personal interests and motivations of young people, and the demands and aspirations of wider society. Where public resources are being committed to these ends, the need for such a balance is not in question. There remains, however, a risk that the pendulum may swing too far towards political agendas and away from the needs of young people, thus defeating at least some of the object of the exercise. This calls for measured development and, for this to be effective, for more incisive evaluation of the benefits and outcomes of such participation; as Stanley notes, there is an urgent need for a deeper awareness of the role and contribution of voluntary activity. Mutz and Schwimmbeck report on one European level analysis outlining some of the key features of voluntary activities if they are to contribute to civil learning. And Shalayeva advances a framework for the kind of qualitative inquiry required if analysis of the impact of voluntary activity is to move beyond the often rather crude description of levels of participation.

Ultimately, the issue is, as Machin tells us, about enabling and sustaining the involvement of young people in voluntary activities. It may still be a "good thing" in and of itself, but there is already considerable embryonic evidence that such experience is an increasingly important platform on which to build personal development, active citizenship and social cohesion.

Conclusion

Clearly the contributions to this publication are more of a first word, rather than a last word, on this complex issue. The book is organised in five sections. The first part is concerned with placing the development of volunteering initiatives within the wider context: of political transformation, labour market change, the promotion of civil society, and the personal development of young people. The second part contributes to mapping the scope of volunteering in Europe (who does what, and where). The third part examines barriers to participation (why engagement in volunteering may be more difficult than it needs to be). The fourth part is about what young people learn through voluntary activities, and addresses issues concerning recognition and evaluation. Finally, in Part 5, the European Commission provides an overview through a presentation of its proposals on common objectives for voluntary services, its analysis of the "voluntary activities" questionnaire responses following consultation with member states through the open method of co-ordination established following the White Paper on youth, and the subsequent resolution on the common objectives that will take this agenda forward.

The contributions to this book provide an analytic commentary on the contemporary landscape of voluntary activities undertaken by young people. They illuminate, from perspectives across Europe, how involvement in such "voluntary activities" has been packed (perhaps even burdened) with multiple expectations and aspirations. The terrain remains, however, rather short of incisive interrogation and critical reflection as to exactly why and how it should be promoted within national and European youth policy development. This is a dynamic contemporary policy context and it is to be hoped that these contributions help to sustain the momentum while, simultaneously, encouraging the reader to engage in some important pause for thought.

References

Council of Europe (1997) *Recommendation No. R (94) 4 of the Committee of Ministers to Member States on the Promotion of a Voluntary Service.* Strasbourg: Council of Europe.

Council of Europe (2003) *European Convention on the Promotion of a Transnational Long-Term Voluntary Service for Young People.* Strasbourg: Council of Europe.

European Commission (1996) "Teaching and Learning: Towards the Learning Society". White Paper, Brussels/Luxembourg: Office for Official Publications of the European Communities.

European Commission (2001) "A New Impetus for European Youth". Communication from the European Commission, COM (2001) 681 final, Brussels.

Gaskin, K. (1998) "Vanishing Volunteers: Are Young People Losing Interest in Volunteering? *Voluntary Action* No.1:1.

Part 1

Voluntary activities in context

1. Youth and voluntary services sector in the context of the Spanish welfare state

Almudena Moreno Mínguez

introduction

In recent years growing emphasis has been placed on non-profit activities in an attempt to promote "active civil citizenship" in democratic societies. In general, this implies a more active role on the part of the various groups that make up society through involvement in a range of activities in the tertiary sector as well as membership of organisations. According to sociologists such as Putnam (2000) and Coleman (1990), citizen involvement in these kinds of activities boosts "social capital", giving rise to more democratically united societies. Debates on citizenship and "empowerment" focus mainly on citizens' contributions to various aspects of civil life through involvement in volunteer associations and organisations.

My goal in this chapter is to present the relevance of the non-profit sector in 22 European countries and in Spain in comparative terms from data gathered in the comparative analysis of the non-profit sector carried out by the Johns Hopkins University in 1998. The final aim of this chapter is to analyse how young Spaniards are contributing to the creation of a "civil citizenship" through volunteer work in a country characterised by the persistence of familiarism, family dependence, and by a poor net in terms of associations coupled with a limited welfare state.

The third sector from a comparative perspective

The growing attention which in recent years has been focused on these organisations is in part due to a widespread crisis of the state, apparent throughout practically the whole world for more than two decades. This crisis has been reflected in a profound questioning of traditional social welfare policies in many developed countries in the northern hemisphere, in a certain disenchantment with state handling of national development programmes in large parts of developing countries located in the southern hemisphere, in the failure of the central and east European state socialist experiment, and in an ongoing concern for environmental destruction that threatens the health and safety of people everywhere. In addition to stimulating support for market – oriented economic policies, this questioning of the state has focused its attention and new expectations on organisations in civil society that also operate in the heart of communities throughout the world. The growth in the number and size of these organisations also helps to draw attention to them. A revolution in this kind of association seems to have been taking place at a world scale, a huge upsurge in both private as well as organised volunteer initiatives in practically all corners of the world (Salomon 1994). In many cases this has been brought about by the growing doubts raised as to the capacity of many countries to deal on an individual basis with problems linked to social welfare, development and the environment, problems which nations must face up to today. This growth in the number of civil organisations has likewise been boosted by the revolution in communications that has taken place over the last few decades and by the rapid spread of middle-class groups with an academic background who feel frustrated by the lack of financial and political expression which they find in many places. Finally, one factor that has recently emerged further highlights the importance being attached to non-profit organisations or to civil society, namely the growing questioning of the neoliberal consensus, sometimes labelled the Washington Consensus, which has been at the forefront of world economic policy for the last two decades. This consensus has basically maintained that the problems which both developed as well as developing societies must face up to at the current time can be dealt with more effectively by simply giving free rein to private markets. Yet, as a result of the global financial crisis and the constant social unrest in many regions, this consensus has come under ever increasing attack, even from its staunchest supporters. As the Chief Economist at the World Bank, Joseph Stiglitz recently stated, "The policies promoted by the Washington Consensus... are not exactly complete and have often been wrong ... the economic results are not only determined by political economy and human resources, but by the quality of a country's institutions" (Stiglitz 1998). Echoing these opinions, political leaders from many areas around the world have begun to seek alternatives which combine the virtues of the market with the advantages of wider social protection. This search is clear in the emphasis placed by Tony Blair on the Third Way in the United Kingdom, in Gerhard Schröder's New Centre in Germany and in the former French Prime Minister Lionel Jospin's summary declaration: "Yes to the market economy, no to the market society". Due to their unique position outside the market and the state, to the fact they are generally smaller, their links with citizens, their flexibility, their ability to exploit private initiative in support of public goals and their recently rediscovered contributions to the creation of social capital, the organisations that make up civil society have emerged as strategically important elements in the search for an intermediate way, between simple faith in the market and faith in the state. However, the non-profit sector's ability to involve itself in this search as an experienced collaborator has been severely restricted by an acute lack of basic information on this sector and how it works. Although huge progress has been made over the last five years, including the culmination of the first stage of the current project and the start of empirical research by Eurostat in response to the European Commission, the non-profit sector is still a lost continent in the social arena of modern society, invisible to most politicians, the business sector and to the press, and even to many within the sector itself. The comparative study project conducted by the Johns Hopkins University has heralded an important step forward in research into the third sector.

This project was set up to bridge this gap in basic knowledge and to place the non-profit sector on the world economy map. To be more precise, this project aims to broaden our understanding of the non-profit sector in various ways. Firstly, it has documented for the first time in solid empirical terms the scope, structure, funding and role of the non-profit sector in a significant number of countries around the world. Secondly, it has attempted to explain why the size of the sector varies from place to place, identifying those factors that would seem to further or delay development. Thirdly, it has assessed the impact of these organisations and the contribution they make and has finally helped to publish the information which has emerged.

To achieve these goals, a plural and comparative approach was adopted. This is a comparative method that covers a wide range of countries. The initial stage of the project, which culminated in 1994, focuses on eight countries (United States, United Kingdom, France, Germany, Italy, Sweden, Hungary and Japan) (Salamon and Anheier 1994). The current stage involves updating the information on many of the original countries as well as widening the analysis to embrace a total of 28 countries, of which 22 have finished gathering basic data and are included in this report: nine west European countries, four other developed countries, four in central Europe and eastern Europe together with five Latin American countries.

This study has helped to make progress in the comparative analysis of the third sector as well as its contribution to different world economies, which in general have neglected this sector.

The third sector in figures

The most relevant findings, the result of research work into the scope, structure, funding and role of the non-profit sector at an international scale, may be grouped into five main sections.

Firstly, apart from its social and political importance, the non-profit sector is a prominent economic force in most of the regions analysed, accounting for a significant share of employment and national expenditure. In precise terms, this is a US$1.1 billion sector. Even when we exclude religious organisations, the non-profit sector of the 22 countries studied moves US$1.1 billion and provides full-time employment to the equivalent of some 19 million workers. As a result, expenditure in the non-profit sector of these countries reaches an average of 4.6% of the gross domestic product, employment in this sector reaching nearly 5% of all non-agricultural employment, 10% of all employment in the service sector, and 27% of total employment for the public sector.

Employment in the non-profit sector in these countries easily outstrips all of the employment in the leading private enterprises in each country, at a ratio of six to one (19 million employees in the non-profit sector compared to 3.3 million for all those employed in the largest private enterprises in each of the 22 countries).

In the 22 countries analysed the number of people registered in the non-profit sector exceeds those in the public service sector, textile manufacturing, the paper industry, graphic arts or the chemical sector in those countries, employing almost as large a labour force as the transport and communications sectors.

Figure 1 : Employment in the non-profit sector for the 22 countries studied (1995) as a percentage

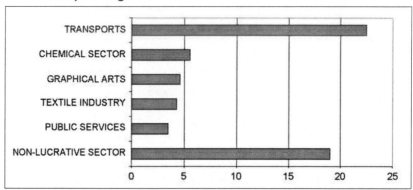

Source: Calculated from the data from the Johns Hopkins University comparative study.

Yet even this does not reflect the full scope of the non-profit sector since a significant number of volunteer workers are also involved. In fact an average of 28% of the population of these countries devote part of their time to non-profit organisations. This is the equivalent of another 10.6 million full-time jobs, taking the total number of full-time jobs in non-profit sector organisations to 29.6 million. Including volunteers, the sector accounts for an average of 7% of total non-agricultural employment in these countries, 14% of employment in the service sector and a remarkable 41% of employment in the public sector (see figure 2).

Figure 2 : Weight of the non-profit sector in the 22 countries studied (1995) as a percentage of employment

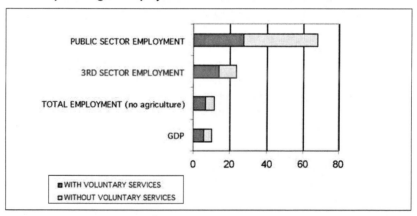

Source: Calculated from the data from the Johns Hopkins University comparative study.

The situation does not alter when we add volunteers. To some extent the gap in fact grows, at least between developed countries and Latin America, as well as between western Europe and other developed countries. Including volunteers, non-profit sector organisations account for 10.3% of total employment in western Europe, 9.4% in other developed countries, 3.0% in Latin America and 1.7% in central Europe (see figure 3). Bearing this in mind, and including volunteers, western Europe appears as the region with the most highly developed non-profit sector and largest amount of volunteer involvement. It is also surprising to note the relatively low level of formal volunteers reflected in our data for Latin American countries.

Figure 3 : Percentage of employment in the non-profit sector by region, with or without volunteers (1995)

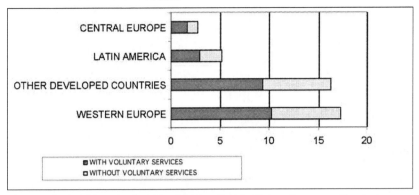

Source: Calculated from the data from the Johns Hopkins University comparative study.

One possible explanation for the discrepancies observed in the development of the third sector by countries is the presence or lack of public systems for social protection. One theory is that the larger the system of public social protection, the smaller the non-profit sector is expected to be. However, our data on the 22 countries analysed do not back up this theory. Of the 11 countries we studied which had relatively high levels of public systems of social protection (above the average for the 22 countries), five have relatively small non-profit sectors (with a level of employment below the average for the 22 countries) and six comparatively wide non-profit sectors. Furthermore, of the 11 countries with relatively low levels of public systems of social protection, eight have fairly small non-profit sectors. By contrast, only three countries have large non-profit sectors. Therefore, as indicated in figure 4, in over half the cases the results contradict the theory. Clearly, something more complex than the relation proposed in this theory is determining the variation in scale of the non-profit sector between one place and another.

Figure 4 : Percentage of the non-profit sector in terms of the total paid employment in Europe

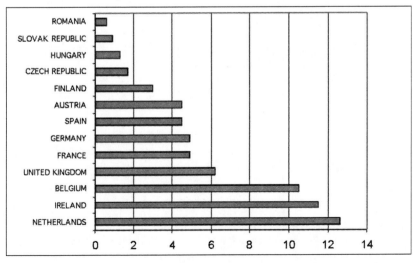

Source: Calculated from the data from the Johns Hopkins University comparative study.

Figure 5 : Relationship between public expenditure on social welfare and size of the non-profit sector

		% OF EMPLOYMENT IN THE NON-LUCRATIVE SECTOR	
		LOW	HIGH
PUBLIC EXPENSE IN SOCIAL WELFARE	**HIGH**	5	6
	LOW	8	3

Source: Calculated from the data from the Johns Hopkins University comparative study.

The report has shown that two thirds of employment in the non-profit sector is concentrated in the three traditional areas of social welfare services: education, with 30% of the total; health, with 20%; and social services, with 8% (see figure 6). The area of recreational and cultural activities is not far behind with 14% of the total for employment in this sector. This pattern changes radically when volunteers are factored in. Around three fifths (55%) of the time devoted by volunteers focuses on two main areas: recreational activities, including sports activities, and social services. Moreover, environmental organisations, those involved in the defence of civil rights and development attract a considerable percentage of volunteers' time. Therefore, including volunteers, involvement in overall employment in the non-profit sector of the three areas (health, education and social services) falls from 68% to below 60%, whereas the share of activities linked to culture and leisure, the environment, development and the defence of civil rights increases from 23% to 30% (see figure 6).

Figure 6 : Percentage of employment in the non-profit sector for several sectors, with or without volunteers (11 countries average) (1995)

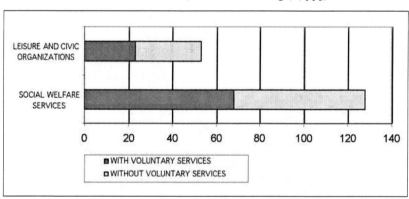

Source: Calculated from the data from the Johns Hopkins University comparative study.

----> The scale of the non-profit sector in Spain

The construction of the institutional net of the welfare state in Spain during the democratic transition presented some lack in the provision of family services and assistance services, which have been compensated with the growth of the non-profit sector, also often designated as the voluntary services sector. The logic of this sector is opposed to the intervention of the public sector (political logic) and also to the participation of the lucrative private sector (market laws), by means of the activities of private agents that altruistically offer services of general interest in an alternative or complementary way to the provision of services carried out by the Spanish public administration (Ferrera 1996, Castles 1998, Naldini 2002).

The fact that the Spanish non-profit sector is smaller than its west European counterparts is due to various reasons that stretch back many years, as well as to more recent events. Spain has a long and complicated history, in which the Catholic Church has played a predominant role. There is on the one hand the late development of industrialisation and the current system of state administration, which has left many conflicts unresolved between state and church, and on the other there is the emergence of civil society. What should also be taken into account is the strong corporate policy during the Franco regime from the end of the 1930s until the mid-1970s and the suppression of civil liberties. These are factors which restricted the social and political space available for the potential emergence of many kinds of non-profit organisations, while at the same time maintaining the social services and educational institutions of the Catholic Church. Another key moment was the transition from an authoritarian model to democracy, which led to a sudden surge in the number of associations, thanks to the freedom existing in the political arena for the development of non-profit activities, a space which was filled by newly fashioned social movements and by citizen involvement. Another factor has been the rapid economic development that Spain has undergone since 1975, which has created a new demand for social services, services which are rendered at least in part by an expanding non-profit sector, a sector that has thus gained ground over the last 25 years in Spain.

As with many of its west European counterparts, the Spanish non-profit sector focuses a large part of its human and financial resources on the areas of social welfare, and particularly social services. However, unlike most other countries in western Europe, Spanish non-profit organisations receive greater financial support from private sources than from the state. Another point that sets the Spanish non-profit sector even further apart is the relatively high level of private donations in mixed income. These conclusions are the result of pioneer work carried out by a research group at the Fundación BBVA in conjunction with the comparative study project of the non-profit sector at the Johns Hopkins University.

According to this study, this is a US$ 22 600 million sector. Even excluding the religious aspect, in 1995 Spanish non-profit sector operating costs amounted to US$ 22 600 million or the equivalent of 4% of gross domestic product in Spain, a highly significant figure. Moreover, this sector is an active driving force for employment, providing jobs for a labour force which is the equivalent of 475 179 full-time paid workers. This figure amounts to 4.5% of the total number of workers in Spain, if we exclude those working in agriculture, 6.8% of service sector workers, and almost a quarter (22.9%) of those employed as public administration staff, whether at national, regional or municipal levels.

This sector attracts a significant amount of volunteer work. In fact, around 9.8% of the Spanish adult population say they devote part of their time to co-operating with non-profit organisations, which translates to another 253 599 full-time jobs, taking the total number of full-time jobs in Spanish non-profit organisations to 728 778, or 6.8% of the total amount of non-agricultural employment in Spain (see figure 7).

Figure 7 : Weight of the non-profit sector in Spain, with or without volunteers (1995)

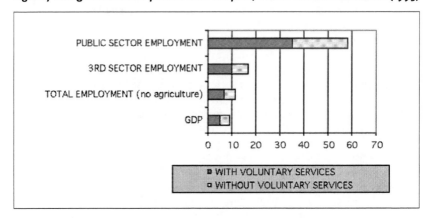

Source: Calculated from the data from the Johns Hopkins University comparative study.

Although non-profit work in Spain is fairly similar to the average of the 22 countries in the study, in comparison to the west European average, the percentage in Spain is quite small. As can be seen in figure 8, equivalent full-time employment in the non-profit sector in Spain, with 4.5% of total employment, is proportionately 35% lower than the European average (7.0%). This low rate of employment is due to the fact that although there is a large number of non-profit organisations in Spain (253 000), most of them are fairly small and create only a limited amount of jobs. The margins increase when volunteers are included. Moreover, the percentage of employment in the non-profit sector increases slightly if volunteers are included. Thus, by including the time contributed by the latter, non-profit organisations make up 6.8% of total employment in Spain, a significantly lower percentage than the west European average (10.3%) (see figure 8).

Figure 8 : Percentage of the employment in the non-profit sector in terms of total employment, with or without volunteers, for Spain and other regions (1995)

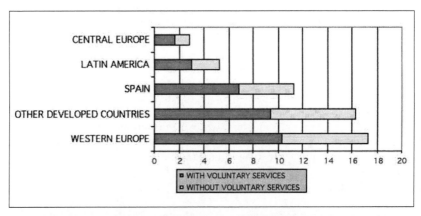

Source: Calculated from the data from the Johns Hopkins University comparative study.

As with other west European countries but unlike the average of the countries included in the study, social services clearly dominate the non-profit scene in Spain. Almost 32% of employment in the non-profit sector is concentrated in the

European youth voluntary activities

area of social services. Of all the different types of non-profit activities in Spain, social services have the highest percentage of non-profit employment. As can be seen in figure 9, 31.8% of the total amount of non-profit employment in Spain is concentrated in this area. This percentage is above the European average (27.0%) and is well above the average of the 22 countries included in the study (18.3%). This situation clearly reflects the dominance of three large networks of non-profit organisations: the National Institute for the Blind (ONCE), the Red Cross and Cáritas, who play a leading role in the rendering and funding of services throughout Spain. By way of just one example, the ONCE alone employs some 40 000 paid workers, representing 8.4% of the total amount of non-profit employment.

Figure 9 : Composition of the non-profit sector in Spain and the 22 countries studied

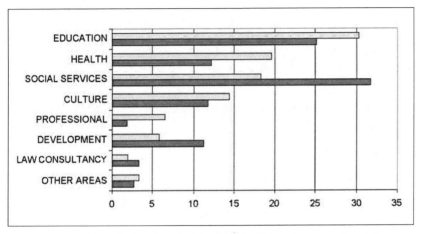

Source: Calculated from the data from the Johns Hopkins University comparative study.

Although quotas and payments for services are the main source of income for the non-profit sector in Spain, private donations account for a larger source of funding than in any other EU country included in this study. The principal source of revenue for Spanish non-profit organisations comes through quotas and payments for services. Alone, this amounts to 49% of the total income in the non-profit sector in Spain. Funding from private contributions is much lower, although it still represents a significant percentage of total income, private donations accounting for 18.8% of total funding in the non-profit sector in Spain.

When taking volunteers into account, the pattern of income in the non-profit sector in Spain changes drastically. After including the contribution of volunteers, private volunteer work increases considerably from 18.8% to 36.3%, thus exceeding contributions from the public sector, which falls from 32.1% to 25.2%. Although the percentage of income from quotas also drops from 49.0% to 38.5%, once volunteers are included, quotas are still the main source of income in Spain.

Participation in formal associations is considered a key activity in establishing social integration in general and civic responsibility in particular. High levels of youth participation in associations are to be considered with favour in that, in all likelihood, it promotes young people's insertion in social networks. The available data suggest that levels of group membership vary significantly among EU countries: in Nordic countries an ample majority of youth belong to at least one association, whereas only a minority do so in most Mediterranean ones (plus Belgium).

The Spanish welfare state

It is worth noting that one reason why membership of associations is higher in Nordic and central European countries is that associations are strongly embedded in the welfare system and in the institutional arrangement of society. Moreover, in many Nordic countries membership of a trade union represents a requirement for getting a job.

In order to better grasp the meaning of formal group participation, one must also consider the types of association which account for such participation. The most important type of association concerns sporting activities, where the same pattern can be found: in Mediterranean countries (plus Belgium) less than one quarter of young people belong to sports associations, whereas Scandinavian countries express the highest rates.

Participation in voluntary and youth associations varies: Luxembourg, where 32% of youth report membership in such associations, displays a participation rate eight times higher than that of Greece. Membership in explicitly youth-oriented associations involve a very low proportion of youths and the Mediterranean areas display the weakest participation, except Italy, since the participation of young people in religious associations is very high in this country.

Figure 10: Percentage of 15-24 year olds participating in/belonging to an association

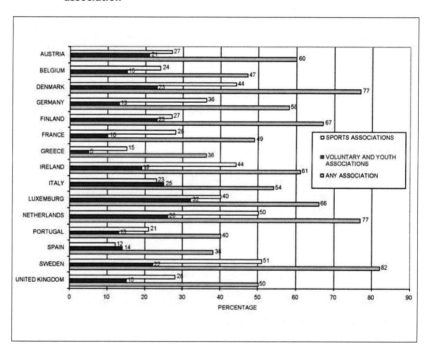

Source: IARD 2001.

For the Spanish case, the participation of young people in volunteers, associations is relatively reduced in comparison with the European average, mainly due to the weakness of the associative net. It highlights the feminisation of volunteering carried out by Spanish youths since 66% of voluntary young people are women compared to 34% which are male.

Figure 11 : Percentage of volunteers aged between 14 and 25, by gender, Spain

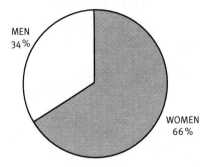

Source: Oficina de Acción Solidaria y Cooperación Estadística, 2004.

The stable or even declining rate of membership north of the Mediterranean countries changes the conditions for youth policy. The importance of voluntary youth work, which used to play an important role in young people's leisure time, has diminished during the last decades. Young people nowadays are more reluctant to bind themselves to organised communities, they move in a "free space" between various youth scenes and institutions and they are no longer permanently organised. Another consequence is that social networks, which used to help youngsters solve problems, disappear.

Associations and volunteers in Spain are turning into a privileged area in terms of civil and political commitment where young Spaniards are concerned. The difficulties they find in the labour market, the lack of housing and dependence on the family that characterises Spanish youth has led within this group to the promotion of non-profit activities such as volunteer work that are only viable in a framework in which the family has become the principal mainstay in both economic terms as well as for social welfare.

In the Mediterranean countries the standard nuclear family still represents a central and stable social institution. Not surprisingly, it is in these countries that the greatest percentages of young men and women, aged between 20 and 30, still live with their parents. This is, in part, an effect of the persistence of traditional culture and traditional gendered division of household labour. In this "familial" context, young people also engage in volunteer work and informal support.

For example, they volunteer for public works projects or provide informal childcare for a relative. These productive activities, however, have been under researched within the household context. There are compelling reasons to examine volunteering and providing informal support (referred to jointly as helping work) in the household context.

Care of elderly parents and volunteer demands generated from children's activities are additional stressors on contemporary families. Researchers should recognise volunteering and informal support as consequential components of intrahousehold labour allocation. Although unpaid labour is not homogenous (Twiggs, McQuillan and Ferree 1999, Hook 2004).

In the case of the countries of southern Europe, factors such as the weakness of the welfare state, the provision of family services and the importance of the family for the Spanish society have reinforced the development of volunteering programmes dedicated to family support (care of children, the elderly and the sick). The available data evidence a remarked participation of youth in programmes of family support volunteering (25%). It highlights the fact that women are mainly the ones who take part in this type of volunteer programmes. It is logical if we keep in mind that the family culture in Spain and the woman's caretaker role continue being the main references of identity for Spanish society.

Figure 12 : Youngsters aged between 14 and 25 in volunteer programmes, as a percentage of the total number of young volunteers, in Spain

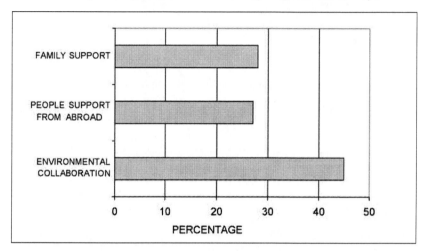

Source: *Oficina de Acción Solidaria y Cooperación Estadística, 2004.*

Figure 13 : Volunteers aged between 14 and 25, by programme and gender

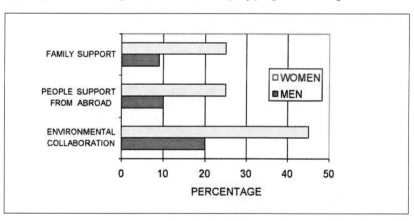

Source: *Oficina de Acción Solidaria y Cooperación Estadística, 2004.*

Finally, the breakthrough of the modern information society is usually described in the Mediterranean countries as reinforcing a process in which the importance of the voluntary sector as a mediating force between the family, market and state has increasing importance.

Studying the relationship between the youth voluntary sector and the development of family policies in Spain over the last fifteen years or so, one might come to the conclusion that there is a negative correlation between the size and scope of family policies provisions and the importance of the youth voluntary sector.

European youth voluntary activities

This chapter has presented some figures related to the size and structure of the youth voluntary sector in Spain, as well as some facts on the relationships between the state and the sector, where an important theme is the emerging importance of voluntary activities in the family policies of the welfare state. These organisations seem to have managed to combine parts of the old mass movement tradition with new demands and new influences.

Conclusions

The data presented in this chapter reinforce the idea that the non-profit sector in Spain is an economic social sector of tremendous importance in which youth plays a key role. From the moment the process of democracy began to take root in the mid-1970s, Spain has made major strides which have paved the way towards the development of a modern non-profit sector. However, there is still a long way to go. One of the key factors to be stressed is that unlike most west European countries, Spain cannot boast a stable policy of relations between the state and the non-profit sector. In fact, misgivings and certain mutual mistrust can often be found between representatives of the authorities and the non-profit sector. This lack of mutual understanding of both the strong and weak points of each of the players involved might stifle the development of relations between the two sectors. Setting up a high-level, broad-based commission to analyse the mission and future of the non-profit sector in Spain might provide the most adequate springboard for establishing the necessary dialogue, above all with a view to greater European integration. To this end, the next urgent task is to create a deeper awareness of the social contribution that the non-profit sector currently makes and might make in the future to the different European societies, a task which is already underway and which constitutes an important part of what the current study aims to achieve.

In the case of youth, it should be underlined that this is a social group with enormous potential to promote the exercise of civil citizenship as is shown by the active and committed involvement of youth in associations and volunteer groups. The apparatus of this institutional mechanism for promoting the civil involvement of youth as citizens can only be achieved through the recognition of individual rights and the neutralisation of all kinds of family as well as institutional and other kinds of dependency. The weakness of the fabric of civil associations and the limited development of the Spanish welfare state in terms of public services to the community contrasts with the active and growing participation of youth in the non-profit sector. We trust that this kind of publication will help to reflect on and recognise the importance this type of volunteer work has for stimulating civil participation on the part of youth and thus furthering the leading role played by civil society as a key element in the democratisation of western societies.

Alonso, L. (1999) "La Juventud en el Tercer Sector: Redefinición del Bienestar, Redefinición de la Ciudadanía". *Revista de Estudios de la Juventud,* 45, pp. 9-20.

Beck, U. (1998) *La Sociedad de Riesgo.* Barcelona: Paídos.

Benedicto, J. and Morán, M.L. (2003) *Aprendiendo a ser Ciudadanos. Experiencias Sociales y Construcción de la Ciudadanía entre los Jóvenes.* Madrid: Instituto de la Juventud.

Bynner, J., Chisholm, L. and Furlong, A. (eds.) (1997) *Youth, Citizenship and Social Change in a European Context.* Aldershot: Ashgate.

Castles, F. (1998) *Comparative Public Policy. Patterns of Post-War Transformation.* Cheltenham: Edward Elgar.

Cieslik, M. and Pollock, G. (eds.) (2002) *Young People in Risk Society.* Aldershot: Ashgate.

Coleman, J. (1990) *Foundations of Social Theory.* New York: Belknap Press.

Ferrera, M. (1996) "The Southern Model of Welfare in Social Europe". *Journal of European Social Policy,* 1, pp. 17-37.

Furlong, A. and Cartmel, F. (1997) *Young People and Social Change. Individualization and Risk in Late Modernity.* Buckingham: Open University Press.

Giddens, A. (1999) *La Tercera Vía.* Madrid: Taurus.

Hall, T., Williamson, H. and Coffey, A. (2000) "Young People, Citizenship and the Third Way: a Role for the Youth Service?" *Journal of Youth Studies,* 3 (4), pp. 461-472.

Halman, L. (2001) *The European Values Study: A Third Wave.* Tillburg: University Press.

Hann, C. and Dunn, E. (1996) *Civil Society. Challenging Western Models.* London: Routledge.

Hook, J. (2004) "Reconsidering the Division of Household Labor: Incorporating Volunteer Work and Informal Support". *Journal of Marriage and Family,* 66, p. 101–117.

IARD (2001) *Study on the State of Young People and Youth Policy in Europe,* final report for the Commission of the European Communities, Directorate General for Education and Culture.

Lister, R., Smith, N., Middleton, S. and Cox, L. (2003) "Young People Talk about Citizenship: Empirical Perspectives on Theoretical and Political Debates. *Citizenship Studies,* 7 (2), pp. 235-253.

Lozano, J. (2000) "Vers l'Empresa Ciutadana?" *Revista de Temes Contemporanis,* 8, pp. 60-76.

Lundstr, T. and Svedberg, L. (2003) "The Voluntary Sector in a Social Democratic Welfare State – The Case of Sweden". *Journal of Social Policy,* 32, (2), pp. 217-238.

Martín Serrano, M. and Velarde, O. (2001) *Informe Juventud en España.* Madrid: Instituto de la Juventud.

Montagut, T., Petrus, A., Orduna, G. and Zubero, I. (2003) *Voluntariado: la Lógica de la Ciudadanía.* Barcelona: Ariel.

Morán, M. and Benedicto, J. (2000) *Jóvenes y Ciudadanos*. Madrid: Instituto de la Juventud.

Moreno Mínguez, A. (2003) "The Late Emancipation of Spanish Youth: Keys for Understanding". *Electronic Review of Sociology* [online], 4, pp. 1-21. Available at: http://www.sociology.org/content/vol7.1/minguez.html (Accessed).

Naldini, M. (2002) *The Family in the Mediterranean Welfare States*. London: Frank Cass.

Oliver, D. and Heater, D. (1994) *The Foundations of Citizenship*. London: Harvester Wheatsheaf.

Putnam, R. (2000) *Bowling Alone*. New York: Simon and Schuster.

Rodríguez, E., Megias, Q. and Sánchez, E. (2002) *Jóvenes y Relaciones Grupales*, Madrid: Instituto de la Juventud.

Ruiz O. (ed.) (2000) *El Sector no Lucrativo en España*. Bilbao: Fundación BBV.

Salamon, L. (1994) "The Rise of the Non-Profit Sector". *Foreign Affairs, 74,* (3), pp. 109-123.

Salamon, L. (2001) "Una Revolució Associativa. *El Correu de la Unesco (Catalan edition),* pp. 36-37.

Salamon, L. and Anheier, H. (1994) *The Emerging Sector: An Overview*. Baltimore: The Johns Hopkins Institute for Policy Studies.

Salamon, L. and Anheier H. (1998) *Social Origins of Civil Society: Explaining the Non-Profit Sector Cross-Nationally*. Baltimore: The Johns Hopkins Institute for Policy Studies.

Salamon, L. and Anheier, H. (1998a) "Social Origins of Civil Society: Explaining the Non-Profit Sector Cross-Nationally". *Voluntas*, 9, (3), pp. 213-248.

Salamon, M., Anheier, H., List, R., Toepler, S. and Wojciech, S. (2001) *La Sociedad Civil Global: Las Dimensiones del Sector no Lucrativo*. Madrid: Fundación BVVA.

Stiglitz, J. (1998) *More Instruments and Broader Goals: Moving Towards the Post-Washington Consensus: Wider Annual Lectures*. Helsinki: World Institute for Development Economics Research.

Twiggs, J., McQuillan, J. and Ferree, M. (1999) "Meaning and Measurement: Reconceptualizing Measures of the Division of Household Labor". *Journal of Marriage and the Family*. 61, pp. 712-724.

Wallace, C. and Kovatcheva, S. (1998) *Youth in Society. The Construction and Deconstruction of Youth in East and West Europe*. London: Macmillan.

Wallace, C., Spannring, R. and Haerpfer, C. (2003) "Jóvenes Ciudadanos: la Integración Política y Social de la Juventud en Europa Oriental y Occidental. In Benedicto, J. and Morán, M. (eds), *Aprendiendo a ser Ciudadanos. Experiencias Sociales y Construcción de la Ciudadanía entre los Jóvenes"* pp. 117-140. Madrid: Instituto de la Juventud.

Wilson, J. (2000) "Volunteering". *Annual Review of Sociology*. 26, pp. 215-240.

Wilson, J. and Musick, M. (1997) "Who Cares? Towards an Integrated Theory of Volunteer Work". *American Sociological Review,* 62, pp. 694-713.

2. Voluntary service in social and political transformations of Europe during the last fifteen years

Maria Sudulich

introduction

The number of people who dedicate themselves to voluntary activities has increased significantly, especially in the last fifteen years. Every year new voluntary associations are formed and existing associations register a growth in new members. This phenomenon is related to changes in society and transformations in the political and civil climate of Europe. The increase in voluntary activities and voluntary services is a complex trend and must be analysed from several different perspectives.

The experiences of voluntary service, observable today, present different aspects, and they represent a variegated universe. The development of voluntary service is a social fact, produced and modified by other social elements, whose growth depends on changes occurring in the civil society. Today the civil society is, in fact, dramatically different from the past and the biggest variation regards the European context.

If, until a couple of decades ago, the sphere of voluntary service, as the largest sector of civil activity, was mainly defined by its national dimension, this no longer presents an accurate picture of reality. Many things have changed such as the volunteer's profile, the kind of activities taking place, supranational work and the age and aims of people employed in this sector. All these developments are causes and, at the same time, effects of the changeable and changed international political and social atmosphere.

For all of Europe the period of most significant change was the year 1989: the fall of communism, the end of the cold war, the growth of European perspectives, the end of an historical era and the beginning of a new one. In 1989 many events took place, many transformations were initiated which set the stage for further "revolutions" which were to take place in the coming years – as such, the date of 1989 is more a conventional indication than an exact starting point (or ending point). In any case, 1989 represents a moment of enormous transformation for Europe and for the whole of European civil society, not only for east European countries, but also for the western ones, deeply affected by the "winds of change". The new European situation dramatically transformed citizens' lives and in less than twenty years, Europe changed shape completely from a divided continent that could not even conceive of reunification, to a union truly attempting to overcome differences and problems in order to guarantee the establishment of a European community. Nowadays, after the enlargement of the 1 May 2004, European civil society is called to new challenges and, at the same time, opportunities are multiplying.

italy and Spain: a sum of crises produces the triumph of the civil society

Moving from Europe in general to specific countries such as Italy and Spain, it should be noted that another watershed in political and social life undoubtedly came into being at the beginning of the 1990s. In both countries the occurrence of certain events contributed to an upheaval in social and political life. This decade was marked by the "experience of crisis" (Muxel 1996), determined not only by the international context but also by domestic factors. The main components of political and social change in Italy were related to the end of the First Republic, wich was brought down by the discovery of spreading corruption in the main political parties, and in the case the resulting collapse of the socialist government and socialist party of Spain. The reaction to the disastrous political situation has been determined by civil society: "Es la epoca de la denominada sociedad civil" (Ortega 2001a).

The ideological vacuum, political disappointment and sense of betrayal felt by many has been overcome by the actions of civil society. For many social actors civil engagement represented a new way for the future and a new hope. In that time of confusion, new ideas for the development of the EU were born and new perspectives appeared; if, on one hand, the transformation left disillusion and a sense of loss, on the other, new doors were opened. Due to the confusion and complexity of that period, analysis could be conducted only *a posteriori*, but today it is possible to discern the roots of important current trends in the upheavals of the early 1990s.

As a component of the behaviour of civil society, voluntary activities have also been affected by these multifaceted changes. Before the crisis, that is before the changes in international affairs in the 1990s which confused many voters and activists, the area of voluntary action was mainly linked with the activities of political parties. In Italy, during the First Republic the most widespread form of social and political participation was activism in a party or in its supporting structures. The biggest parties could count on a strong base of activists, whose activity consisted not only of involvement in election campaigns, but also ongoing participation, voluntary and unpaid. The Radical Party was built upon volunteer activities and this became one of its strongest aspects politically. The Italian Communist Party (PCI), the Italian Socialist Party (PSI) and the main governmental party, the Christian Democratic Party (DC), had an apparatus of volunteers, which amounted to millions of people for almost fifty years. Volunteers' activities and political engagement operated in many different spheres, from strict party support to civil actions, such as activities for youth, environment protection, international exchanges and many others.

The deep crisis in the party system at the beginning of the 1990s resulted in a huge decrease in volunteer-based engagement. The distrust of ideologies and of the political system in general modified not only party structures, several historical parties were dissolved, and involvement suffered a lack of interest and a decrease in popularity. The experience of the Italian green movement is particularly interesting in relation to the disaffection with politics: ecological movements emerging between the end of the 1970s and the beginning of the 1980s have reached huge dimensions and can count on the work of an enormous number of volunteers. In the past there were many attempts to attribute a political affiliation to this movement, however, while the green movement has been channelled into a political party in many countries, the concept of the "green volunteer" is today, at least in Italy, more transnational and independent from the party system. The experience of the Italian Green Party is paradigmatic; in an attempt to form a political party in the first half of the 1980s, several green candidates did fairly well in the national and European elections. When the Green Party reached a kind of unity during the second half of the 1980s, it could count on a strong base of adherents, even if the majority of green activists refused to be politicised. The passage from the First to the Second Republic also deeply affected the Green Party, whose electoral share fell from 6.1% in the European elections of 1989 to 2.8% in the national elections of 1992. The crisis in faith in the political system also affected the newest group, and green militants began again to dedicate themselves to forms of engagement outside the party system. The leadership of the party decided to rediscover its roots and encourage a form of militancy based more on ecological issues than on political change (Biorcio 2000).

People started or, in some cases, began again to dedicate themselves to other forms of activity and discovered other meanings of voluntary involvement on a different basis. It was not a quick or real substitution but a change of perspectives and values in the civil society, a transformation detectable only some years later. The change in involvement did not happen all at once; voluntary service was already in existence with a long history, but the deep crisis in the political sphere contributed to many people becoming involved in forms of engagement different from the past, divorced from political activity.

The crisis of traditional political channels also had a profound effect in Spain, where from the first part of the 1980s to the middle of the 1990s, interest in politics fell by 13% among young people (Orizo 1996). Young people refused to become involved in the traditional channels of political activity[1] and preferred to try to institute new forms of action. Notwithstanding the fact that, when looking at the Spanish population as a whole, the number of people working as volunteers in areas such as ecology, human rights and pacifism is still quite low, the interest showed by the majority of youth is growing, and incidents such as the *Prestige* disaster testify to youth sensitivity to these types of issues.

Another comment that might be made concerning the new face of voluntary service in Italy and Spain concerns the Catholic Church, as in the past voluntary service had a largely religious connotation. During the dictatorship in Spain, every volunteer activity fell under the control of the Catholic Church, and only in the mid-1970s, when the dictatorship was at its end, was a form of diversification introduced in the voluntary sector, which was consolidated when Spain finally established democracy.

Today, the influence on religion in voluntary service is still strong, and many volunteer organisations refer to Catholic institutions and promote Christian values, however, secular organisations are emerging and the inspiration for their work derives from different roots. The main difference from the past concerns the relationship

1. Traditional channels are in fact not so traditional in Spain where democracy has a rather short history.

between politics and religion; today voluntary service is free from political and/or religious control and constraint. In addition to voluntary associations classified as "confessional" or "a-confessional", a third category has appeared comprising all "voluntary organisations without any explicit matrix". The birth of this third type of organisation indicates both the relative lack of politicisation of civil society and the heterogonous face of voluntary service, no longer linked with traditional political channels but, on the contrary, completely open. Something similar is happening in former communist countries, where under the communist regime civil activities were fully under the Communist Party's control: today a process of "ideological liberalisation" of voluntary service activities is under way.

In Italy, the crisis of political and ideological beliefs, especially among young people, is deep. Only 3.9% of Italian youths are members of a political party similar data have been recorded in Spain. On the other hand, data regarding youth involvement in voluntary activities and youth organisations indicate a trend in the opposite direction. Only by considering both categories of data can we have a complete picture of youth society: young people seem to prefer forms of civil engagement totally divorced from any political affiliation, but to interpret these data as a proof of civil disengagement would be a grave misunderstanding. The data show a new manner of civil involvement not linked with party affiliation, but somehow still "political". It is a different way of understanding politics and acting politically and represents the best part of politics, being social action with the aim of building a better society, without reference to competition for power.

Figure 1 shows the period during the twentieth century when voluntary associations were constituted in Italy. As we can see, 48.4% of Italian voluntary organisations were formed after 1990. The graph shows that after 1990, in the crisis period, there was an enormous increase in the number of voluntary service organisations, whereas before the 1980s the existence of such organisations was marginal. As stated, the growth of civil service organisations did not begin exactly in 1990, but reflected changes in society occurring during the 1980s. The ecological and pacifist movements are important to consider here. The crisis mentioned above, in addition to social changes and social movements, led to many young people turning away from mainstream politics, and one of the most significant signs of social change has been the growth of voluntary service. Civil society had its golden era in the 1990s during which it was in a state of constant flux; today we can observe the changes which took place and, looking back, we can say that civil service represented a significant part of the civil revitalisation of that era. Also, if we think in terms of numbers, the size of voluntary service today is impressive: 4 861 600 people were involved in voluntary service activities in 2001 (FIVOL 2001). This means that almost 5 million people took part in voluntary service activities, a number not even thinkable twenty years ago; referring again to the numerical dimension, we would note the rapid growth in the number of volunteers: from 3 221 722 in 1997 to almost 5 million in 2001. A recent survey about what Italians trust showed voluntary service as one of the most trusted institutions in Italy, with 85%; political parties, in line with tradition during the last ten to fifteen years, got just 20%.

In the 1990s novel aspects of a newly revitalised civil society were apparent in the affirmation of the role of civilian service in the place of military service. The majority of European countries have decided on the creation of a professional army, not only for budgetary reasons, but also because of the enormous number of young men who preferred civilian service to military service.

Civilian service is not a form of voluntary activity, being only an alternative to obligatory military service, but its popularity among young people testified to a major
change in values in European society. Further, on 14 February 2001, it became possible for young Italian women to perform civilian service. As women in Italy are not
bound by any military duty, for them the choice to enter civilian service is a real
form of voluntary service. Italy is not the only country to have instituted optional
civilian service for women, but the Italian results have been particularly positive.
Data regarding civilian service in Italy are fairly astounding: a force of 17 930 in
2003, and 37 880 at the end of 2004.[1]

Figure 1: Formation of voluntary organisations by periods (as at 1999)

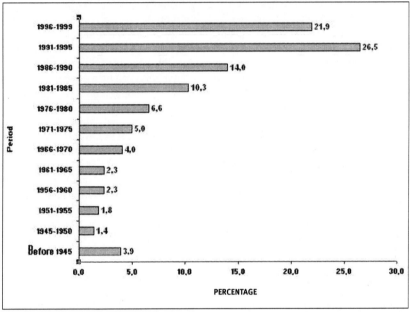

Source: Istituto nazionale de statistica (ISTAT) 2001.

Spain does not have quite as many volunteers; in fact, data indicate there were
1 073 636 in 2000. Compared to the Italian numbers this figure is quite low, but the
Spanish Ministry of Social Affairs did not include in its survey almost 300 000
people doing unpaid labour for NGOs. The significance of the number becomes
more evident if we compare the data with the previous survey from 1996 when the
number of people working as volunteers was "only" 300 000 (Rodríguez Cabrero
and Montserrat Codorniú 1996).[2] It would appear there was an extremely rapid rate
of growth in voluntary service in Spain over four years. It is easy to predict a similar
pattern of growth in the period from 2000 to 2004.

1. These data do not include numbers of people who choose civilian service instead of military service
(conscientious objectors). If these figures were to be included, almost 18 000 people who performed
civilian service in 2003 could be rightly considered as volunteers.

2. The difficulty in collecting data about volunteers has been noted by many sources. This results from
the fact that many volunteer associations are not registered in the regional registers; in Italy it is thought
that a greater number of voluntary associations exist than are accounted for due to this difficulty. In
Spain the same difficulties exist, and for both countries the most precise data refer to the local and
regional levels. In Italy data from FIVOL and Censis are quite different and the gap is justified by the fact
that Censis collected data only on registered associations whereas FIVOL estimates that 50% of voluntary organisations are not registered in the regional registers.

Given these two countries as a case study, it is also interesting to check data about a neighbouring country, France, and quickly reference French conditions in the field of voluntary service. France certainly comes first in terms of the number of people involved in voluntary service. The data indicate an incredible growth, from 7.9 million in 1990 to 10.4 million in 1996 and finally 12 million in 2003. The numbers are impressive and clearly show that France as well has followed the trend of the other two countries in the last fifteen years; participation in voluntary service has increased significantly, especially among young people.

The growth in voluntary service lends credence to the idea of a "revolution" in civil society and indicates a trend for the future. In fact, the changes happening in this sector are important not only in terms of numerical growth and an increase in civil engagement, but also, and maybe more importantly, in relation to structural factors. The social and political changes at national and international level at the beginning of the 1990s also affected the shape taken by voluntary service. One of the biggest changes relates to the profile of the volunteer: in recent years the number of young people involved in voluntary activities has increased dramatically. In Spain, for example, 49% of volunteers are young people under 25 years of age, generally speaking, looking at France at the national level, the number of young people engaged in voluntary service is not particularly high, but from a regional point of view, the results indicate a good level of participation where the information systems for the promotion of voluntary activities are adequate. A study conducted in several regions of France demonstrates that the national average depends on the communication and information infrastructure: in the Ile de France almost 50% of young people have volunteered, and the numbers are even higher in Champagne Ardenne, where more than half of the youth population has been engaged in voluntary activities- in Midi-Pyrénées, the figure climbs to two thirds of young people in the region.

The situation in Italy is defined by a variance in the data of recorded participation levels of young people in voluntary activities that range from 10% up to 30%. Even though data come from various authoritative sources (FIVOL, Abacus, Doxa), they present a considerable gap which could have been caused by different methodologies in conducting surveys or, even more, by the fact that many Italian surveys about voluntary service have been conducted on a regional base. The low level of accuracy of Italian surveys about young people and voluntary service is compensated for by the availability of data about volunteers' profiles. In Italy 50% of people engaged in volunteering have stable employment, whereas the other 50% fall into other categories such as "retired", "student" or "unemployed". These data seem to lead to the conclusion that the majority of Italian volunteers, more than 50%, are around 40 or 50 years of age, whereas the minority is composed of young people (who fit into the categories of "unemployed" and "students") and old people (who fit in the category of "retired").

The most recent surveys on the profile of volunteers found that the average level of education of Italian volunteers is increasing; the majority have a secondary school degree and the number of graduate volunteers is growing. This increase may be a result of the growth in the number of students taking part in voluntary activities thanks to good effective campaigns for the promotion of volunteerism being organised in Italian schools and universities.

In terms of women in the voluntary service, Spain comes out on top with 61% of volunteers being women, whereas in Italy women comprise only 50.8% of volunteers. The involvement of women and young people in voluntary service merits particular attention as this would suggest that this aspect of civil society is attractive to these demographics, who likely find here a broader space than in other sectors, like politics, where women's engagement is still low.

With regard to young people, it has been noted in Italy and in Spain that youth prefer to be active in voluntary activities for brief periods and with different levels of intensity. However, the main news in youth engagement in voluntary service regards the experiences of international voluntary service and especially the opportunities granted by the European Union. In this regard, the importance of the changed international context can be seen. As a result of the development of the European Union and the dissolution of borders, the voluntary sector has truly entered a new era.

A new Europe produced new voluntary service

Much like the end of the dictatorship in Spain, the fall of communism in eastern Europe represented a crucial moment for civil society. The democratisation and the "explosion" of civil society have not only had a direct effect on the former communist countries, but have also heavily influenced the civil life of western Europe. East European countries actually experienced volunteering only after the fall of communism. During the communist regime every kind of civil association was owned or controlled by the state/party, and the concept of civil society had no real role, as the party deeply discouraged all civic activity. Hence, the situation in eastern Europe changed dramatically after 1989 when volunteerism came there in the form of NGOs and international agencies and became a recognised social value. The current situation in eastern Europe shows an increase in the number of people volunteering and countries such as the Czech and Slovak republics have reached levels of "volunteerism" higher that those in many western countries (Voicu and Voicu 2003). It is not possible to generalise about the level of volunteerism for western or eastern countries as major differences exist within these two groups – Scandinavian countries used to volunteer more than Latin ones – and to create a level of incidence of volunteering for the said categories could give an inaccurate picture of the reality. In any case, what emerges is that many former communist countries that experimented with voluntary service practices during the 1990s seem to be likely to carry on in this way and in doing so have reached very high levels of participation in volunteerism. It is possible to check also by looking at data about experiences of international or European voluntary service where the level of participation of young east European people is constantly increasing.

Especially at the moment, following the recent enlargement and the prospect of additional EU states in the not too distant future, attention should be drawn to the European dimension in every aspect of civil life, including voluntary service. In this field an important experience of international voluntary service has also been experimented for several years. Individuals with dual citizenship often forget this big advantage, on the other hand many people, especially young people, are exploiting the advantages of being European, as well as being citizens of individual member states.

One of the opportunities offered by the European Union is the possibility to approach voluntary service in a new way. The EU programmes for voluntary service, the most important being the European Voluntary Service, are different from the majority of national programmes, because they promote a form of action not based on free time, but on a full-time schedule for long or short periods. This represents a

Social and political transformations

new way of living the voluntary experience and appeals to many young people who have never before been involved in voluntary service associations. The main aim of the programme is

> to help young Europeans become more mobile and, hence, more active citizens, provide them with a formative experience in several areas of activity and encourage them to make an active contribution to building Europe and to co-operation between the Community and non-member countries by taking part in transnational activities of benefit to the community. (http://europa.eu.int/scadplus/leg/en/cha/c11602c.htm)

The fundamental objective of the programme is to give young people the opportunity to become familiar with the meaning of active citizenship at an international level through practical experience which is useful not only for the beneficiaries of the volunteers' work but especially for the volunteers themselves.

Between 3 000 and 4 000 young people enrol with the European Voluntary Service each year. It was established on 20 July 1998 and has been one of the most successful programmes promoted by the European Union. The experience of voluntary service is coupled with an intensive experience of life abroad and not only promotes values such as solidarity and philanthropy but also supports a culture of brotherhood and knowledge of diversity. The opportunity of living in another country, of doing altruistic work, improving skills and experimenting with another way of life is appealing to many young people throughout the EU. One of the most attractive aspects of the EVS is the choice offered amongst a vast range of different experiences, such as activities aimed at integration and combating racism, cultural activities for youth, helping the elderly, helping the homeless and many others.

It stands to reason that a project that offers its participants such a wide variety of experiences has gained the interest of many young people. This kind of "open" experience seems to be favoured by European youth. The choice of taking part in voluntary service programmes is a sort of challenge the young set for themselves, a passage to adulthood and a first step towards an independent life. For these reasons a project like EVS represents a phenomenon different from previous forms of voluntary service, and thanks to European citizenship it is possible to enlarge the dimension of voluntary service. The growing desire to test a new manner of engagement is also indicated by the success of programmes such as "With Helmets" which is becoming more and more popular, and many other voluntary service programmes promoted, directly or indirectly, by the United Nations; today more than 10 million volunteers are involved in such programmes all over the world. Generally, there is a flow of volunteers from richer countries to poorer ones, evidence of the civil culture of co-operation between nations promoted by voluntary service. The spread of the voluntary service culture, especially among young people, shows the existence of transnational solidarity and results in useful services for communities.

An open experience with open media

There is another remarkable aspect of the renewed diffusion of the voluntary service especially regarding the recent forms of engagement in this area: the use of new media. If new technologies brought many advantages to the everyday life of communities as well as to citizens' private lives, they have also contributed to the spread of civil engagement and voluntary service programmes. The extreme ease of logging on to the Internet and of disseminating information via the Internet has transformed and enlarged the approach to voluntary service experiences. Thanks to new technologies, word about the EVS programme has spread more widely and many websites exist about the personal experience of volunteers. Therefore young people interested in this experience can easily determine what impressions previous volunteers have of the programme. The Internet is helping not only "virtual volunteers", the previous volunteers, but also the associations wanting to take part in the programme. The UK is a vanguard in this field but the level of "connectivity" of many other European countries is growing and websites dedicated to voluntary service are registering an impressive number of visitors (www.hacefalta.org and www.do-it.org.uk are just two successful examples). It has been demonstrated that the level of connectivity of each country depends mainly on the monetary capacity of voluntary associations. The first problem for voluntary associations is to be able to pay to set up a website and for an Internet connection, because even though many associations would like to get a certain level of presence on the web, they are still not always able to pay for it. Another factor significant in establishing the level of connectivity of voluntary associations is the age of their managers; a French study (IRIV 2003) proved that managers under 55 years of age are more likely to be disposed to get an Internet connection and a website than their older colleagues. Hence, voluntary associations managed by young people have a greater chance of being known on the web and gaining opportunities from that source.

Even though the Internet could provide many services to voluntary associations and can help in improving the diffusion of voluntary activities, there are some problems which need to be sorted out. There is an Italian study in which the authors conducted an inquiry based on the use of IT in the Italian world of voluntary service. They concluded that voluntary associations are not yet able to exploit the potential of the Internet, and they point out some problems they consider prevalent in the use of the Internet. Firstly, there are some cases of voluntary organisations' websites which not only provide useless information but also frustrate visitors to the sites. This kind of website is at the lowest level of a continuum from best to worst in terms of exploiting IT. Many Italian websites of voluntary associations occupied a middle position on the line, and only few reach the top. This would indicate there is still a lot of work to do in improving the use of the Internet in the voluntary sector, and in so doing associations must be very careful otherwise they run the risk of producing problematic effects (Ferraris and Paltrinieri 1998).

The use of the Internet has helped in developing another important experience of voluntary service: work camps. This form of volunteering has already been experimented for several years, but the web has facilitated its spread thanks to the ease with which information can be obtained and applications made online. The concept of work camps comes from the beginning of the twentieth century, the first experience in Europe goes back to the 1920s after the First World War when work camps were set up for reconstruction. This form of volunteering has developed during the second half of the twentieth century and is quite well known today. Generally, it is a form of international co-operation based on a short period of volunteering which has a definite goal as its object. Many work camps concentrate on environmental or historical protection but a vast range of choices is now available. Even if their aim is to work on a single project, one of the most important characteristics of work camps is to promote the culture of volunteering and international co-operation, especially among young people.

Overall there are many forms of volunteering today, for short periods, for long periods, during free time or on particular occasions. The European Union has started to assist in the diffusion of voluntary service and has instituted some special programmes for its implementation. Young people seem to enjoy the experience and the opportunities offered by it. Today, it seems young people are interested in getting involved in these kinds of activities for the personal improvement they can gain.

Conclusions

The forms of civil engagement and civic participation as well as voluntary service have deeply changed in the last fifteen years. The European civil society of the 1980s was a fragmented entity; it was divided into national civic societies with an underdeveloped web of international connections. Political parties, in many west European countries, and the state or the only single party in eastern Europe, were largely responsible for managing civil society. The forms of voluntary service and voluntary associations were in existence, and some had a long and successful history, but the element of European cohesion did not yet exist. On the contrary, today civil society and voluntary service are getting more and more European every day. The phenomenon has strong support and massive levels of participation and the opportunities given by the European Union are appealing to young people. The shape of voluntary service has changed and its popularity is growing thanks also to the Internet and new media, even though the use of the Internet in this sector is still problematic in certain respects. European civil society is acquiring an open connotation which is the real new element compared to the past.

Although here we have mainly looked at the situation in Italy and Spain, similar trends have been noted in other European countries. Italy and Spain passed through the experience of governmental corruption and failure; and although the former is an old democracy and the latter a relatively new democracy, the populations of both countries experienced the same disillusion and crisis in political beliefs, especially on the left. Despite these problems, civil society was able to reinvent itself and become proactive in the 1990s. If trust in politics has decreased, voluntary service, voluntary activities and the number of voluntary associations have grown. In spite of the difficulties experienced by volunteers, the popularity of voluntary service has risen and its international element has become a stable characteristic.

Overall, the trends discerned provide hope for the future, not only of the voluntary service, but in general for the further growth of civil society, although many problems must still be addressed, such as the dissemination of information and voluntary service culture, and the establishment of a clearer definition and recognition of the status of volunteers and related legal implications.

European youth voluntary activities

References

Borcio, R., "The Italian Greens' Participation in the Centre-Left Government", joint sessions of the ECPR, Grenoble, 6-11 April 2001.

European Commission (2000) *Summaries of legislation* [online]. Brussels: European Commission. Available at http://europa.eu.int/scadplus/leg/en/cha/c11602c.htm (accessed 30 June 2005).

Ferraris, D. and Paltrinieri, A. (1998) "Studio Esplorativo". Terza Conferenza Nazionale del Volontariato, 11-13 December 1998, Foligno.

Fondazione Italiana per il Volontariato (FIVOL) (2001) *Terza Rilevazione sulle Organizzazioni di Volontariato, a Cura di Renato Frisanco – Settore Sudi e Ricerche.* Rome: Fondazione Italiana per il Volontariato.

Institut de recherche et d'information sur le volontariat (IRIV) (2003) *Accès et Utilisation d'Internet par les Asssociations.* Paris: IRIV.

Istituto nazionale di statistica (ISTAT) (2000) *Le Organizzazioni di Volontariato.* Rome: ISTAT.

Muxel, A. (1996) *Les Jeunes et la Politique.* Paris: Orchette.

Ortega, F. (2001) "Cambio Politico y Imagenes de la Juventud Politica Española". In Giovani, J. (ed.) *Jóvenes.* Florence: Florence University Press.

Ortega, F. (2001) "Real o Virtual? La otra Participacion Politica Juvenil". In *Jóvenes,* op.cit.

Orizo, F. (1991) *Los Nuevos Valores de los Españoles.* Madrid: Ediciones SM.

Pisu, R. (1999) "Inchiesta/Oltre il Volontariato". *La Repubblica,* 25 February.

Rodríguez Cabrero, G. and Montserrat Codornú, J. (1996) *Las Entidades Voluntarias en España. Institucionalizacion, Estructura Económica y Desarrollo Asociativo.* Madrid: Ministero de Trabajo y Asuntos Sociales.

Rossi, G. and Boccacin, L. (2001) "Que es el Voluntariado". *Revista del Ministerio de Trabajo y Asuntos Sociales.*

Voicu, B. and Voicu, M. (2003) *"Volunteering in Eastern Europe: One of the Missing Links",* Paper for the round table "Globalization, integration and social development in central and eastern Europe" held at the University Lucian Blaga. Silu: University Lucian Blaga.

3. What's it worth?
How valuable is volunteering?
Young people and volunteering
in Birmingham

Alun Severn and Terry Potter

Introduction

Throughout the course of this project we have sought to gain a more informed view about voluntary activity in Birmingham and how best interventions might be designed that can support and promote volunteering. Our earlier desk research and public attitudes survey compared the state of volunteering in Birmingham with that nationally (Severn and Potter 2003).

This indicated that:

- The level of volunteering in Birmingham – whether considered as "formal" volunteering or "informal" voluntary activity – may be as low as only one half to one quarter of that nationally. This may indicate that Birmingham is a volunteering "cold spot", but there is also some evidence to suggest that by failing to distinguish adequately between respondents' past and present volunteering, national surveying methods may historically have tended to overstate volunteering levels.

- When the numbers of people indicating they had volunteered in the past were compared with those who said they were still engaged in voluntary activity, there was a consistent falling off across all activities – in some cases by up to two thirds.

- While greater numbers of people were engaged in informal volunteering and for increasing periods of time, the evidence suggested that formal volunteering – i.e. that conducted under the auspices of an established voluntary or community organisation – was more sustainable, with volunteers maintaining their involvement consistently in the longer term.

- Birmingham has an ageing volunteer force, with voluntary activity highest in the 45-60/64 age group. In the 16-29 and 30-44 age groups there was the biggest falling away in numbers between those volunteering in the past and those volunteering currently.

While important for the detailed picture of voluntary activity in Birmingham that this provides and for its implications for the volunteering support infrastructure, it also serves to illustrate some of the fundamental difficulties – and contradictions – in how volunteering is identified and subsequently valued.

Although models of assessing and valuing voluntary activity have over the past few years become more sophisticated, they remain essentially statistical, seeking to measure either the numbers volunteering, the duration of this activity, or its notional economic value. There is no doubt that the mass of statistical data generated by periodic surveys of volunteering – such as those conducted every six or seven years by the Institute for Volunteering Researching (IVR) – has been instrumental in convincing government of the importance of volunteering, it is also the case that the public policy agenda regarding volunteering has shifted. Government now places much less emphasis on calculating the financial "worth" of volunteering and instead locates volunteering in the very broadest sense as one of a range of community-based actions that can contribute to stronger communities and a more active and engaged citizenship. This is perhaps nowhere more clearly stated that in the Home Secretary's two recent pamphlets explaining and promoting the "civil renewal" agenda (Home Office 2003a and 2003b).

The purpose of this chapter, then, is to look more critically at the whole issue of ascribing value to volunteering. What do we mean by "value"? Value to whom and according to whose value system? And why, exactly, do we need to ascribe value to volunteering in the first place – what does this help us to decide or do? It is also a timely point at which to revisit some first principles – this may aid us in considering the often complex array of interlocking issues that are involved in volunteering. Why do we think volunteering is worthwhile? Why does it have such a central, defining role in this thing called the "voluntary sector"?

This chapter was originally a paper commissioned by Birmingham Volunteer Action (BVA) as a contribution to the Volunteering Development in Birmingham project funded by the Active Community Directorate. It was written by Alun Severn of Third Sector Services, Gail Walters and Terry Potter of Birmingham Voluntary Service Council (BVSC) Research, Information and Sector Intelligence (RiSi).

What has become increasingly evident during the course of this research project is that assessing the value of volunteering is the tip of the iceberg. What at first appears a reasonably straightforward aspiration in fact rests on top of a complex mass of questions – of the value, worth and contribution of volunteering, the wider social benefits it creates, its relationship to the state, and the role played by the personal attitudes and value systems of those who volunteer or, indeed, choose not to volunteer. In setting the broader context of this chapter it is necessary to at least touch on these briefly.

Let us pose the question again in the same way that the title of this chapter does: "What is volunteering worth?" Perhaps more accurately, where does its worth derive from? Why do we consider volunteering to be good?

We would argue that there are at least four quite distinct areas for examination in volunteering:

- First, there is our essentially "political" commitment to the concept of voluntary action. A core value of the voluntary and community sector, it can be stated and adhered to as a guiding principle, but is not very amenable to measurement.

- Second, there is the impact achieved by and the effectiveness of the volunteering infrastructure – the support and promotion mechanisms, interventions, campaigns and activities to foster the growth and good health of volunteering.

- Third, there is the wider social or community benefit attributable to voluntary activity. (Indeed, we might also add to this the personal gains attributable to volunteering – for both the donor and the beneficiary – but we will consider this briefly in the section on the "Volunteering contract".)

- Fourth, there is the as yet largely unexplored, we believe, dimension of a cost-benefit comparison of voluntary and statutory provision.

While the latter three are more amenable to measurement this, as we argue later in the chapter, would be at significant cost, inevitably raising the issue of resource allocation and priorities. In passing, however, this serves to illustrate the complexity of the issues involved in ascribing value to volunteering.

Volunteering – A core value

Let us look a little more closely at the central role that volunteering plays in our conception of what the voluntary sector is about. As an expression of neighbourliness and mutual aid, volunteering is central to the values of the voluntary sector. Freely given and elective, volunteering is a personal choice that comes down on the side of social solidarity. It emphasises collective aid and reciprocity and because volunteering, by definition, is non-commercial, it favours mutuality over individual consumerism. It is inconceivable, then, that volunteering would not be central to the ethos of the voluntary and community sector.

Volunteering's elective nature must also be emphasised: organisations may be committed to volunteering, but it is individual volunteers who choose to involve themselves in the personal transaction of volunteering, freely donating their time, energy and effort. In this sense, the freely chosen voluntary nature of volunteering is a crucial value underpinning the act and strongly informs our views about how closely or otherwise volunteering can or should be tied to the aims of the state. We would argue that while it is legitimate to utilise the benefits of volunteering to help achieve some greater, overarching good – more cohesive communities, for example, or more widespread active citizenship – anything that detracts from or compromises the voluntary nature of the act will tend to be viewed unsympathetically by those most likely to engage in volunteering.

What this suggests to us is that while the voluntary sector and government do indeed share some common interests in extending and maximising the benefits of volunteering, these interests are not strictly co-terminus. The voluntary sector also has a duty to safeguard the voluntary nature of volunteering and ensure that in any closer harnessing to the state's social policy objectives it does not become expected or required. We must also be vigilant in avoiding any blurring which might occur between voluntary services freely given for community good and the potentially punitive notion of community service. These concerns are brought into sharper relief by the Chancellor's recent call for the establishment of a commission to report on the way forward for a National Youth Volunteering Strategy. This he clearly sees as a key instrument for building notions of civic responsibility in the longer term (Brown 2004, Fabian Society 2004).

Writing in its Manifesto for Change 2003, BVSC highlighted the dangers that exist for the voluntary sector in its ever closer relationship with the state: "The more the sector wins the arguments, the more it finds itself incorporated into the fabric of social provision it evolved to challenge." This is as true of volunteering *per se* as it is of the wider sector, but with an added danger. Many voluntary organisations are equipped to handle any such debate robustly; they have many years experience of "fighting their corner" and will never simply walk away from the complex relationships modern society demands of them. But this is not true of volunteers, of the millions of individuals who, propelled by a complex set of motivations and attitudes, volunteer every day of the year. For them it would at least seem plausible that there is a tipping point, a step too far in state intervention which could simply switch off the volunteering impulse.

It is against these wide voluntary sector responsibilities that we consider the role and worth of volunteering in the rest of this chapter.

······> What do we mean by "value"?

Over the past few years, efforts to assess the value or impact of volunteering have tended to focus on those things that can be counted: the numbers of people volunteering, the duration of their volunteering and the notional financial worth of this voluntary activity. Few would doubt that this effort has been instrumental in raising the profile of volunteering and in establishing the central role that volunteering can play in adding value to statutory and voluntary services and more widely to communities themselves.

As a consequence of the periodic national surveys carried out by the Institute for Volunteering Research (IVR) and more recently by the Home Office (Home Office 2002), we now have a better picture of national trends in volunteering than ever before. But such surveys are extraordinarily costly. IVR, for example, is usually only able to conduct a national volunteering survey every six or seven years – the last was 1997 – and is currently trying to raise the funding necessary to conduct the first twenty-first century survey.

Similarly, more sophisticated economic models for assessing the contribution of volunteering within individual organisations – such as IVR's "VIVA": the Volunteer Investment and Value Audit – while clearly useful to larger volunteer-using organisations that want to know the economic contribution that volunteering makes to their own operation, are unlikely to be within the budget or capacity of those at the smaller and poorer end of the voluntary sector spectrum.

And yet, it is not surprising that quantitative surveying and audit methods such as these have predominated. Measuring anything beyond numbers, duration and economic value – the social contribution of volunteering, for instance, or the personal gains experienced by volunteers and beneficiaries, or the community-building contribution of voluntary work – is methodologically complex and may in addition be open to wide interpretation. Underlying social and community benefits are resistant to measurement. They do not lend themselves to standardisation or repetition and may depend to a large degree on personal testimony.

Perhaps for these reasons, social indicators which would enable a more thoroughgoing evaluation not just of volunteering but also of a wide array of social policy objectives have become a kind of holy grail. While at a national level they may be of crucial importance, at a local level amongst cash-strapped voluntary organisations whose primary aim is direct service delivery, they will rarely be perceived as the most pressing priority for investment.

Value or values — A personal matter?

It must also be emphasised that value means different things to different people: personal motivation cannot be dismissed from the equation because to a great extent it determines how people view their voluntary effort.

Our findings from amongst focus groups carried out with Birmingham volunteers, for example, show that few if any think of the monetary value their volunteering might represent, but they do consider the values on which their volunteering is based. And while some volunteers may talk about "giving something back to the community", or of "wanting to make a difference" it is perhaps not surprising that few if any speak of their volunteering in terms that have now become familiar in public policy – community empowerment, for example, active citizenship, or civil renewal.

This is not to say that these concepts have no broader validity, of course, merely to acknowledge that they are not generally speaking for popular consumption. But there are important implications in this for how volunteering is promoted – for how we ensure that the right messages reach the right people. At "street level" it is vital that the volunteering message reflects and speaks to the values of volunteers and potential volunteers themselves.

As the Birmingham survey illustrated, most volunteers do so out of personal or family experience. They respond to an often fairly simple desire to put something back into the community. Some volunteer in support of a specific service, illness, condition or disability that they have some personal or family experience of. Others volunteer because of experience gained in a period in their own past – raising children as a lone parent, for instance, or homelessness, or sight or hearing impairment. Personal experience is a powerful motivator and most volunteers we spoke with seemed to consider volunteering an essentially personal choice, even when conducted under the auspices of an organisation or volunteer agency of some description.

Volunteers, then, respond most positively to the one-to-one relationship of voluntary help – the real, tangible freely given service. And they respond most powerfully to its voluntary nature: proscription is inimical to volunteering's good health.

Segmentation

It is possible that a quite different picture might be gained if one were to examine a specific sector of volunteering, such as that attached to regeneration programmes such as New Deal for Communities. Here, it might be argued that a much clearer relationship exists between personal volunteering and community benefit and it may be the case that volunteers in these kinds of situations do in fact make a stronger connection between their voluntary effort and the wider community good.

Indeed, as we discuss later in this chapter, in operational terms there may be a case for drawing a much clearer distinction between volunteering that is primarily personally motivated – such as one-to-one care, support or befriending, for example – and that which arises primarily as a response to conditions in a particular community. It may be that the latter does have a clearer "community empowerment" dimension to it, but again this is to argue for a greater precision, a greater segmentation, in thinking about voluntary effort. While very different kinds of volunteering have shared characteristics, not all voluntary effort arises from the same motivation and the respective values and perceived consequences of different kinds of volunteering will appeal to very different types of people.

What do we want to measure and why?

Although we can observe that communities which have a well-developed voluntary and community sector, where volunteering and community activity are frequent and levels of good neighbourliness high, are somehow more robustly cohesive than neighbourhoods where these things are underdeveloped or in decline, the precise contribution that volunteering makes to the overall health of communities remains an extraordinarily complex question. More sophisticated counting or measuring of voluntary activity obviously gives us a clearer picture of what and how much is going on, although whether this helps us better understand the contribution that volunteering is making to the overall social or community mix, especially at a local level, is another matter. More importantly, perhaps, quantitative surveys of volunteering rarely help us to understand how best voluntary activity can be encouraged, or supported when the need arises, or most effectively be helped to flourish in those communities where it is absent. These are pressing issues, especially for agencies involved in the voluntary sector infrastructure.

But the messages we wish to project about volunteering may also determine what we seek to measure or assess. At a local level, for example, organisations may wish to assess the value, effectiveness and impact of particular volunteering projects or interventions, perhaps within a specific community or neighbourhood in mind. There may also be an argument for as yet untried cost-benefit analyses of volunteering that seek to assess the respective voluntary and statutory costs and benefits of service provision. This would be demanding and methodologically challenging research; it would also be costly. But it would also bring to the volunteering debate a dimension that at present is missing.

Alongside this, however, it must also be emphasised that volunteering is not just about money. There are personal gains for the donor, quality of life gains for the beneficiary, community and neighbourhood gains and – as government now increasingly emphasises – broader social gains in the form of social cohesion and active citizenship.

The "volunteering contract"

"Value" is spread across what we have called the "volunteering contract". Not only will all parties to this contract be unlikely to share the same notion of value, it is also quite possible that they will have different value systems.

There are three main parties to the volunteering contract: the donor, the beneficiary and the commissioner of the volunteering (at least in cases where the activity is formally organised by an agency). We have already seen that for the donor, there is a strong likelihood that the motivation will be primarily personal – as much to do with what they get out of and put into volunteering and how this makes them feel as it is any broader notion of community benefit.

For the beneficiary, value will be much more likely to revolve around what the help or assistance they get means to them – how it affects them, how it improves their quality of life, the degree to which they can depend on its availability, and what would happen if this voluntary service ceased. The value – or values – of the transaction are strongly informed, therefore, by personal circumstances.

Organisations that commission volunteering will again take a different perspective on value and it is here that the social significance of volunteering in its wider context might be considered and longer-term strategic objectives come into play. Again, a very different interpretation of value.

There are other partners to the volunteering contract, however, and these have been of increasing importance over the past few years. A fourth category might be funders of volunteering initiatives, where again different expectations will prevail. In some cases, funders may be synonymous with a fifth category – the local or national state. It is here that voluntary activity will most clearly be harnessed to broader social policy aims – as can be clearly seen in the Home Secretary's writings on civil renewal.

The notion, then, that the value of volunteering changes according to one's place in the volunteering contract is an important one, with implications that go far beyond how we value volunteering and touch on all aspects of the volunteering debate – the language we use to describe volunteering, how (and where) volunteering is promoted, what people think their voluntary action is for and is meant to achieve, and the role they feel the state can legitimately claim to play in the volunteering arena.

In this context it is important that we again remind ourselves of a few key facts:

- The last IVR national survey of volunteering (1997) showed a decline in the numbers volunteering of around a million – despite the proliferation of new routes into volunteering and nationally backed volunteering campaigns.

- The single most effective means of promoting volunteering is word of mouth: people respond most readily to direct appeals to volunteer and this is especially the case when the appeal is made by someone they know or someone already involved in voluntary activity.

- And research has shown that public awareness of volunteering agencies of all kinds is abysmally low.

We still need to find effective ways of reconciling broad social policy aims with popular messages about volunteering; we still need "street level" messages that "sell" the volunteering experience, reflecting and speaking to the values that volunteers and potential volunteers consider most important. These are vital considerations for an organisation such as Birmingham Volunteer Action and for the wider network of volunteer placement, referral and brokerage agencies.

The social policy environment

Although since 1999/2000 there has been a plethora of government initiatives to support or encourage volunteering, particularly amongst specific age groups such as young people (Millennium Volunteers) and the over-50s (Experience Corps), it is evident that government thinking on volunteering, certainly as regards programmes directly engaging with or supporting individual volunteers, has changed markedly. Some 90 volunteering schemes supported by the Home Office are currently under review and at the time of writing a number of these look set to lose all or some of their funding, including Experience Corps (the government ceased funding in March 2004), and Time Bank, the skills/service exchange scheme targeting the most disadvantaged communities.

This does not indicate that volunteering *per se* has fallen from popularity, however. Rather, it is the emphasis that is changing – and nowhere is this more evident than in the Home Secretary's two recent pamphlets to promote his vision for "civil renewal" (2003a and 2003b). Voluntary community action lies at the heart of this vision.

But it is an extraordinarily broad and sweeping vision. Its central thesis is that renewal of civil society and the public realm demands a new contract of active citizenship – a contract between a "progressive, activist state" and empowered communities that are "increasingly capable" of "defining the problems they face and then tackling them together".

While individual volunteering is certainly not absent from these policy statements, a clear shift in emphasis is none the less apparent – away from programmes to support and encourage individual volunteers and much more towards communities of volunteers, "active citizens" engaged in a mutual effort to build community solidarity and work for the common good.

This is perhaps most clearly expressed in the later of the Home Secretary's pamphlets, *Active Citizens, Strong Communities: Progressing Civil Renewal*. Where there is specific mention of voluntary activity – as opposed to civil renewal's key notion of the engaged citizen acting for the common good – it is noticeable that rather than generic volunteering this tends to be voluntary activity in quite specific civic contexts: within the youth justice system, schools, hospitals, fire stations and prisons, for example (Home Office 2003a).

Alongside this emerging civil renewal agenda, the government is still pledged to increase voluntary and community sector activity amongst socially excluded groups by 5% by 2006. But more recently the Chancellor has added his voice to the volunteering debate with a controversial and much longer-term aim of establishing a youth community service scheme, the assumption being that voluntary activity in youth will grow into active citizenship in later life – a continuum of engagement measured in decades rather than simply the here and now.

There is little doubt, then, that a new perspective on volunteering is emerging within government. The scattergun approach to funding numerous volunteer support programmes – which broadly coincided with the UN International Year of Volunteering in 2001 – would seem to be over. In its place is an emphasis on active citizenship and the role of engaged communities, what we might call a kind of "civic volunteering", in which there is a much clearer relationship between voluntary effort and the building of civil renewal and community solidarity.

Overarching values?

One of the most interesting things about the Home Secretary's civil renewal agenda is that it is recasting a set of social ideas – solidarity, mutuality and co-operation, for example – in what has become New Labour's characteristic language of civic rights and responsibilities. The agenda, then, is not significant necessarily for its newness; what is significant is the determined detachment of these particular social values from the old municipal socialism which would previously have been their most likely political underpinning.

There is also a further significant dimension to this attempt to formulate a new and more widely understood language of social solidarity, however. One of the problems that has bedevilled such attempts previously has been the tendency to fall back on "imported" and often highly contested concepts such as "social capital". Although *Active Citizens, Strong Communities: Progressing Civil Renewal* does use this term, it is used on only three occasions and then somewhat in passing. Blunkett says that new forms of social capital should be recognised and supported by government, that government has a role to play in assisting communities to "build social capital" and, in the longest reference, that the social capital lost during the forced march of industrial restructuring under Thatcherism in the 1980s must be restored and reinvigorated. There is no attempt to locate social capital in a more theoretical or academic context, as some other commentators have done (Putnam 2000) and it is used almost as a synonym for "community spirit" or simply "sense of community". What emerges with a much higher profile – a central notion in civil renewal – is community cohesion.

Community cohesion has risen up the political agenda in the wake of Ted Cantle's report on the race riots that took place in some northern former textile towns during the summer of 2001 (Home Office 2001) and is seen as central in Blunkett's vision for civil renewal. The pursuit of civil renewal, he says, must "be backed by a resolute commitment to break down barriers to the realisation of our shared citizenship": communities that are cohesive, that are not divided by "mutual suspicion or misunderstanding of diverse cultures", are seen as a prerequisite platform for progressing civil renewal.

And community cohesion is being resourced. The Home Office has committed £6 million to funding Community Cohesion Pathfinders in 37 local authorities, aimed at driving community cohesion measures into the mainstream of service delivery; the Department for Education and Skills is making funding available to support community cohesion in schools, enabling them to take action which will build bridges, especially in areas where there are "clear fractures within the community"; and the Connecting Communities grants programme – which includes proposals for race equality support programmes – is supporting 75 projects from 2003 to 2006 (Home Office 2003b). It is only, says Blunkett, "by setting a clear legal framework for citizenship, and developing practical initiatives to promote its realisation that we will strengthen communities through strengthening their cross-cultural relationships."

Does this begin to suggest a different approach towards thinking about volunteering and community activity and how their value should be judged? We think it does and discuss this more fully in the next section.

Valuing volunteering – The characteristics of cohesion

This shift in emphasis now taking place in government policy suggests that gauging the duration, frequency and notional financial value of volunteering may no longer be the most important objective. Rather than quantitative measurement, we now need something that can assist us in understanding the broad contributions that volunteering can make in pursuit of civil renewal's core objectives of:

- community cohesion;
- active citizenship;
- cross-cultural working.

And yet this also highlights the difficulties. While efforts to develop community cohesion indicators, for example, are ongoing – the Home Office, the Community Cohesion Unit and the Local Government Association have all published guidance of various kinds – large-scale community cohesion surveys are beyond our capacity and resources to implement in Birmingham, specifically for the volunteering sector. (This is to set aside for a moment the widely acknowledged difficulties that exist in designing successful methodologies for measuring community cohesion.)

In any case, we would question whether attempting to replicate such surveys on a smaller scale in Birmingham is necessarily a useful investment of resources. If policy-driven indicators do have a role to play in helping to assess the contribution of volunteering at a local level, then it may be more useful to use them as the basis for developing a volunteering framework that can be used to guide the kind of interventions that are made to support, promote and encourage volunteering.

What this would suggest, rather than a set of measurable indicators to enable the counting of units of volunteer activity, is a framework linked back to key policy objectives (and these could be national or local objectives – the approach is inherently flexible), which will help in identifying voluntary activity which has particular characteristics. By looking for volunteering that has particular characteristics we can begin to manipulate the interventions made in support of key policy objectives. For example, it would be possible to design a volunteering framework linked specifically to civil renewal, as in the table below:

A volunteering framework to contribute to civil renewal	
Headline policy objectives	**Identify activities with the following characteristics**
Cross-cultural working	• Activity that encourages people from different backgrounds and/or different communities to meet and help each other* • Activity that encourages cross-cultural volunteering – namely groups assisting people from a different community to themselves
Community cohesion	• Activity that helps people to identify more strongly with their local area • Activity that helps people from different backgrounds and communities to live together more harmoniously • Activity that draws in and/or involves excluded groups
Active citizenship	• Activity that adds to the overall sum of community engagement • Activity that promotes more effective or more direct engagement with broader community issues

* The LGA guidance (LGA 2002) recommends "Using the networks of statutory and voluntary agencies to develop cross-cultural contacts at all levels and reviewing the funding of VCOs in order to provide incentives to promoting community cohesion and cross-cultural contact and understanding."

While far removed from a quantitative or measuring approach to valuing volunteering, this is a means of ensuring that local interventions in volunteering support and development are informed and guided by key policy objectives (wherever they might derive from). This is very much in keeping with the kind of "segmentation" approach we advocated in earlier papers, but takes the process a stage further. This is a logical point at which to consider in more detail the implications of such an approach for BVA.

Role of BVA

We have long argued that BVA should take a more segmented view of volunteering and that this, when linked back to key policy objectives, will assist significantly in modelling interventions that make a more critical contribution to supporting and developing voluntary activity in Birmingham. Nothing that we have so far advanced in this chapter contradicts that view; however, there are one or two areas in which further thought is required in order to fine-tune BVA's operational priorities.

Developing a strategic framework for volunteering interventions

We have seen the shift that has taken place in public policy regarding volunteering away from individual volunteering programmes in favour of communities of volunteers – the emergence of the active citizenship and civil renewal agendas. We have also highlighted the Home Secretary's emphasis in *Active Citizens, Strong Communities: Progressing Civil Renewal* on what we have called civic volunteering. This clearly has implications for how BVA operates.

One possible operational change that BVA could consider is whether its volunteering priorities should be themed. (Let us emphasise again that this is for BVA's internal operational guidance and is not necessarily amongst the messages it would project to the outside world and especially to prospective volunteers.) We have so far in this chapter drawn a distinction between personal volunteering, community volunteering and Blunkett's vision of civic volunteering (police, health, fire, schools, youth justice system and so forth). It might assist BVA to focus on specific strategic objectives if its own priorities were similarly "themed", so that effectively it had three "departments":

- Personal volunteering – for all activities that involve personal service delivery to a beneficiary or group of beneficiaries (most care, befriending, visiting, elderly support and the like would come under this heading).

- Community volunteering – activities with a direct relationship to the wider community good, such as tenant/resident groups, regeneration, community groups, local campaigns, development trust-style activities, environmental activities and so forth.

- Civic volunteering – specifically aimed at voluntary activity in statutory or civic services (health, education, police, justice system, fire services, etc).

While there would probably be some overlap and also some grey areas – is volunteering to read to children in a local school in one's own community "community volunteering" or "civic volunteering", for example – these would be no worse and certainly no more of an obstacle than the overlaps and grey areas that have persisted over the years with just about any definitions or categorisations of volunteering one might choose to examine.

The advantage of such an approach, however, is that it could be very neatly linked with the "framework" approach outlined above, thus enabling strategic or policy-related objectives to be set within each volunteering category.

Measuring volunteering — is it over?

One other matter that we should comment on at least briefly is the future need for further local volunteering surveys in Birmingham. Our view is that the kind of "generic" volunteering survey conducted as part of this research has, in the longer term, only limited utility and is perhaps not the best use of resources, certainly on a repeated basis.

While the data gathered provided a greater level of intelligence specifically about Birmingham volunteering than has ever before been available, the potential of such surveys to inform and shape strategic interventions in volunteering is actually very limited – partly because the response rates across cohorts (age, gender, ethnicity; formal or informal volunteering) or across volunteering activities are very much smaller than in a national survey and therefore drawing conclusions based on these can be problematical.

But having said this, there is also an issue about the level of data on city-wide volunteering trends that other parties expect BVA to be able to furnish. Many automatically make BVA their first port of call in seeking facts and figures about volunteering in the city and BVA therefore needs to consider how it meets this expectation and the relative priority it should have within its operational budget.

There is a further consideration, of course, and this is that in future BVA may choose to be partner to research without necessarily conducting it itself. Indeed, there might be an argument to say that such a division of labour would be both logical and effective, leaving BVA free to focus on what it has developed as core activity – being an action-based placement, referral and brokerage volunteer agency, challenging the boundaries of "formal" volunteering and providing organisations who host volunteers with key infrastructural support.

However they might be handled, we have identified four priorities for research and activity:

- The development of effective strategic interventions in volunteering support and development.

- Assessment of the effectiveness and/or impact of such interventions.

- Assessment of the contribution made by volunteering against specific policy or strategy objectives (as outlined in the volunteering framework concept, for example).

- And investigation to see whether research adopting a cost-benefit analysis approach (comparing volunteer provision with statutory service provision) can be viably developed and carried out.

In our view, the usefulness of this approach is that it focuses on covering the key operational concerns that BVA and BVSC share:

- The design and delivery of effective volunteering interventions – namely, improving and strengthening the support infrastructure.

- Evaluation of the effectiveness and impact of such interventions.

- Development of a policy-linked volunteering framework as a guide to prioritising action.

- And the more innovative notion of cost-benefit analysis of volunteer provision.

The "customer relationship"

Finally, something should be said about BVA's continuing role as a promoter and advocate of volunteering directly to the public and its signposting, referral and brokerage role to the wider voluntary and community sector. While a more strategic volunteering framework that can inform the nature and intention of BVA's volunteering interventions is crucial, the direct delivery elements of BVA's work – its support, signposting, referral and brokerage roles – are also vital to the continuing health of volunteering in Birmingham. These should be seen as complementary, each reinforcing and informing the other.

However, while it is clearly important that BVA's interventions are guided by a strategic framework, at "street level" it is crucial that volunteering is presented – as we suggested earlier – in a way that resonates with, and plays to the values of, volunteers and prospective volunteers. BVA is uniquely well situated to combine these roles and adopting a more "departmentalised" approach – distinguishing, as suggested, between personal, community and civic volunteering – could play an important part in ensuring that the right kind of messages reach the right kinds of volunteers.

Conclusions

In the final analysis, then, certainly as far as BVA and BVSC are concerned, available resources will to a large extent determine the future of both volunteering interventions and research. But there is a broader point to be made here. We have said that those supporting and promoting volunteering from within the sector share a common interest with government in seeking to spread the benefits that derive from volunteering, but that these interests are not strictly co-terminus. The voluntary sector also has a duty to safeguard the voluntary nature of volunteering and to ensure that it does not become proscriptively attached to the state's social policy agenda. This is not only necessary, it is a legitimate role of the sector.

A fruitful relationship has been developed in Birmingham between BVSC and the Active Communities Directorate and this has enabled us to think more systematically, more critically and more creatively about volunteering in the round than has ever previously been the case. It has facilitated the instructive process of utilising research to inform and modify the actions and priorities of Birmingham's main volunteer agency and has enabled us to examine a number of different options for BVA's future work.

But how government fosters, resources and keeps open the channels of this debate present something of a challenge. There must be room for dissenting views and for the healthy scepticism that comes so naturally to the voluntary sector.

There must also be space to develop new ideas rather than fall back on the comfort of preconceived ones. Indeed, without a wider debate conducted in this spirit, it is unlikely that government can rise to the biggest challenge of all: how to harness volunteering to its longer-term social policy goals without compromising the very principles and values on which it is founded and which to a great degree motivate individual volunteers.

References

British Government Home Office (2001) *Community Cohesion: Report of the Independent Review Team, Chaired by Ted Cantle.* London: Home Office Communication Directorate.
Available at: http://image.guardian.co.uk/sysfiles/Guardian/documents/2001/12/11/communitycohesionreport.pdf (accessed on 1 August 2005).

British Government Home Office (2002a) *Initial Findings from the 2001 Home Office Citizenship Survey.* London: Home Office Communications Directorate. Available at: http://www.homeoffice.gov.uk/rds/pdfs2/acuactcomm.pdf (accessed on 1 August 2005).

British Government Home Office (2002b) *Connecting Communities: Proposals for Race Equality Support Programmes.* London: Home Office Communications Directorate. Available at: http://www.homeoffice.gov.uk/docs/conncomsconpaper.pdf (accessed on 1 August 2005).

British Government Home Office (2003a) *Civil Renewal: A New Agenda, The CSV Edith Kahn Memorial Lecture.* London: Home Office Communications Directorate. Available at: http://www.homeoffice.gov.uk/comrace/active/civil/index.html (accessed on 1 August 2005).

British Government Home Office (2003b) *Active Citizens, Strong Communities: Progressing Civil Renewal.* London: Home Office Communications Directorate. Available at: http://www.homeoffice.gov.uk/comrace/civil/index.html (accessed on 1 August 2005).

Brown, G. (2004) *Speech to the NCVO National Conference, 9 February 2004.* Available at: http://www.ncvovol.org.uk/asp/search/ncvo/main.aspx?siteID=1&subSID=206&sID=18&documentID=1942 (accessed on 1 August 2005).

Fabian Society (2004) *Fabians Present Chancellor with a Blueprint for his National Community Service Scheme.* London: Fabian Society. Available at: http://www.fabiansociety.org.uk/press_office/news_latest_all.asp?pressid=296 (accessed on 1 August 2005).

Local Government Association (LGA) (2002) *Guidance on Community Cohesion.* London: LGA. Available at: http://www.homeoffice.gov.uk/docs2/cc_guidance.html (accessed on 1 August 2005).

Putnam, R. (2000) *Bowling Alone.*

New York: Simon and Schuster.

Severn, A. and Potter, T. (2003) *Because We Want To ... Volunteering Development in Birmingham BVSC RiSi Report (Birmingham Voluntary Services Council and Research Information and Sector intelligence).* Birmingham: BVSC.

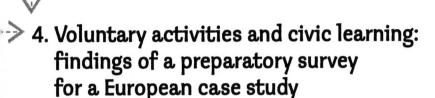

4. Voluntary activities and civic learning: findings of a preparatory survey for a European case study

Gerd Mutz and Eva Schwimmbeck

Introduction

On the basis of biographical data of young people in seven European countries (United Kingdom, Denmark, Netherlands, Germany, Poland, Hungary, Spain) we examined social and civic learning processes in the wake of voluntary activities. The following observations are preliminary findings for the research is still in progress, though we do believe we are in a position to elaborate the most significant differences on country-specific particularities.

With reference to the actual state of the respective academic debate, it is safe to say that the effects which are generated by voluntary engagement of young people are not well understood. Only a few studies concentrate on the question of how learning in this special sphere is structured and whether or not learning processes of any kind do take place at all. The question of what it is exactly, that might be learned in the wake of voluntary activities, is disputed as well.

First of all we have to point out that there is a difference between social and civic learning. On the one side it is stated that voluntary activities bring about processes of social learning, meaning the advancement of informal social competences. The other side points to the civic aspects of voluntary activities, aiming at the promotion of abilities to engage with civil society, thus contributing to community and societal cohesion and integration. This form of learning can be called civic learning. While social learning in the sense of social competences refers to the private sphere, civic learning alludes to the public or societal dimension – in a wider sense to the constitution of social capital.

The proclamations of the European Union often intermingle these meanings and, as a result, do not make clear the distinctions between the individual profit through personal development and the public advantages of an active citizen. The prominence of voluntary activities is furthermore regularly diminished by its understanding as a labour market or socio-political resource only. In the following commentary, we will focus on the social and civic dimension of learning processes in the context of voluntary activities of young people. On the basis of our preliminary empirical surveys we can demonstrate that voluntary activities generate learning processes conducive to social solidarity, social affiliation and to the strengthening of social capital. In this sense we can affirm that the voluntary engagement of young people does engender civic learning processes.

Three different dimensions, which can vary regionally or at national level, are of importance in this respect:

- Learning processes within the framework of voluntary activities differ from learning processes in other spheres. There are specific characteristics of social and civic learning.

- If we take voluntary activities as a particular framework for learning processes, we can distinguish beneficial and constraining conditions for social and civic learning.

- It is of eminent relevance how the proximal social environment influences and reacts to the voluntary activities of young people and how societies transmit appreciation and recognition of voluntary activities.

If we look at civic activities and learning in the different countries there are significant differences concerning social and civic learning.

The specific characteristics of social and civic learning

Learning processes in the context of voluntary activities follow a genuine "logic", discerning them from other social contexts and featuring a number of particularities.

a) Learning in the scope of voluntary activities is not formalised. This implies that the barriers to these learning processes are relatively low – which boosts the willingness of young people to engage in this field.

b) We are confronted with a type of learning that is centred on practical activities and everyday life experiences. This marks a great difference to learning processes in the education and schooling context where learning is (in general) more theoretical and less practical in its orientation and conveyance. Young people do not expect a specific learning potential in their voluntary activities. For them, voluntary activities are more about "learning for life" in the sense of a general attitude towards life and normative orientations.

c) Learning within the limits of voluntary activities is self-initiated and on one's own responsibility.

d) Of special interest is the finding that – from young people's perspective – the learning processes are not of an individual kind. In the wake of voluntary engagements activities are implemented together and collective experiences take place, resulting in respective learning processes. This means the young people do not ascribe these experiences to personal efforts or their individual learning capacities but rather to common activities. We find a clear case of collective learning within a group of young people.

Learning conditions in the context of voluntary activities

Independent of the individual faculties of the young people, the general conditions of voluntary activities are pivotal in determining whether or not these experiences lead to social or civic learning. The following dimensions have to be kept in mind.

a) Our empirical findings point out that the duration and intensity of the engagement are decisive. The longer and more intense the engagement, the more sustainable learning process. These aspects are substitutable: we were able to observe fields of voluntary activities in our study where people were only engaged until a certain goal was reached – the accompanying experiences were so intensive, though, those sustainable learning processes were ignited. For example, this is the case with citizen's initiatives or action committees. Social and civic learning remains almost ineffective, however, when the engagement provides deep but overwhelming experiences, which cannot be properly reflected.

On the other hand, long lasting and constant engagement can foster social and civic learning as well, even if the field of action does not offer a great depth of experience. This is the case with forms of engagement oriented more towards sociability or companionability, such as in some sectors of voluntary activities associated with sports, entertainment and diversion.

b) It is fundamental, whether the civic activities allow for an active participation and the chance of a self-determined intervention by the young people.

c) The field of voluntary action also has to provide opportunities to bring out the experience of responsibility for young people. This placing and assuming of responsibility seem to represent the vital variable for the question of whether a truly social and civic learning is initiated and whether a continuing voluntary engagement is sustained.

The social environment

The voluntary engagement of young people requires social flexibility. It is often a big step to enter the world of voluntary activities and to tolerate learning processes under unfamiliar conditions. It takes courage for young people to discover this world and to expose themselves to these unfamiliar experiences. But young people do not get involved in these matters with the overriding goal in mind to gain social skills or to create social capital. Instead, the successful application of the newly acquired experience depends heavily on the social environment, though civic experiences have to be transferable to other spheres of living in order to support social skills, cohesion and social capital building processes. Therefore, a transformation mechanism between the voluntary activities and other spheres of living has to be established.

It is because of these interrelations that the reaction of the proximate social environment – family, friends, teachers and colleagues – to young people's voluntary activities is of such great importance. It is absolutely crucial as to whether the respective voluntary activities are regarded as socially acceptable forms of engagement in this social context. The importance of these interrelations becomes obvious in the following illustration. It demonstrates the process of sustainable learning in civic activities.

The first step in the process of effective learning requires an acknowledgment of the civic experiences by the private network. This confirmation is bound to two conditions. It results on the one hand from attention from the proximate social environment, and on the other from access to mutual communication about civic experiences which is performed in an arena of discussion. Talking about experiences is the basis for sustainable learning. Until such an exchange has taken place, there will not be a development of a consciousness of experience which in turn can then lead to self-confidence.

Both reflection and self-confidence are necessary to enhance sustainable social and civic learning which can be applied in another social context. In addition, it is better if they are embedded in external institutions, which also have to provide support for reflection.

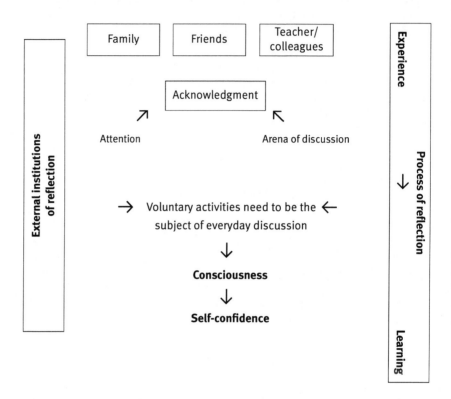

In order that the experiences of voluntary activities can be transformed and that civil society can benefit from them, further attendant support is necessary. Only with professional assistance can social and civic learning processes be sustainable. The intense experiences of voluntary activities alone, especially when they touch the young people emotionally and constitute unforgettable adventures, are not sufficient. Experiences in an unfamiliar world, which are not deliberated and reflected upon, may even have an opposite and counterproductive effect. On their own, experiences deriving from voluntary activities cannot enhance social skills and deploy a civic impact. Personal as well as societal recognition and acknowledgment is a key variable for the effectiveness of voluntary learning.

International comparison

At the current stage of our empirical research (which is yet to be completed), we can state significant differences between four types of countries concerning social and civic learning from experiences in voluntary activities. The most significant dimensions of learning processes and their distinctive characteristics in the respective country type are given below.

United Kingdom		Poland, Hungary	
Character of civic activities and learning	Idea of associations, idea of community oriented learning: chance for networking	**Character of civic activities and learning**	Civic activities with strong reference to individual usefulness
Acknowledgment	High value on community participation	**Acknowledgment**	Accepting of group membership in "secret societies"
Citizenship/civic learning	Model of active (modern) citizenship	**Citizenship/ civic learning**	Model of passive citizenship
Social skills/ social learning	Implicit knowledge	**Social skills/ social learning**	Deliberated learning in order to get social skills
Denmark, Netherlands, Germany		**Spain**	
Character of civic activities and learning	Experiences for personal fulfilment, importance of getting together	**Character of civic activities and learning**	Emphasis on productivity, importance of family structures
Acknowledgment	Importance of having a distinguished position	**Acknowledgment**	High significance of cohesion in family networks
Citizenship/ civic learning	Model of citizenship in transition	**Citizenship/ civic learning**	Model of traditional citizenship
Social skills/ social learning	Necessity to bridge different spheres	**Social skills/ social learning**	Implicit knowledge

The idea of community learning is important and prevalent in the UK. It is the ideology of associations which shape the background for civic activities. This makes it possible to network in a broader sense, including connections into the business world. The idea of engaging in the community is about getting everyone involved and having an impact within civil society. Being an active citizen means participation and contributing to public welfare. In this type of country we can observe a modern and societal form of citizenship. Engaged young people get attention because they are involved in community activities. Their civic experiences are memorised like implicit knowledge. Implicit knowledge cannot be acquired consciously and cannot simply be transferred into other spheres of living, though it is potentially knowledge which can be activated if required (for example at the workplace).

In east European countries like Poland and Hungary, learning in civic activities has an instrumental character. Learning processes are oriented towards employment needs. Learning takes place in interest-oriented environments. There is no community affiliation or solidarity in a communitarian sense. Therefore young people do not feel as though they are active citizens as they are in the UK. There is boundary diffusion between individualism and public orientation. In fact they act as "secret societies" which have the effect of socially closed organisations. Young people get recognition because of their social power which is solely based on group membership in these secret societies. As a consequence of the instrumental character of civic activities young people get engaged in order to get social competences meeting their particular interests. We rarely find distinct forms of civic learning.

In countries like Denmark, Netherlands and Germany, the characteristic of civic learning is ambiguous. On the one hand, civic activities are self-centred which means that engaged young people look for personal fulfilment and growth. On the other, young people just want to club together while doing socially good actions. This characteristic of civic activities holds specific difficulties for learning processes in general. In these countries the state of being an honourable volunteer is important. Civic activities which are associated with responsibility and respect receive most attention. This special character of civic activities causes problems because there is a need for bridging these to other areas of life. There seems always to be a gap between volunteer activities and other parts of life.

In the southern countries, namely in Spain, civic activities mean productive activities in a more economic sense. Engaged young people try to be creative. The central concern is the cohesion of traditional family organisations and community structures. Young people get attention from other people because they are influential members of these strong relationships. Learning in civic activities and communities is quite traditional. It is not a modern form of citizenship like in the UK. Engaged young people get social skills in the form of implicit knowledge, which can be activated if required.

Conclusions

Through an empirical study we examined the impact of civic activities in seven European countries. The question was whether active EU citizenship and employability can be achieved through various forms of civic activities among young people. First, we can state that empirical evidence shows that young people get important experiences while involved in civic activities. But we do not know much about the learning processes in these activities and whether it is possible to transform these experiences into habits and skills. Without further evidence it is not sufficient to state that civic activities are good for enhancing civic habits and social skills. Therefore we have to learn more about the transformation process and the usefulness of these experiences. Beyond this we have to distinguish between civic learning (to enhance social capital and to grow into a civic habit) and social learning (to get social skills in order to use them at the workplace).

Focusing on the learning process itself we can say there are specific characteristics and a genuine logic when we look at civic activities as a learning field. As opposed to formal learning, young people who practicipate in non-formal learning civic activities need greater time for reflection on the experiences and greater professional support from external institutions. These institutions should provide assistance for young people to reflect their experiences in order to apply what one has learnt in other social contexts. From our findings we are convinced that civic activities avail social and civic learning processes but there is still the problem of its transformation in other spheres of life. To achieve this, it is most important they get attention and encouragement from family, friends and teachers (at school) or colleagues (in the workplace). We can state there is a need for a framework to supply sustainable learning. In this sense it becomes obvious that learning in civic activities must become a subject of everyday conversation in the private network.

Looking at the various European countries and their very different living conditions we found that the process of reflection and transformation is dependent on the national or cultural characteristics of civic activities and which concepts of citizenship predominate. It makes a difference whether people live in modern or traditional concepts of citizenship and whether a society has developed an active or a more passive citizenship. Therefore, there is still clearly a need to analyse further the national and cultural differences that evidently exist within Europe, in order to understand the place and impact of voluntary activities within them.

Part 2

Mapping the landscape and framing the debate

1. Young people in Scotland: those who volunteer and those who do not

Diane Machin

introduction

A UK-wide National Survey of Volunteering in 1997 indicated that 43% of 16-24 year olds were involved in volunteering, a decrease from 55% in an earlier survey conducted in 1991. The report caused concern with its conclusion that there had been a "sharp reduction in levels of participation by young people aged 16-24" and that young people "were considerably less likely to be involved on a regular basis" than they had been in previous years (Davis-Smith 1998). Subsequent research in Scotland sought to explore whether volunteering is sufficiently user-friendly for young people (Volunteer Development Scotland 1999b). The study found that while the experience of young volunteers in Scotland is primarily a positive one and levels of satisfaction are high, a number of areas of concern existed. These included:

- a failure of adult society to present volunteering to young people as a realistic and attractive option;

- under-representation of young people who are not white, female and in education;

- outwith the voluntary youth sector, some organisations struggling to have any meaningful involvement of young volunteers;

- unequal treatment of young volunteers compared to older volunteers in some organisations, and tacit barriers to their full participation.

Volunteering agencies also faced problems with high turnover rates of young volunteers and were having to compete with increased demands on young people's time and resources (Volunteer Development Scotland 1999b).

Similar research in England and Wales explored the conditions and incentives that attract young people to voluntary work and the most effective ways of publicising and marketing volunteering opportunities to young people (Gaskin 1998). This study concluded that the essential requirements of volunteering for 16-24 year olds are flexibility, legitimacy, ease of access, experience, incentives, variety, organisation and laughs (or "FLEXIVOL").

Being young in Scotland

In 2003 YouthLink Scotland commissioned MORI Scotland to undertake a major survey of a representative sample of 3 000 11-25 year olds across Scotland. The survey explored young people's characteristics, the things they like to do and their attitudes and opinions on a range of issues. The opportunity was taken to ask a number of questions about young people's involvement in volunteering and the data provide some insights into what can facilitate and what appears to hinder their involvement.

11-16-year-olds in Scotland

Young people aged 11-16 (n=2 124) were asked what they are most likely to do in their spare time. While listening to music and visiting friends' houses were the most popular activities, 11% of respondents said they were most likely to "give up some time to help others (that is, volunteering)". Young people aged 11 and 12 were significantly more likely than those aged 13-16 to say they were likely to volunteer in their spare time and girls (13%) were significantly more likely than boys (9%) to say they volunteered.

The data suggest that young peoples' perceptions of their academic ability may influence their participation in volunteering – those who expected to leave school with Standard Grade qualifications were significantly more likely than those who expected to leave with Highers to say they were likely to volunteer in their spare time. Similarly, those who thought it was "very" or "fairly likely" that they would go to further or higher education college were significantly more likely than those who thought it was "very" or "fairly likely" that they would go to university to say they volunteered. This suggests two things:

- among the 11-16-year-old age group, volunteering might be regarded as being a predominantly vocational activity that is particularly suitable for people with average academic aspirations; or

- those with higher academic aspirations may feel that they have less time to devote to volunteering because they have to devote more time to their studies.

Support for the former suggestion comes from the finding that young people who believe they do not "have good job prospects in the future" are significantly more likely than those who feel they have good job prospects, to say they volunteer.

Over one quarter of 11-16 year olds (28%) stated they would like to do more volunteering in their spare time, with girls (35%) being significantly more likely than boys (20%) to want to do more. Those who expected to leave school with Highers and those who thought it was "very" or "fairly likely" that they would go to university were significantly more likely than those who thought they would leave school with standard grades and those who thought they would go to college to say they would like to give up more time to help others. This finding supports the suggestion that those young people who are more academically orientated have less time for voluntary activity. Table 1 shows the proportions of young people saying they would like to give up more of their spare time to help others.

↑ European youth voluntary activities

Table 1: Young people who volunteer and who would like to volunteer in their spare time

	Expect to leave school with Standard Grades	Expect to leave school with Highers	Very/fairly likely to go to FE/HE College	Very/fairly likely to go to university
Most likely to give up some spare time to help others	216 12%*	166 11%	188 13%*	158 11%
Would like to give up more time to help others	532 29%	461 30%*	432 29%	448 31%*

* Difference significant at p<0.05 level.

Over one quarter of 11-16 year olds (29%) thought it was "very" or "fairly likely" they would "take a gap year/do voluntary work" when they left school. However, just 6% hoped to work overseas as a volunteer. The data show that aspirations change with age, as 15 and 16 year olds were significantly more likely than 11-14 year olds to say they hoped to work overseas as a volunteer. Girls in Scotland were significantly more likely (7%) than boys (4%) to say they hoped to volunteer overseas but this appears to arise from girls being more outward focused rather than from them being more inclined to volunteer – that is, girls were also significantly more likely than boys to say they hoped to study and work in another European country.

Volunteering appears not to feature highly in young peoples' information needs – just 13% of 11-16 year olds said they would find it useful to have information or advice on volunteering. Young people aged 11-12 were most likely to say they would like information on this issue and girls were twice as likely as boys to want information.

One in five 11-16 year olds (21%) believe that volunteering to do things is one of the most important things that make someone a good citizen. This proportion is greater than that believing voting in elections makes someone a good citizen. Again, age is influential, with 11-12 year olds being significantly more likely than 13-16 year olds to say that volunteering makes someone a good citizen.

In addition to exploring what young people aged between 11 and 16 like to do in their spare time, the survey asked specifically whether they would consider doing some voluntary work. Chart 1 shows that almost half (47%) said they would consider doing voluntary work during school time (that is, within the school's curriculum and organised by the school). One quarter of young people (26%) said they would consider doing voluntary work in their own spare time in their community. Taken together, two in three 11-16 year olds (61%) said they would consider doing voluntary work.

Chart 1: Proportion of 11-16 year olds who would consider doing some voluntary work

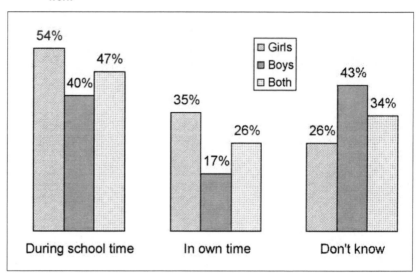

Again, girls were significantly more likely than boys to say they would consider doing voluntary work in both scenarios. The data suggest that household composition might have an impact on young people's perceptions of the amount of free time they have available for volunteering. Those from households in which both parents work were significantly more likely (48%) than those from households where one (42%) or no parents (40%) worked to say they would consider doing voluntary work during school time.

A young person's family can have a substantial impact upon their attitude towards volunteering. Research by MORI in England and Wales shows that while school is a highly influential factor in encouraging young people to volunteer, family influence is also crucial. Three quarters of adults who had participated in voluntary work in the previous year said they encourage their children to undertake voluntary work and half said they themselves had been encouraged to undertake voluntary work by their own parents (MORI 2000).

The Being Young in Scotland survey shows that a willingness to help others outside of the family and to engage in activities that could be construed as contributing to active citizenship is firmly established by the time young people reach their teenage years. Chart 2 shows that around half of 11-16 year olds (51%) had given money to charity in the previous six months and around half (49%) had given up their seat to someone else on public transport. The chart shows that helping others is more common amongst girls than boys and this difference is significant in all activities with the exception of "taking part in a sponsored walk or other fundraising event". The chart also shows that encouraging proportions of young people had taken direct action to help specific people, for example by visiting someone to make sure they were all right or by shopping for someone who could not manage for themselves.

Overall, just 5% of 11-16 year olds claimed not to have taken part in any of these activities, a finding that does not correspond with earlier questions on whether young people were likely to give up some of their spare time to volunteer. This

European youth voluntary activities

Chart 2: Things done by 11-16 year olds to help others outside their family in the previous six months

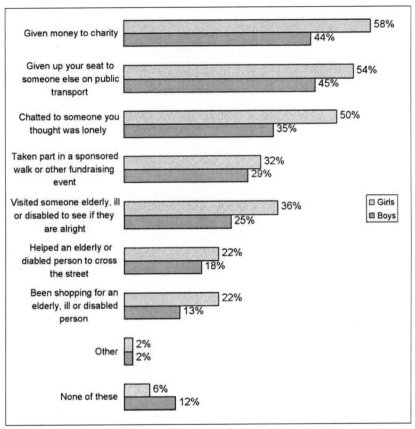

difference may be accounted for in part by the question of whether young people see ways of helping others such as donating money to charity and giving up their seat on public transport as forms of volunteering. Irrespective of whether these activities amount to volunteering, however, engaging in them arguably amounts to active citizenship by young people and contributes to the development of social capital. Young people aged 11-16 are clearly willing to help others but this willingness appears not to be capitalised on to the maximum extent and translated into formal volunteering.

17-25 year olds in Scotland

The Being Young in Scotland survey also sought the views of a representative sample of 972 17-25 year olds across Scotland. Watching television and listening to music are again the most favoured spare time activities but one in ten of this age group said that in a typical week they are most likely to give up some of their spare time to help others (that is, volunteer). Again, females and those at the younger end of the age spectrum (17-20 year olds) were more likely than males and 23-25 year olds to give up their time to volunteer. However, the differences were not significant.

For this age group household composition appears to have an important influence on volunteering – those who are married or living with a partner and those who are home owners are much less likely to give up some of their time to volunteer than those who live with their parents or in rented accommodation and those who are single or of other marital status. It is important to recognise, however, that employment status may also have an influence here – those who are homeowners are more likely to be in full-time employment and, therefore, may have less time to give to volunteering. Indeed, the data show that those 17-25 year olds who are employed are less likely than those who are unemployed, in government work or training or in further/higher education to say they are most likely to give up their spare time to help others.

The relationship between volunteering and 11-16 year olds' expectations of their school leaving qualifications was explored earlier in this chapter and the data indicated that those with higher academic aspirations were less likely to volunteer. This tendency appears to be carried through to actual academic attainment among 17-25 year olds. The data show that those who have a degree and/or professional qualification are less likely to say they will give up some of their spare time to volunteer than those who have vocational qualifications, Highers or School Leaving Certificates. However, the important influence of time should be borne in mind again – those with a degree may be more likely to be in full-time employment and feel they have less time to give to volunteering.

One in ten 17-25 year olds (11%) said that they do not currently volunteer in their spare time but would like to. Again, females (13%) were more likely to express this view than males (9%). Neither marital status nor household tenure appear to have any influence on desire to undertake voluntary work among those 17-25 year olds who do not currently do any.

Those living in urban areas are significantly more likely (16%) than those living in rural areas (9%) to say they would like to volunteer but do not currently do so. However, there is no difference between urban and rural areas in the proportions who say they are likely to give up some of their spare time to help others or those who have volunteered in the past six months. In this respect the profile of 17-25 year olds is different to that of adults who volunteer in Scotland. Data from the Scottish Household Survey, a continuous cross-sectional survey, commissioned by the Scottish Executive, show that rates of volunteering by adults are highest in rural areas and lowest in large urban areas (Scottish Executive 2002, Dudleston et al. 2002).

The survey explored whether 17-25 year olds had "done anything unpaid (that is, volunteered) to help others in the past six months". One in four young people (24%) said they had. Chart 3 shows that there was little difference in the proportions of males and females saying they had volunteered but those at the younger end of the age spectrum (17-18 year olds) were significantly more likely than those at the older end (21-25 year olds) to say they had volunteered. For this age group, however, the relationship to academic aspirations is less clear – 17-25 year olds who were still in education (that is, at school or in further or higher education) were significantly more likely than those who were not in education to say they had volunteered in the past six months. There was little difference between those with different levels of qualification, although those with a degree and/or professional qualification were slightly less likely to say they had volunteered than those with lower qualifications.

European youth voluntary activities

Chart 3: Characteristics of 17-25 year olds who had volunteered in the previous six months

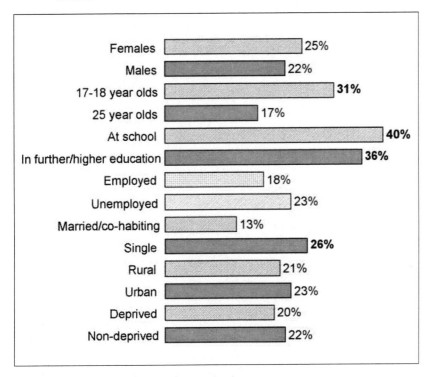

Females	25%
Males	22%
17-18 year olds	**31%**
25 year olds	17%
At school	**40%**
In further/higher education	**36%**
Employed	18%
Unemployed	23%
Married/co-habiting	13%
Single	**26%**
Rural	21%
Urban	23%
Deprived	20%
Non-deprived	22%

NB Figures in bold are significant at the p<.05 level.

For those in employment, time may have been an issue, but the incidence of volunteering was also lower among those who were unemployed and who were not available for work. These findings reflect those for the adult population. The Scottish Household Survey shows that in 2000 18% of unemployed adults volunteered, compared to 28% of adults in employment, 36% of students and 35% of school pupils (Scottish Executive 2002).

Interestingly, one quarter (26%) of those who felt their job prospects were good had volunteered in the past six months compared to just 15% of those who felt their job prospects were not good, a difference that is significant. It is not clear from the survey whether participation in voluntary activities enhances young peoples' positive feelings about their job prospects. However, 17-25 year olds were asked how they would like their volunteering to be recognised and two in five (38%) said they would like a job reference. This was slightly more important to males (39%) than it was to females (37%) and significantly more important to 17-20 year olds than it was to 25 year olds. This suggests that the link between volunteering and employment is of greater importance to young people who are at the start of their careers or work history than it is to those who are established in employment. Those who agreed that their job prospects were good were significantly more likely than those who disagreed to say they would not want any reward or recognition for volunteering. Chart 4 shows the ways in which young people said they would like their volunteering to be recognised.

Chart 4: Ways in which 17-25 year olds would like their volunteering to be recognised

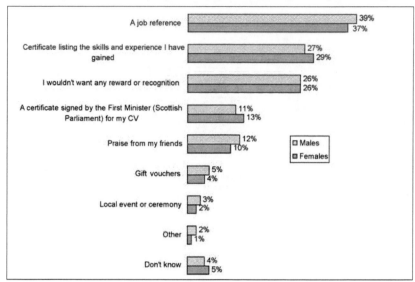

Noticeably, there was little support among 17-25 year olds for financial recognition of volunteering in the form of gift vouchers. This finding concurs with that of an earlier study by the Institute for Volunteering Research (Gaskin 1998) which found that while young people were keen that volunteering should offer the incentive of a reference, certificate or qualification, there was very little support for the idea of financial reward. However, it is at odds with the approach of Young Volunteer Challenge in England and Wales and with the approach recommended for the recently launched Project Scotland (Scottish Executive 2004b).

The survey explored young peoples' awareness of a range of volunteering opportunities available to them. Chart 5 shows that nine out of ten 17-25 year olds had heard of the Prince's Trust, a UK charity that helps 14-30 year olds realise their potential and transform their lives, focusing in particular on those who have struggled at school, been in care, been in trouble with the law, or are long-term unemployed. One quarter of young people (24%) had heard of Voluntary Service Overseas, but just 6% had heard of European Voluntary Service.

Chart 5: Volunteering opportunities heard of by 17-25 year olds

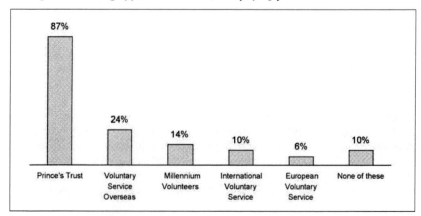

As with the younger age group, volunteering does not feature highly in 17-25 year olds' information needs – just 12% of this age group said they would find it useful to have advice or information on volunteering.

One in ten 17-25 year olds said they hope to work overseas as a volunteer, a higher proportion than among 11-16 year olds. Young people in further or higher education were significantly more likely than others to have this aspiration, as were young people who were single.

One in five 17-25 year olds (19%) thought that "volunteering to do things" is one of the most important things that make someone a good citizen, a slightly lower proportion than among 11-16 year olds. This suggests that the perceived importance of volunteering as a measure of good citizenship decreases with age. However, this perception is not confined to volunteering – fewer 17-25 year olds than 11-16 year olds regard "respecting others"; "having a say in what goes on"; "voting at elections" and "looking after the environment" as being important aspects of good citizenship.

The survey shows that over half of all 17-25 year olds (55%) had given money to charity in the past six months. The proportions of 17-25 year olds who said they had undertaken direct action to help people outside their family are lower than the proportions of 11-16 year olds. However, the greatest decline is in respect of fundraising activities – just 13% of 17-25 year olds said they had taken part in a sponsored walk or other fund-raising event in the previous six months, compared to 31% of 11-16 year olds. Clearly this particular type of voluntary activity is more attractive to young people at the younger end of the 11-25 year old age spectrum. Information from other surveys, however, indicates that interest in this type of activity may pick up again – the Scottish Household Survey shows that almost half of adults who volunteer in Scotland (45%) are involved in fundraising (Dudleston et al. 2002). Overall, 13% of 17-25 year olds said they had not taken part in any activities to help others in the last six months, more than twice the proportion of 11-16 year olds. Chart 6 below shows that males were more likely than females to have not done any of the things mentioned, a trend that continued from, but is less pronounced, than that among 11-16 year olds.

Chart 6: Things done by 17-25 year olds to help others outside their family in the previous six months

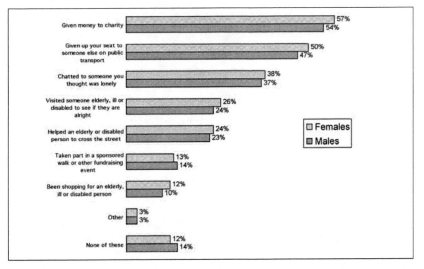

The survey sought to explore the attitudes of 17-25 year olds on a number of social issues. Analysis of the data shows that those who had done voluntary work in the last six months appear to be more conservative in their views and have a stronger environmental conscience than those who had not done voluntary work and than all 17-25 year olds. Chart 7 shows that 29% of those young people who had volunteered either tended to disagree or strongly disagreed that "on the whole television is more of a good influence than a bad one". This compares to 19% of people who had not volunteered and 25% of all 17-25 year olds. Those who had volunteered were more inclined to agree that the Internet will have a detrimental effect on moral values and that sex and violence on television should be subject to greater control. They were also more inclined to disagree that the environment is the subject of too much concern and that there is little ordinary people can do to protect the environment.

Chart 7: Social and environmental attitudes of 17-25 year old volunteers and non-volunteers

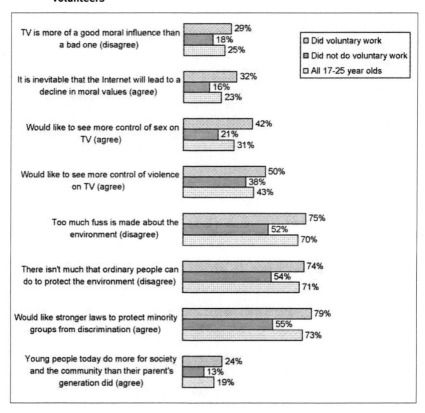

Conclusion

The Being Young in Scotland survey shows that 24% of 17-25 year olds have undertaken voluntary activity in the past six months. It is not clear from other data available on Scotland whether this is a healthy proportion or not – the Institute for Volunteering Research 1997 UK Survey of Volunteering found that 43% of 16-24 year olds across the UK and 50% of adults in Scotland were engaged in formal volunteering; however, data from the Scottish Household Survey showed that in 2001

25% of adults in Scotland had volunteered through a group, club or organisation in the previous year. Research commissioned by Volunteer Development Scotland in 2002 showed that 20% of the adult population in Scotland had volunteered in the past year, but a subsequent survey (that used different wording in the questions) put the proportion at 38%.

It is clear, however, that the proportion of 17-25 year olds, who say they have actually volunteered, is substantially lower than the proportion of 11-16 year olds who say they would be willing to consider volunteering (61%). The Scottish Executive launched a new Volunteering Strategy for Scotland in May 2004 and one of its four key strands focuses on young people. The strategy aims to "increase the range of young Scots aware of volunteering and the benefits it brings to volunteers, communities and organisations, as well as improving awareness amongst young people of how to access volunteering". The results of the Being Young in Scotland survey suggest that many 11-16 year olds are already aware of volunteering. What appears to be of greater importance for the future of volunteering in Scotland is ensuring that we capitalise on the willingness of young people to volunteer by enabling them to readily access appropriate volunteering opportunities, and retain their interest and involvement in volunteering as they make the transition to adulthood. The Scottish Executive's newly launched "Project Scotland", based on the AmeriCorps model, aims to encourage 16-25 year olds to undertake one year of full-time voluntary work on a modular basis by providing quality-assured placements of three to four months duration, for which volunteers will be paid basic living expenses. The project will make "a concerted effort to attract those from traditionally under-represented groups" into volunteering (Scottisch Executive 2004b). Future sweeps of the Being Young in Scotland survey will provide an opportunity to explore whether Project Scotland has impacted on young peoples' volunteering at a national level.

References

Dudleston, A., Hope, S., Littlewood, A., Martin, C. and Ormston, R. (2002) "Scotland's People. Results from the 2001 Scottish Household Survey". Volume 5, *Annual Report,* Scottish Executive.

Davis-Smith, J. (1998) *The 1997 National Survey of Volunteering.* Berkhamsted: The National Centre for Volunteering.

Gaskin, K. (1998) *What Young People Want From Volunteering.* Berkhamsted: The National Centre for Volunteering.

MORI (2000) "Charitable Giving and Volunteering". *Nestle Family Monitor,* No. 10, Nestle UK Ltd., p. 9. Available at: http://www.nestle.co.uk/about/familyMonitor (accessed 27 July 2005).

Scottish Executive (2002) *Volunteering in Scotland: Evidence from the Scottish Household Survey 2000.* Edinburgh: Astron.

Scottish Executive (2004a) *Volunteering Strategy 2004-09.* Edinburgh: Astron.

Scottish Executive (2004b): *Working Group Report into a National Youth Volunteering Programme.* Edinburgh: Astron.

Volunteer Development Scotland (1999a) *Volunteering: User-friendly for Youth? A Study of Volunteering by Young People in Scotland.* Stirling: Volunteer Development Scotland.

Volunteer Development Scotland (1999b) *Volunteering: User-friendly for Youth? A Study of Volunteering by Young People in Scotland. Executive Summary.* Stirling: Volunteer Development Scotland.

Volunteer Development Scotland (2003) *Research Findings Scotland No 2. Research on Volunteering in Scotland.* Stirling: Volunteer Development Scotland.

2. Youth civic service in Europe: comparison of policies and programmes – France, Germany, Italy, Czech Republic, Poland and at European level

Regine Schröer [1]

Introduction

Voluntary and civic service programmes provide a wealth of evidence confirming the contribution of voluntary service to society and the young people themselves. But until now, international voluntary service in the EU has been restricted to a small number of young people. The European Voluntary Service (EVS) programme of the European Commission is by far the largest source of financial support. In 2003, 3 500 young people performed voluntary service in a European country other than their own for periods of between three and twelwe months. Under the current Youth programme (2000-06) there is little prospect of any significant increase in the number of participants. The number of privately funded programmes[2] does not at all satisfy the demands of young people.

This research study has been carried out at a time when several European countries are in transition from compulsory military service to a professional army. In this context, they are in the process of establishing legal frameworks which set the conditions in which volunteers and organisations can receive state support. All frameworks foresee opportunities for youth civic and voluntary service abroad and some offer the possibility of receiving foreign volunteers.

Interest in the development of civic service is growing – youth voluntary service being one of several forms – not only in Europe, but also worldwide (McBride, Benitez and Sherraden 2003). Civic service is considered a means of active citizenship and non-formal education. This article presents only the first results of the research study.

1. First results elaborated by Regine Schröer (MA). Co-ordination of the research by Regine Schröer and John Stringham (Association of Voluntary Service Organisations). Academic Supervision by Holger Backhaus-Maul, Martin Luther University of Halle-Wittenberg, Germany, and Gisela Jakobs (Ph.D.), Fachhochschule Darmstadt, Germany. National research carried out by Valérie Becquet (Ph.D.) in co-operation with Eric Sapin, Comité de Coordination pour le Service Civil (France); Wolfgang Schur (MA), Ost-West Institut für Sozialmanagement e.V. (Germany), Prof. Pierluigi Consorti (Ph.D.), University of Pisa – Interdepartmental Centre of Sciences for Peace, and Licio Palazzini, National President of Arci Servizio Civile (Italy).

2. Foundations and international voluntary service organisations.

The study aims to understand the legal, financial and administrative frameworks for youth voluntary and civic service that are developed in France, Germany and Italy. The reports on Poland and the Czech Republic illustrate the situation in two new member states from central and eastern Europe in the enlarged European Union. The study compares the national policies and programmes in order to identify the major incompatibilities regarding international youth voluntary service.

The development of policies and programmes at European level is also explored in addition to the comparative approach of the different youth and civic service programmes at national level. The special status created for the EVS programme in most countries and its impact on national youth policy development is an example of the interaction between both levels.

The parallel analysis of the national and European frameworks, as well as research into how the different levels interact, aims to identify the incompatibilities for international voluntary service programmes and how they can be overcome. Despite bilateral declarations to develop international volunteer exchange programmes,[1] the legal frameworks for civic and voluntary service in the countries are very different and present many practical and administrative obstacles to their implementation. This study aims to identify the challenges and possibilities to significantly increase the number of international voluntary service opportunities for young people in Europe.

------> Methodology

Methodological approach

The research began in May 2003 and was completed in July 2004. The methodological approach was developed and continually reviewed in three meetings by a research team composed of practitioners from the voluntary service sector and academics from the social and political sciences. The study was co-ordinated by the Association of Voluntary Service Organisations (AVSO), an umbrella for organisations involved in managing full-time, long-term voluntary service programmes.

Originally, there were four countries: Italy, France, Germany and Spain. They were selected because all of them had either recently ended the compulsory military service for young men, or were discussing its end. Each country had established new, or amended existing frameworks for national civic and voluntary service for young men and women. It was also suggested that the development of civic service programmes in three large EU member states would be relevant to the possible development of international programmes at European level. The research in each of the three countries was carried out by the national research partner (and member of the research team) and supported through national funding.

In view of the EU enlargement, the team agreed to explore developments in two countries from central and eastern Europe. Poland and the Czech Republic were selected as both countries had adopted legal frameworks to promote volunteerism in 2003. The research was carried out by the study co-ordinator.

1. Such as *Déclaration sur le volontariat civil* during the summit on 10 November 2001 between France and Germany.

↗ European youth voluntary activities

The research comprises four components:

1) National reports for five countries with an analysis of the political background and the current system of youth voluntary and civic service programmes according to a common structure.

2) Validation through case studies in Italy, France and Germany with experiences of international voluntary service from the perspective of different national stake-holders from a government body and from NGOs using a common questionnaire.

3) Analysis of EU policy, legislation and programming with a focus on European political or legislative instruments and the impact on the development of national political and legal frameworks for volunteers.

4) Comparative analysis and recommendations explaining differences in the countries. Recommendations aim to give practical suggestions on how co-operation between the stakeholders at national and at European level can be facilitated.

Limitations

The study is broad, and the limited time and resources did not allow for an in-depth investigation of all the issues that could affect the development of youth service in the five countries. The study on Poland and the Czech Republic relies only on English and German documents and on interviews with several stakeholders due to the language limitations of the author.

Other limitations are the lack of comparative quantitative data as well as the dynamic situation in each one of the countries. The five countries involved are all in a policy transition period regarding youth voluntary service. The impact of recent legal changes in the countries is examined until April 2004.[1] The research project is considered to be a starting point for the development of comparative research in a new field. Hopefully, it will stimulate similar research on the subject in other countries.

Terminology

The research team agreed in the first team meeting to change the term "trans-national" into "international". According to the typology developed by the Global Service Institute "transnational" programmes are defined as "co-operative pro-grammes between two or more countries where the servers are expected to serve in a host country as well as their country of origin (during the programme)" (McBride et al. 2003:9) while "international" service programmes send people from the home country to another country. According to the definition of the Global Service Institute, the term "civic service" defines "an organised period of substantial engagement and contribution to the local, national, or world community, recognised and valued by society, with minimal monetary compensation to the partici-pant" (McBride et al. 2003:1). "Civil service" or "civilian service" in the five European countries researched is defined as an alternative to compulsory military service for young men and therefore not voluntary.

1. The reports on Italy and the Czech Republic cover developments until August 2004, the other reports present the situation until April 2004.

Youth civic service in Europe

The definition of "voluntary service" can vary according to the organisations or networks active in this field. According to AVSO (2001:7), a "volunteer engaged in long-term voluntary service is someone who:

- is active in an unpaid activity, full-time, for a defined period of time, on the basis of an agreement between her/himself and the voluntary organisations involved;
- serves at home or abroad following a free and informed personal decision without compulsion (direct or indirect) by the state;
- serves in projects which promote the common good and are non-profit making. Projects may be run by non-governmental associations, by religious groups, local authorities, communities, etc.;
- engages in a personal, social and (in the case of international voluntary service) intercultural learning process both individually and in interchange with other volunteers, throughout their period of service."

The group agreed to focus on full-time "international voluntary and civic service" programmes according to the following criteria:

- that they involve young people aged 16-28 who are carrying out a full-time voluntary or civilian service for at least six months in another country;
- that the volunteer is not expected to have special training or skills in advance.

In order to understand the differences in the countries, the research had to look at voluntary civic programmes in the country as well as at the history and the current national civilian service. The age range of the young people recognised in national policies in the five countries differs slightly in regard to the minimum and the maximum ages: 18-28 (Italy), 16-27 (Germany), 16-26 (France), 18-26 (Czech Republic) and 15-25 (Poland).

National reports: an overview

The following section provides a summary of the different national reports on youth voluntary and civic service. They briefly introduce the legal basis for youth voluntary and civic service and other programmes that operate outside the specific legal framework (for a list of legal and administrative documentation, see Appendix 1). They also serve as an anchor for subsequent analysis and recommendations for voluntary activity at an international level, of which the European Voluntary Service programme has been a notable pioneer. Table 1 provides detail of participation in EVS in the respective countries in 2002, in relation both to those young people from those countries who did their voluntary work elsewhere (sending), and those young people from elsewhere who did their voluntary work within those countries (hosting).

Table 1: Implementation of EVS in the five countries 2002

	France 2000-02	Italy	Germany	Czech Republic	Poland
Sending	1373	209	580	46	185
Hosting	924	393	330	28	101
Rejected applications	No information	62 sending/ 157 hosting	367 for sending/hosting in 2001	16 sending/ 12 hosting	No information

France

The tradition of full-time voluntary service in France focused on sending people abroad through organisations officially recognised by the Ministry of Co-operation and Development.[1] Full-time voluntary service on French territory was, due to the high rate of unemployment, always viewed with ambivalence and the fear of introducing low paid jobs. A "new" national service was adopted in France in 1997 together with the transition to a professional army. National service has been replaced by voluntary military and civic service.

The recent adoption of the Law on Voluntary Civic Service *(Volontariat Civil)*[2] further complicates the legal framework. It allows young French people, or citizens from another EU country (18-28 years old), to perform a full-time service in areas of civil defence and security, social cohesion and solidarity, international co-operation, development and humanitarian aid, for a period between six and twenty-four months. The service is regulated by a public-law contract. Civic volunteers are under the responsibility of French ministries. They receive pocket money (exempt from taxes and social security contributions) and basic health care insurance. Their period of service is taken into account for their pension and may contribute to certain diplomas of further education or professional titles. The law also foresees possibilities for a service abroad although these programmes are highly selective.[3]

On 28 July 2003, the French Government published the long awaited Circular DIES No. 2003-001 in order to implement the *volontariat* for social cohesion and solidarity, which was closest to the idea of a national youth civic service. Although originally foreseen, this legal framework does not offer the possibility of performing voluntary service abroad.[4] To date, the government has made no financial commitment to the programme, so its uptake by organisations and volunteers has been slow to develop.

Italy

Until 2001, full-time voluntary service only existed in the field of international co-operation and development work and foresaw services of up to twenty-four months outside of Italy (Law No. 49/1987). The *Decreto del Presidente del Consiglio dei Ministri* (DPCM) of 10 August 2001 created a voluntary civic service and the volunteer status in Italy, preparing the way for the end of the military service in 2004.[5] The transition is legislated in Article 5 of the Law for National Civil Service. Only women and men who are exempt from military service for medical reasons can apply for voluntary service. The programme will be open to all women and men aged between 18 and 28 after the end of the draft. Volunteers can be placed in civic

1. These volunteers benefit from social insurance from the *Caisse des Français à l'étranger,* comprising retirement benefits, civil liability insurance, a lump sum for reinsertion in France plus monthly allowances.

2. Law No. 2000-242 of 14 March 2000.

3. These *volontariats civils* in the field of economic, social and cultural co-operation in French embassies, consulates, Alliance Française or commercial enterprises, are strongly promoted as professional international experience.

4. The law mentioned EVS and the voluntary civic service as a possible combination for young EU citizens doing a service in France. No legal provision has been set up by decree or circular so far to integrate EVS in this context.

5. The Italian Government decided to accelerate the process (see Law No. 77 of 6 April 2002). The draft of compulsory military service will end in December 2004.

service projects in Italy or abroad, either in Europe or in developing countries. EVS remains outside the law. After the service, for pension purposes, it counts as the equivalent of one year's work in a state or governmental office. In 2003, 22390 young volunteers used the possibility to perform national civic service in Italy and 539 abroad.

Germany

Germany is one of the few countries in the EU that has developed the concept of full-time voluntary service within youth policy. Its two laws on voluntary service[1] were amended in 2002.[2] The current law offers greater flexibility in the length of the service (varying between six and eighteen months, in general twelve months)[3] and extends the programme to include conscientious objectors who can perform a twelve-month voluntary service in Germany or abroad instead of their civilian service (ten months). The FSJ can be performed worldwide, but organisations abroad have to fulfil the same criteria as those at national level. Around 15100 volunteers were involved in 2003 in the FSJ/FÖJ programme as well as 3200 conscientious objectors. Nearly 200 volunteers were sent abroad as well as 600 conscientious objectors.

Two international programmes exist in Germany for full-time volunteers abroad outside the framework of these two laws: EVS and "Learning Services Abroad". The latter is organised by churches, social welfare and voluntary service organisations and offers placements between six and twenty four months to people over 18 to develop international exchange and understanding, solidarity, peace and reconciliation. Organisations are not required to contribute to unemployment or pension costs as in the case of the FSJ programme. The parents of the volunteers do not receive any family or child allowance.

The commission on "Impulses for the civic society – Perspectives for volunteer and civilian services in Germany" launched by the Minister for Family, Senior Citizens, Women and Youth in May 2003 put the future development of both services high on the agenda and involved all the major stakeholders in the area of voluntary and compulsory civil service. The report focused on the German situation and asked for state support in the case of the end of the compulsory military service. The abolition of 92000 compulsory civil service placements could only partially be compensated by new volunteer programmes involving men and women of all age groups with flexible service periods, new activity fields and the involvement of new organisations. Pilot programmes will test the new concepts.

Czech Republic

The image of volunteerism in Czech society is still tainted by former experiences of the so-called "volunteering" under the communist regime. The Czech Act on Volunteer Services (zákon o dobrovolnické sluzbe) effective from 1 January 2003 is unique among the countries of central and eastern Europe.[4] Influenced by the

1. Voluntary social year (Freiwilliges Soziales Jahr – FSJ) adopted in 1964 and the voluntary ecological year (Freiwilliges Ökologisches Jahr – FÖJ) adopted in 1993.

2. Law to amend the law promoting the voluntary social year and other laws (Gesetz zur Änderung des Gesetzes zur Förderung eines Freiwilligen sozialen Jahres und anderer Gesetze) came into force on 1 June 2002.

3. Completion of education is required instead of minimum age, enlargement of the range of activities to the cultural and sports fields, enlarging of the programme worldwide.

4. Act No. 198 of 24 April 2002 on volunteer services amending certain regulations (volunteer services act).

design of EVS, the act introduces new terms (volunteer, voluntary services, sending organisations, receiving organisations), which have no historical roots in the Czech legal system. The law is not conceived as a comprehensive framework law for volunteerism. Other forms of voluntary activity may take place outside the law. The law requires written contracts between the volunteers and the sending organisations. Specific requirements are compulsory for long-term service or short-term service abroad.[1] Volunteers must have insurance coverage for health, accident and civil liability. Contracts may stipulate provisions for the pension insurance of the volunteer paid by the sending organisations as the minimal basis, if the service exceeds twenty hours per week. Some 51 projects from 34 organisations had been accredited by 10 August 2004.[2] The majority of recognised project activities are in the field of social services: inclusion of disadvantaged youth, hospitals and centres for disabled persons, integration of ethnic minorities. Volunteer programmes at national level are mostly part time in the social field tackling social exclusion, but also run in the area of environment and cultural heritage.

The "Volunteering of Unemployed People" programme is the only programme at national level involving young unemployed people for four days/week in an NGO. The focus of the programme is less on the development of civic society than to find a job in the labour market.

The end of military and alternative military service announced for December 2004 may strongly influence the development of full-time voluntary service in the country, as organisations need to look for alternative solutions to replace 48 000 conscientious objectors.

Poland

In the context of the struggle for recognition of NGOs by the state and by society, the adoption of the Law on Public Benefit Activity and Volunteerism in April 2003 is very important for the future development of the third sector. The law provides the procedural framework for co-operation between local governments and NGOs, and ensures the protection of volunteers working with accredited organisations regarding health and social security. Volunteers are entitled to receive reimbursement of expenditure for costs like travel and training, as well as a daily allowance exempt from taxes.

The law does not distinguish between part-time and full-time volunteering. The application of this law is very wide and foresees volunteer activities in all the areas of public benefit. The law contains provisions for international voluntary services programmes sending Poles abroad and/or receiving foreign volunteers from other countries. Volunteers are entitled to benefits and reimbursements of their costs "generally acknowledged for the situation" (for example, board and lodging). Besides the "First Job" programme, no official programme specifically promotes full-time voluntary service in Poland. Most organisations work with part-time volunteers who are active in a wide range of fields: youth unemployment, social inclusion, civic society development and lifelong learning. The possible abolition of compulsory military service expected for the years 2006-08 will not have a strong

1. With regard to nature, location and duration of service, preparatory training, specification of food and accommodation conditions for the volunteer, reimbursement of costs linked to preparation, international and local transport costs, payment of pocket money, etc.

2. The list on accredited organisations is available on the website of the Ministry of the Interior: http://www. mcv.cz/Akreditované dobrovolnické organizace.htm.

impact on the development of full-time voluntary service in Poland due to the small numbers of conscientious objectors.

Voluntary service at European level

Alongside these national developments, several activities are currently ongoing at a European level related to youth participation in society and the role of voluntary service. In the follow up to the White Paper on youth policy (European Commission 2001), the Youth Unit of the European Commission send out a questionnaire on "voluntary activity" as one of its priority areas for the Open Method of Co-ordination.[1] The answers of each member states' government (European Commission 2004) were compiled in a synthesis report[2] and the European Commission proposed common objectives for national and EU co-operation in this field in a communication (European Commission 2004) to the Council in April 2004. The report asks all member states to apply the EURecommendation on Mobility of July 2001[2] with regard to volunteers in order to remove obstacles to the freedom of movement in educational and vocational training programmes with a European dimension.

The conclusions of the first Intergovernmental Conference on Civic Service and Youth on 28 and 29 November 2003 in Rome highlighted the need for the systematic and regular exchange of information and good practice for strengthened co-operation between civic services and youth policy, as well as enhanced co-operation among the member states, the acceding countries and the EU in the field of civic service for young people.

In March 2004, the Commission published two communications outlining its general ideas for the future programmes. EVS will be part of the future Youth Programme. Major changes foresee the extension of the target group (13-30 year olds) as well as the simplification and strong decentralisation of the programme. EVS will target 10 000 volunteers per year – compared to 3 500 currently – a total of 70 000 for the duration of the programme. The European Commission is currently discussing how the EVS programme could be linked to a voluntary humanitarian aid corps as declared in the draft constitution. The consultation of all member states in the above-mentioned survey on voluntary activity with regard to this perspective resulted in the general interest of most countries, while several stressed the importance to maintain the educational value of the EVS programme.

Comparative analysis

The comparative analysis is based on the findings of the national reports of the five countries, the analysis of policy and programmes related to youth voluntary service at European level as well as the experience expressed by stakeholders in the interviews in Italy, France and Germany. The comparative analysis has two parts. In all countries, international voluntary service (with the exception of development aid) is a sub-category of voluntary service policy. Therefore it can only be examined once the differences in the national voluntary service schemes are understood. The com-

1. The Open Method of Co-ordination was introduced by the Lisbon European Council 2000 in order to develop a European Union action plan for combating poverty and social exclusion. It offers a means of benchmarking national initiatives, in order to develop a coherent EU approach while respecting the principal of subsidiarity.

2. Recommendation of the European Parliament and the Council of 10 July 2001 on mobility within the Community for students, persons undergoing training, young volunteers, teachers and trainers, *Official Journal* L 215, 09 August 2001.

parative analysis focuses on the different understandings of voluntary service, their history and the political motives behind the development of youth voluntary service in each of the countries concerned, as well as on the differences in implementation of the programmes.

Understanding of voluntary service

(I) Voluntary service, the abolition of obligatory military service and conscientious objection

The development of the legal basis for youth voluntary service programmes in France, Italy and Germany is inextricably linked to the suspension of compulsory military service. The fact that national legal frameworks for youth voluntary service are so closely tied to the phasing out of civilian service performed by conscientious objectors has enormous impact on the nature of the voluntary service programmes. In both Germany and Italy, the public sector and well-established social welfare organisations are still responsible for hosting the bulk of volunteers. In France, associations are more active in the solidarity and social cohesion programme. However, the actual number of young people involved is much lower. Although both the Czech Republic and Poland are considering phasing out compulsory military service, their recent laws on voluntary service are not an attempt to replace the activities of conscientious objectors. The laws are more closely linked to the development of civic society (see below).

(II) Voluntary service and the provision of social welfare services

As mentioned above, the countries with large numbers of conscientious objectors (Italy, Germany and to a lesser extent the Czech Republic) face a significant loss of manpower in the social welfare sector when military service is no longer obligatory. The promotion of youth voluntary service in these countries is therefore partly motivated by the need to retain young people in the social welfare sector. None the less, even where the involvement of conscientious objectors in the social welfare system has been less important, voluntary service is increasingly seen as a means of improving the delivery of services in the face of growing economic pressure and demographic changes. There is a trend in all countries towards giving greater flexibility and autonomy to NGOs in the delivery of social welfare services, and supporting the increased involvement of volunteers. This vision of voluntary service is a strong motivating factor behind the new laws in Poland and the Czech Republic where the legal framework offers a means of facilitating greater co-operation between the government and NGOs.

(III) Voluntary service and youth unemployment

The unemployment rate among young people is more than double the national average in all countries except Germany. In Poland, over 41% of young people under 25 are without work. Governments in all five countries consider the integration of young people into the labour market as a major political priority. Volunteering has been loosely interpreted as a means of providing professional experience and training in the social or non-profit sector. Germany launched the "voluntary social training year" – targeted at young people from disadvantaged backgrounds. Poland initiated the "first job" programme in which voluntary engagement is one of several options. The Czech Government supports a specific programme for young unemployed people through which they work four days/week as volunteers in an NGO or a public institution. The main motivation behind each of these programmes is the professional integration of young people. Training options may be referred to as "volunteering" because they are within the non-profit sector. The criticism of voluntary sector organisations to this motive is that what are essentially training or make-work programmes will be referred to as "volunteering" simply because they focus on work in fields that are within the non-profit sector and that the motive of civic participation will be lost. Table 2 illustrates, across the five countries, levels of youth volunteering and youth unemployment in the context of the overall unemployment rate.

Table 2: Voluntary service and youth unemployment

	France	Germany	Italy	Czech Republic	Poland	EU-15
Number volunteering in thousands/ percentage of young people aged 15-24 (2002)	7726 (13.0%)	9395 (11.4%)	6602 (11.4%)	1496 (14.6%)	6540 (16.9%)	46821 (12.4%)
Total unemployment rate First quarter 2003	9.0%	8.6%	8.9%	6.8%	20.2%	7.9%
Unemployment rate of young people under 25 First quarter 2003	20.6	9.5%	26.8%	16.1%	41.4%	15.3%

Note: data for Italy 2002. *Source: Eurostat news release 35, 20 March 2003.*

(IV) Access to voluntary service

The national frameworks for youth voluntary service are open to all young people. In two countries participation is limited – only to EU-citizens in France and to young Italians in Italy. None of the programmes requires the young person to make a financial contribution, so as to avoid excluding young people on economic grounds. However, in all countries the majority of participants in the national as well as the international programmes are well-educated young people. In the case of Germany and Italy, the demand for placements exceeds supply so organisations can select candidates with the effect of excluding less academic candidates.

The European Voluntary Service programme is the only programme so far with an explicit inclusion policy with regard to young people from disadvantaged backgrounds. However, the percentage of these young people in the programme remains low for a number of reasons.[1] The German law was amended in 2002 to attract new target groups like young people with a migrant background or with low education. The minimum age was lowered and new activities were introduced (like the voluntary social year in sports associations).

(V) Voluntary service and young people

International voluntary service is an attractive option for many young people because it combines individual development (language, international and professional experience) with the feeling of "making a contribution". Demand for EVS placements has increased steadily since the launch of the YOUTH programme in 2000. Many national agencies now have to reject applications. Demand is also high for international placements in the frame of the German voluntary social and eco-

1. Complex administrative procedures at national level, delay of approvals, lack of knowledge of sending and hosting organisations how to deal with these youngsters and insufficient financial support of organisations for preparation, subversion and follow up, see: Schröer, R., Voluntary Service: Opening doors to the future, AVSO, Brussels and AVSO et al, 2003.

> European youth voluntary activities

logical year and many candidates are rejected, even the programmes outside the legal framework, which imply a participation fee and the loss of certain financial benefits (for example, family allowance), are heavily oversubscribed. The French civic programmes abroad, especially the "volunteers in enterprises" have a high number of well-qualified candidates[1] (15 000 since 1 January 2004 and 130 on average every day). While the programme is increasing (2001: 984 volunteers, 2002: 1790 including 194 extensions), available places cannot meet the demand. Organisations in Poland and the Czech Republic are still in the phase of accreditation and the focus of implementation is within the country. The number of accreditations for international youth voluntary service in the Czech Republic is increasing. Four organisations for six programmes are currently registered. Two of them are youth organisations, one of them is a catholic organisation and the fourth is accredited as the Czech focal point of UNV volunteers in the framework of development aid. While demands increase among Italian organisations and volunteer candidates to develop the civil service abroad, the numbers are so far limited due to administrative procedures.

(VI) Voluntary service and international understanding

All countries provide frameworks for young people to go abroad under programmes of international solidarity. All countries mention catastrophe relief, development and humanitarian aid as activities for international service. In contrast, volunteer programmes for international understanding – the focus of this research study – are less well known by politicians and the general public, though the concept of this kind of international voluntary service predates that of national voluntary service. They are accessible to young people on the same basis as national service. Two forms are predominant: international work camps for groups of people living and working together for two to three weeks and individual placements for six to twelve months (sometimes longer). Both give equal weight to the learning experience of the volunteer and the service for international understanding. The duration of recognised international service varies. All the countries studied allow for service abroad from six to twelve months and all programmes require some preparation and training of the volunteers. Beyond this, however, standards vary considerably.

(VII) Voluntary service and European citizenship

It is striking that – with the exception of France – none of the five countries has integrated EVS into their national volunteer frameworks, all of which, however, promote international voluntary service. Only France identifies EVS as compatible in the law on civil service. At least, the hosting part of the EVS programme in France could be integrated in the programme for social cohesion and solidarity as the activities and projects are similar. The implementation is at stake as no legal provision has been yet set up in France to allow associations to combine the two programmes for the hosting of volunteers coming from other EU member states. Only young Italians aged 18-26[2] can participate in the Italian voluntary service programme. Access to the French voluntary service programmes is limited to EU citizens. The restrictive access to both programmes does not allow the participation of third country citizens legally living in the two countries. The three other countries (Czech Republic, Poland and Germany) do not limit participation in their programmes with regard to nationality.

1. Some 56% have spent five years or more in higher education, 28% have three or four years, 10% have two years and 6% have no 18+ education, see Becquet 2004.

2. From 2005: 18-28.

Implementation of voluntary service schemes

(I) Government responsibility

Different ministries are in charge of voluntary service and responsible for the implementation of the laws: the Ministry of Social Affairs in Poland; the Youth Ministry in Germany; the Ministry of the Interior in the Czech Republic; and the Presidency of the Italian Council of Ministers in Italy. In France, the responsibility for the four different forms of civic voluntary service is distributed according to the competences in the relevant sectors. In the area of social cohesion and solidarity (Ministry of Social Affairs), 12 ministries are concerned with its further implementation. While the variety of areas have a lot of potential for the further development of volunteering, it will be more difficult to ensure the co-ordination and the development of common visions for society or for example, international youth voluntary service. All countries have specific legal frameworks for the different forms of voluntary service/activity rather than a general law integrating all forms of voluntary service. Initiatives in Germany and France to set up a more general legal framework have failed so far.

A major challenge will be the development of a common approach, which simplifies administrative procedures but still allows for a diversity of international programmes. Current experience at multilateral or bilateral level is less promising. The administration of the national programmes reflects the limited vision of all five countries in youth voluntary service. EVS and national programmes are managed by separate administrations and rarely tend to communicate or co-operate. The Youth Unit of the European Commission will change the current management[1] of the EVS programme[2] in order to simplify procedures. Administration costs are too high for 3 500 volunteers per year and procedures do not guarantee secure time planning for the organisation of the exchange programme. The French-German agreement on mutual recognition of youth voluntary service has so far failed to facilitate exchanges between organisations in both countries. As the French law is now enforced, it will be interesting to track if the number of French-German exchanges increases.

(II) Programme management: relationship between state and civic society

In Italy, the contract is signed between the National Office (the state) and the volunteer. In France, the contract is signed between the volunteer, the state and the associations.[3] This involves the Italian and the French state more actively in the organisation and supervision of the programmes than in the three other countries where volunteer agreements are based on private contracts signed between the volunteer and the organisation. In all countries the state accredits organisations

1. All EVS projects have to be accredited after submission of a host expression of interest. Application for EVS has to be submitted to the two national agencies in the sending and hosting country. A common decision on the application is not certain as national agencies have set up in each country national priorities for activities, partner countries and are confronted with a limited budget. Organisations are regularly confronted with delays on decision of at least one side and several experienced an approval for one side and a rejection from the other side. The project needs to be approved from both sides to take place.

2. The European Commission decided to introduce "more collective forms" – of EVS namely, funding/ approval for several volunteers together. From September 2004 on, the approval of one national agency may be sufficient to realise the project.

3. If young people from abroad combine the French service with EVS, the European Commission signs the contract with the associations.

either for sending and/or hosting according to specific requirements for the domestic or international voluntary service.

Eligible sending organisations tend to be international NGOs. In addition, French law identifies different beneficiaries for the different programmes. The type of hosting organisations varies from country to country, while all countries recognise the variety of organisations in the non-profit sector (NGOs, municipalities, local authorities, associations, etc.). While the majority of countries (and EVS) restrict placements for volunteers in the profit sector, the French understanding sees it as a co-operation partner for the development of international youth voluntary service.

(III) Activity areas of voluntary service

Some countries have specific requirements for international projects. In Italy, projects have to either support foreign countries or Italian communities abroad. The international frames of the two German programmes focus on reconciliation, international solidarity and understanding. The Czech act refers to the assistance in the implementation of development programmes and Poland mentions activities for the sake of European integration and development of relations and co-operation among nations.[1] The French programme for international volunteering in enterprises identifies other tasks for young people: the research for and the prospecting of new international markets, the technical or commercial reinforcement of local teams, the search for partners, agents or distributors and the creation or set up of local structures.

(IV) Accreditation of organisations

The process of accreditation of sending and/or hosting organisations is different in each country. While the Czech Republic and Italy (for the transition phase until 2005) have central institutions to deal with the applications, the other countries focus on decentralised implementation. The role of the Italian regions and the self-governing provinces will strongly increase in the process after January 2005 with the implementation of the new service. The regions and provinces will have decisive power on the legal and financial aspects of the future programme and the extension of working hours from the current twenty-five hours/week to a possible thirty or thirty-six hours/week.

(V) Pedagogical support

All programmes require preparation and pedagogical training for the volunteers. However, the pedagogical standards vary considerably. Italy, Germany and EVS offer financial support for the pedagogical dimension through lump sums per volunteer. The requirements for seminars for German volunteers abroad[2] represent an obstacle for developing the programme in other countries.

(VI) The legal status of volunteers

The emphasis in all the legal frameworks is, understandably, on the legal status of the volunteers in the country. However, this leaves a hiatus for those volunteers performing voluntary service abroad. None of the legal frameworks gives legal status to EVS volunteers. EVS is incompatible with the national systems. The EVS

1. Poland defines in the law 24 areas of public tasks where volunteers can work. No distinction exists between domestic and international volunteering.

2. Some twenty-five seminar days during twelve months, preparation and evaluation seminars compulsory in Germany during the twelve months and language training in Germany.

programme covers private insurance to all participants. While optimal social protection is desirable for volunteers during their service, this becomes particularly complex and difficult if the provisions for international volunteers (volunteers sent abroad/hosted from abroad) with regard to social security differ from country to country. Differences appear regarding the protection requirements for volunteers' insurance. While all countries specify requirements for health insurance, accident and civil liability are not required for volunteers in Poland.

While pocket money for EVS (€140-220) is at a similar level in Germany (€153 on average),[1] the fixed allowances in France (€570.86) and Italy (€433.80 and €600 abroad) are significantly higher. While the state pays the allowances in Italy, the situation is completely different for French organisations that are requested to cover the amounts. The law in the Czech Republic does not entitle the volunteer to any remuneration, but to the reimbursement of costs for accommodation, food and travel, if they arise in connection with the voluntary activity. Poland defines the reimbursement of expenditure in the same way, but also grants per diems without specifying the amounts.

France, Poland and the Czech Republic declare that the payments are exonerated from taxation, however, Germany and Italy ask that volunteers declare their allowances. In both countries, the amounts remain under the threshold.

Other allowances like child or family benefits are maintained in some countries while in others they are suspended or lost if young people go abroad.[2] The differences apply in similar ways if the young people participate in the EVS programme. The loss of allowances is often a major disincentive to participate for young people with low financial means. Others who ignored the situation encountered the problem on return after the service. In most countries the allowances are no longer paid because the activity is not considered similar to formal training or education.

The situation regarding contributions to pensions and unemployment is also quite problematic and highlights the different status of volunteers in the different countries. While in Germany the volunteers are treated in the same way as workers and vocational trainees, organisations have to cover contributions to the German social security system. Italy and France recognise voluntary service as counting towards for the pension schemes and the state covers the costs, although volunteers are not considered as workers or trainees and therefore, no unemployment contributions are requested from the organisations. The Czech state partly refunds the pension payments for volunteers working more than twenty hours per week. While the act does not require hosting organisations to pay an unemployment contribution, unemployed people involved in accredited volunteer programmes can maintain their unemployment benefits. These volunteers maintain their social status as unemployed because the state considers the activity similar to job seeking.

1. Legislation considers a sum of pocket money appropriate if it does not exceed 6% of the contribution assessment limit valid for the Workers' and Employees' Pension Insurance (Article 159 of the Sixth Book of the Social Code). The contribution limits were fixed in 2002 at a monthly rate of 4500 (in the western part of Germany) and 3750 (in the eastern part). The amount paid to volunteers by the host organisation/project should not exceed this amount and is generally lower, see Schur 2004.

2. While the situation is particularly difficult for young volunteers abroad, the problem is more general: the suspension or loss of benefits occurs also for volunteers in domestic programmes that remain outside the law. In some countries organisations are obliged to remain outside the law because they are not able to pay social security conditions like in Germany or cannot apply like Czech associations membership-based activities of their volunteer members.

(VII) Validation of experiences

The national as well as the European certificate in the frame of EVS are not suffi-ciently recognised in the EU. The problem is partly due to the lack of visibility of international volunteers. Employers and institutions do not know the programmes and experiences in the non-formal sector of education and in most countries these do not have the same value as a formal diploma.

(VIII) Financial support

While all countries recognise the value of voluntary service for society, the state financially supports the national programmes in different ways. In all countries except Poland the support has increased, but is insufficient. In France the support differs from programme to programme, while reimbursing the cost of social insur-ance and counting the time of service for an individual's pension entitlement. Social insurance costs are in most countries covered by the state, except in Poland and in Germany. The latter finance social security costs for conscientious objectors but not for "real volunteers" under the social or ecological year. Only Germany and the Czech Republic, and to a lesser extent Italy, support the costs for pedagogical preparation and training, while the other countries give low importance to the ped-agogical quality of the programmes. Italy is the only country to finance the monthly allowance for the volunteer as well as international travel costs, as the EVS pro-gramme does. These amounts represent significant support for small organisa-tions, which are already struggling for support of their own activities. The Czech Republic is the only country to recognise volunteering as an equal activity to job seeking, maintaining unemployment benefits for that period of time. State support at this stage is important to stimulate programme development as well as to guar-antee quality standards. The general recognition of the value of the programmes needs to be better known and acknowledged in order to allow projects to look for alternative funding resources to state funds since the budget for volunteering will always be limited.

Recommendations

Only those aspects relating to international voluntary service are considered. The examples of best practice are identified to deal with the factors which obstruct the significant development of international and transnational programmes. Sug-gestions are also made for European level co-operation.

Understanding voluntary service

(I) Voluntary service for international understanding

The best policy context is that contained in the EVS enabling legislation. The national policies studied give little or no context for international voluntary service. The exception is when their legislation deals with development aid voluntary service, usually within the foreign policy aspects of foreign aid. In the case of France, the legislation also deals with the context for volunteering in enterprises in other countries (defending and promoting French interests), but in the researchers' opinion, this kind of service should not be included in a definition of voluntary service for international understanding.

(II) Access

International voluntary service is a concept that should be open to all and indeed needs to allow many more to participate in it. There are formal and practical barriers to open access. A good policy deals with both.

(III) Citizenship – Nationals and non-nationals

Germany allows its citizens, foreigners with resident status and refugees allowed to stay in Germany to participate in the programme, as well as nationals of all other countries who come for the purpose of doing a voluntary social or ecological year. This is the most comprehensive framework of the countries studied. Having such a visa status for the voluntary social/ecological year greatly simplifies the process for all concerned. Similarly there are no limits on what countries a German volunteer may go to within the voluntary social/ecological year. They can serve in an OECD country or a less-developed one.

(IV) Minorities, less-educated, lower income, physically disabled, unemployed

The EVS policy of allowing organisations to apply for additional funds for young people with fewer advantages is the only programme which acknowledges explicitly that getting youth who are marginalised to participate in international voluntary service will require additional resources. It suffers, however, from two national agencies needing to agree and from the uncertainty engendered by the "each person is a project" micromanagement approach. The approach does not allow organisations to develop strategies for reaching large numbers of such young people. This is especially difficult because research conducted on less-advantaged youth in EVS shows that close co-operation between youth workers of both sending and hosting organisations and allowing networks of sending and hosting organisations to develop expertise through working with numbers of less-advantaged youth are keys to success.

Where governments express the wish to have a broad participation in civic service and provide monies to enable it to happen, then it does happen. In Germany, the reduction of the minimum age for the Voluntary Social Year and the creation of the Voluntary Social Training Year have resulted in less-advantaged youth and youth at risk participating. However, neither of these approaches has been expanded to international placements. In Italy, the decision to provide a generous monthly stipend and other benefits make the programme attractive to youth from regions of high unemployment. These measures are producing results for service within the country. The effect on applications from less-advantaged youth for international service are not known yet. However, given the experience in EVS of the need for extra support to enable youth with less opportunities even to consider international service, special measures will be necessary for the five national policies for their international service dimensions to be inclusive too.

Implementation

(I) Legal framework

The best general legal framework for voluntary service for international understanding at the moment appears to be that of the Czech Government. It explicitly covers both Czechs serving in their own country and abroad, and foreigners coming to the Czech Republic. It does not set an upper age limit, and so deals with issues such as taxation, etc. that are not age-specific. Further, since state subsidies never cover all costs and organisations must look for additional funding, public policy frameworks must allow for this and exempt such contributions from private individuals and business from taxation. This dimension is not often considered within voluntary service policy.

(II) Government administrative responsibility

Best practice is to have a lead ministry responsible for all framework legislation relating to voluntary service, both national and international. Best practice here appears to be in the Czech Republic where the Ministry of the Interior is responsible for all accreditation issues, with an advisory body from other ministries and NGOs. Ministries can develop promotion policies to encourage volunteering projects in their respective areas. The EVS does not fall within the act or the jurisdiction of the Ministry of the Interior, however. In most other countries, responsibility is more blurred with several ministries and/or regional entities responsible. In France and to a lesser extent Italy, where the relevant framework for national civic service is still national defence and the Ministry of Defence still has a leading role, the confusion is likely to continue. But given the clear profile and relatively autonomous status of the National Office on Civic Service in Italy, the problem there is not so great.

(III) Duration of voluntary service

The Czech and Polish legislations set no minimum and maximum periods. This allows different forms of international service to be covered within one frame. This is helpful for organisations offering international service of different lengths and types. It may also enable more coherent approaches to residency and visa issues.

(IV) Activity areas

The Polish legislation and the French under social cohesion and integration provide examples of the broadest range of social, cultural and environmental activities. Although the activity areas were perhaps not defined with international service specifically in mind, such definitions allow for maximum diversity and flexibility in finding placements for foreign volunteers and in sending volunteers abroad.

(V) Accreditation of organisations

Best practice appears to be the Czech Republic, providing a clear and detailed process for accreditation at national level, including an advisory body with third sector representation to make recommendations. In the other four countries studied, responsibility for accreditation is or will be at a regional level to some extent. At the European level, decision making has been decentralised to the national agencies in the EVS. With regard to regionalisation, the question is unanswered whether an organisation working in more than one region will have to be accredited in all the regions where it places volunteers or only in the region where it has its headquarters.

A key value for good administration anywhere and especially for a policy that sets a high value on accessibility must be simplicity and speed in processing applications and placements. Systems that try to control each volunteer and each placement directly cannot be cost efficient (European Voluntary Service, France). The German and Italian approaches focus on accrediting co-ordinating organisations with the possibility of spot checks on placements the organisations co-ordinate. A similar approach is being started in the Czech Republic.

(VI) Non-formal education and pedagogical support

The German voluntary year legislation sets broad objectives and controls these predominantly through prescribing the number of days volunteers must be in training as a group. The EVS also indicates core themes to be dealt with. A combination of the two would seem to be the most appropriate. However, rigidity about form as in Germany can exclude the development of different approaches to non-formal education and ways of doing projects. The absolute power of national agencies of EVS to decide who will do a training event (some allow the organisations to do their own, others insist on all training being done by trainers they appoint) prevent international networks developing their own concepts and delivering their own training. It also prevents the development of new networks of national or regional organisations that could do the same. A more conciliatory and effective approach is that of the EVS national agency in Germany. It allows organisations to do their own training subject to them meeting minimum criteria in terms of numbers of volunteers and countries represented, subjects covered, etc.

(VII) Legal status

There is no one country that has the best practice here. There seems to be a consensus that voluntary service is not work, therefore unemployment contributions should not have to be made, and that someone who is receiving unemployment payments at the start of her/his service should have them suspended during the service but be entitled to receive them again upon termination. Another point of consensus seems to be that family and other allowances should continue on the same basis as if the person were a student or family dependent. But taxation and other laws are still often applied as though the volunteers were salaried workers.

(VIII) Validation and recognition

Recognition of voluntary service is most established in Germany but only in terms of internships in certain fields. The Italian national office's efforts to have voluntary service recognised for university credits through the Ministry of Education and the university rectors seems a good way forward. Recognition of service for public sector jobs is done in Italy and France. Recognition in business and in other professions is a challenge in all the countries.

(IX) Financial support

It is hard to determine an optimal level of state funding. Obviously, a part of the success of the Italian national voluntary civic service and the EVS is the amount of funding provided per volunteer. However, if the demand greatly exceeds the funding available in the scheme (as in EVS at present), the principle of access for all changes to a more and more exclusive project and volunteer selection. A practical solution used in Germany with regard to distributing limited youth plan funding for training for international voluntary service was to divide the money available on an equal basis among all the accredited applicants for that year. No organisation received 100% of what it had requested, but the equitable treatment provided enough security for most of the organisations to exert themselves to find other funding to continue their programmes.

(X) Information and publicity

Both EVS and the Italian National Civic Service show that a constant multimedia campaign carried out over several years can establish a programme image in the public eye. But without careful management of funds so that demand is more or less met, public support can be lost if the principle of open to all who want to serve becomes contradicted by the numbers refused because of lack of money. What is promoted must be deliverable.

(XI) Developing a European policy on civic service

The analysis shows the necessity to have an exchange of practice and understanding between EU member states and European institutions. Governments need to think of how there could be common national and European recognition/certification of voluntary service experiences. For example, international voluntary service could be certified as a period of intercultural education. Incompatibilities in legal status and the treatment of volunteers going from one European country to another with regard to social insurance and benefits issues need to be identified and solutions found. The development of common standards and procedures could be helped by European level training events of civil servants from the national ministries/administrations. A common approach would also include clarification of terms and values for youth voluntary service. Programmes using the term "voluntary service" for training placements in the for-profit sector should be renamed as internships or traineeships in order that similar approaches can be effectively compared.

(XII) The creation of an independent European observatory on civic service

A network of experts on national and international voluntary service is needed to track the developments in different countries, identify incompatibilities and report on implementation and impact of programmes. Data about and from volunteers should be collected under conditions of anonymity of both individual volunteers and organisations. Such an observatory might also initiate systematic research on the long-term impact on volunteers, hosting placements (clients, local communities) and co-ordinating organisations. Aspects could be the impact on the personal and professional career development of volunteers, the level of volunteers' participation in civic society after their service, the effect on residents' attitudes in communities that host foreign volunteers, etc.

(XIII) Validation of existing European instruments and implementation in the national context

Several measures on recognition of voluntary service, legal status, etc. have been created at European level, but their appropriation and implementation at national level have not taken place. The instruments are either unknown or their value is ignored. Even in recent national legislation they have not been taken into account. For example the EVS was not considered in the 2003 amendment of the German voluntary social/ecological year law.

The Council of Europe's European Convention on the Promotion of a Transnational Long-term Voluntary Service for Young People prepares a proper legal status for volunteers in Europe. Except for France, none of the five countries studied has signed it. Another example of a tool not used is the EU recommendation for transnational mobility aimed at removing legal obstacles to freedom of movement within educational and vocational training programmes with a European dimension.

Further research

Research in the sector of voluntary and civic service is just emerging. International terminology of the key notions of volunteering should be established to clarify terms and concepts. Cross-national comparisons especially need to be further developed in order to get a complete picture of developments in the European Union as countries like the UK and the Netherlands are also setting up initiatives. The development and comparison of voluntary and civic service in the new EU member states is of particular interest for the common development in the enlarged EU. Legal initiatives are also undertaken in Lithuania and Romania. In the Balkans, comparative research has started in order to allow the development of legal proposals.

There is a need to set up European criteria for gathering quantitative data from the countries allowing comparison. An important issue would be the comparative analysis of the financial costs of voluntary and civic service programmes. Research on international voluntary service should question the effects on European civic society development, European citizenship and the contribution of voluntary and civic service to bridge social and human capital. A matter of further research will be to define criteria to measure these developments.

Appendix 1: Legal and administrative documents relating to the five countries and to the international context

National laws

- Law on Public Benefit Activity and Volunteerism, dated 24 April 2003, Poland.
- Act No. 198 of 24 April 2002 on Volunteer Services, amending certain regulations (Volunteer Services Act), Czech Republic.
- *Loi n° 2000-242 du 14 mars 2000 relative aux volontariats civils institués par l'article L. 111-2 du code du service national et à diverses mesures relatives à la réforme du service national,* France.
- *Décret n° 2000-1159 du 30 novembre 2000 pour l'application des dispositions du code du service national relatives aux volontariats civils,* France.
- *Décret n° 2002-1527 du 24 décembre 2002 modifiant le code du service national et le décret n° 2000-1159,* France.
- *Circulaire DIES n° 2003-001 du 28 juillet 2003 relatif au volontariat de cohésion sociale et de solidarité,* France.
- Law No. 49/1987 on Volunteering in International Co-operation and Development Work, Italy.
- Act No. 60/2001, Italy.
- Act No. 64/2001 of March 2001 on the Establishment of National Civil Service, Italy.
- Decree No. 77/2002 of 5 April 2002 on Management of National Service, Italy.
- *Gesetz zur Änderung des Gesetzes zur Förderung eines Freiwilligen sozialen Jahres und anderer Gesetze* of April 2002, Germany.

Council of Europe

- Council of Europe, European Convention on the Promotion of a Transnational Long-Term Voluntary Service for Young People, ETS No. 175, 11 May 2000.

European Commission

- European Commission, European Commission White Paper, "A New Impetus for European youth", Com (2001) 681 final, Directorate General Education and Culture, Brussels, 2001.

- European Commission, Recommendation of the European Parliament and of the Council on mobility within the Community for students, persons undergoing training, volunteers, teachers and trainers, PE-CONS 3627/01, Brussels, 2001a.

- European Commission, "Implementation of Education & Training 2010, Work Programme, Progress Report", Directorate General for Education and Culture, Brussels, 2003.

- European Commission, "Youth Programme, Directorate General Education and Culture Activity Review 2002", Brussels, 2003a.

- European Commission, questionnaire on "Voluntary Activities" addressed to the governments of the member states and future member states of the European Union as well as to the candidate countries, Directorate General Education and Culture, Brussels, 2003b.

- European Commission, "Analysis of the Replies of the Member States of the European Union and the Acceding Countries to the Commission Questionnaire on Voluntary Activities of Young People", SEC 628, Brussels, 2004.

- European Commission, "Building our Common Future, Policy Challenges and Budgetary Means of the Enlarged Union 2007-2013", communication from the Commission to the Council and the European Parliament, Com (2004) 101 final, Brussels, 2004a.

- European Commission, "The New Generation of Community Education and Training Programmes after 2006", communication from the Commission, Com (2004) 156 final, Brussels, 2004b.

- European Commission, "Report from the Commission, Interim Evaluation of the Youth Programme 2000-2006 (covering the period 2000-2003)", Com (2004) 158 final, Brussels, 2004c.

- European Commission, "Communication from the Commission, Making Citizenship Work: Fostering European Culture and Diversity through Programmes for Youth, Culture, Audiovisual and Civic Participation", Com (2004) 154 final, Brussels, 2004d.

- European Commission, "Follow-up to the White Paper on a 'New Impetus for European Youth'. Proposed Common Objectives for Voluntary Activities among Young People in Response to the Council Resolution of 27 June 2002 regarding the Framework of European Co-operation in the Youth Field", Com 337 final, Brussels, 2004e.

European Council

- European Council (2001) "Meeting within the Council, on the Added Value of Voluntary Activity for Young People in the Context of the Development of Community Action on Youth". Draft resolution of the Council and of the representatives of the governments of the member states, 13461/01 JEUN 60 SOC 410, Brussels.

United Nations

- United Nations, "Improving the Status and Role of Volunteers", a contribution by the Parliamentary Assembly to the IYV 2001 (Doc. 8917), 2000.
- United Nations, "Improving the Status and Role of Volunteers in Society", a contribution by the Parliamentary Assembly to the IYV 2001 (Recommendation 1496), 2001.

Acknowledgements

This research was supported by a grant from:

- Global Service Institute (GSI) of the Center for Social Development, Washington;
- University in St Louis, with funding from the Ford Foundation;
- Federal Ministry of Families, Seniors, Women and Youth, Germany;
- Robert Bosch Foundation, Germany;
- Action Committee Service for Peace, Germany;
- Arci Servizio Civile, Italy, Comité de Co-ordination pour le Service Civil, France;
- Ost-West Institut für Sozialmanagement e.V.

References

AGDF and Katholischen Bundesarbeitsgemeinschaft mittelfristige internationale soziale Freiwilligendienste (2004) *Impulse für die Zivilgesellschaft, Stellungnahme zum Kommissionsbericht.* Bonn, Düsseldorf: AGDF.

ARCI Servizio Civile (2004) *The 2000 Civil Service: A Resource for the Society, an Opportunity for the Young.* Available at: http://www.arciserviziocivile.it/engver/CS2000.htm (accessed on 25 April 2005).

AVSO (2001) *European Induction Programme, European Youth Forum, Step-by-Step to Long-term Voluntary Service.* Brussels: AVSO.

AVSO (2003) *Reflections and Recommendations on Working with Young People from Disadvantaged Backgrounds in Transnational Volunteering.* Brussels: AVSO.

AVSO and CEV (2003) *Legal Status of Volunteers: Country Report Poland.* Brussels: AVSO.

AVSO and CEV (2003a) *Legal Status of Volunteers: Country Report Czech Republic.* Brussels: AVSO.

AVSO and CEV (2003b) *Legal Status of Volunteers: Country Report France.* Brussels: AVSO.

AVSO and CEV (2003c) *Legal Status of Volunteers: Country Report Italy.* Brussels. AVSO.

Bastide, J. (1995) *Les formes civiles du service national. Rapport presenté devant l'Assemblée nationale et le Sénat.* Paris: Conseil économique et social.

Becquet, V. (2004) "Youth Civic and Voluntary Service in France". In AVSO (ed.) *Youth Civic Service in Europe,* Pisa: Edizioni Plus – Pisa University.

Berninger, M. et al. (1998) *Youth Renewing the Fabric of Society: a Call for Voluntary Service in Germany and Europe.* Stuttgart: Robert Bosch Foundation.

Bernal de Soria Martínez, A. and Martínez-Odría, A. (forthcoming) *Voluntariado de Los Jóvenes y Formación de Competencias Profesionales.* Madrid: GECI.

Bruneau, C. (2003) *Consultation européenne, les activités volontaires.* France.

Bundesministerium für Familie, Senioren, Frauen und Jugend (2004) *Perspektiven für Freiwilligendienste und Zivildienst in Deutschland, Bericht der Kommission Impulse für die Zivilgesellschaft.* Berlin: Bundesministerium für Familie, Senioren, Frauen und Jugend.

Busson, V. (1997) *Le volontariat à moyen et long terme.* Paris: Cotravaux.

Chauveau, G.-M. (1990) *Le service national, rapport au ministre de la Défense.* Paris: La documentation française.

Consorti, P. and Palazzini, L. (2005) "Youth Civic and Voluntary Service in Italy". In *Youth Civic Service in Europe,* op. cit.

Co-ordinating Committee on International Voluntary Service (CCIVS) *National Services – What are the Choices?* Paris: CCIVS.

ECOTEC Research & Consulting Ltd (2000) *The Evaluation of the European Voluntary Service Programme. Report to the YOUTH Unit of the European Commission.* Brussels.

European Bureau for Conscientious Objection and Heinrich Böll Foundation (2000) *European Union without Compulsory Military Service: Consequences for Alternative Service.* Brussels: Heinrich Böll Foundation

European Commission (2001) "A New Impetus for European Youth". White Paper, Communication from the European Commission, Com 681 (2001) final, Brussels.

European Commission (2004) "Follow-up to the White Paper on a 'New Impetus for European Youth'. Proposed Common Objectives for Voluntary Activities among Young People in Response to the Council Resolution of 27 June 2002 regarding the Framework of European Co-operation in the Youth Field", Com 337 (2004) final, Brussels.

Guggenberger, B. (ed.) (2000) *Jugend erneuert Gemeinschaft, Freiwilligendienste in Deutschland und Europa.* Baden-Baden: Nomos.

Halba, B. et al. (2001) *Volunteering an Opportunity for Youngsters in Europe.* Paris: Institute for Research and Information on Volunteering (IRIV).

Hestia (2003) *Voluntary Activities in the Czech Republic – Review for European Commission.* Prague: Hestia.

Innovations in Civic Participation (ICP) (2004a) United Kingdom: Government to Implement AmericCorps-Type Volunteer Program. *ICP Newsletter,* Issue 6, April 2004 Washington: ICP.

Innovations in Civic Participation (ICP) (2004b) *Worldwide Youth Service Policy Scan.* Washington: ICP.

Lopez-Lotson, A. (2001) *National Country Reports on the Position of Volunteers in Spain, Italy and France.* Brussels: AVSO.

Marsaud, A. (1994) *Rapport sur les formes civiles du Service National.* Paris: Mission parlementaire auprès du Premier ministre.

McBride, A., Benitez, C. and Sherraden, M. (2003) *The Forms and Nature of Civic Service: A Global Assessment, Research Report.* St Louis: Center for Social Development, Washington University.

McBride, A., Lombe, M., Tang, F., Sherraden, M., and Benitez, C. (2003) *The Knowledge Base on Civic Service: Status and Directions, Working Paper.* St Louis: Center for Social Development, Washington University.

NOV and Community Partnership Consultants (2000) *Volunteering into Participation: A Strategy for Social Inclusion.* Amsterdam.

Presidency of the Council of Ministers, National Office for Civic Service (2004) *Building Europe alongside Young People, European Conference on National Voluntary Civic Service: Conference Proceedings,* Rome, 28-29 November 2004.

Rahrbach, A. et al. (1998) *Untersuchung zum Freiwilligen Sozialen Jahr. Schriftenreihe des Bundesministerium für Familie, Senioren, Frauen und Jugend* (BMFSFJ), Vol. 157, Stuttgart: Kohlhammer.

Schröer, R. (2003) *Voluntary Service: Opening Doors to the Future.* Brussels: AVSO.

Schröer, R. (2005) *"Youth Civic and Voluntary Service in Poland".* In *Youth Civic Service in Europe,* (2005) op. cit.

Schröer, R., "Youth Civic and Voluntary Service in the Czech Republic". In *Youth Civic Service in Europe,* op. cit.

Schröer, R., (2005) Voluntary Services at European and International Level. "In *Youth Civic Service in Europe",* op. cit.

Schur, W. "Youth Civic and Voluntary Service in Germany". In *Youth Civic Service in Europe,* op. cit.

Sieveking, K. (ed.) (2000) *European Voluntary Service for Young People: Questions of Status and Problems of Legal Policy.* Frankfurt: Peter Lang GmbH.

Steering Group of Voluntary Service Organisations (1994) *Potential Development of Voluntary Service Activities: Steps to Realise a Legal Status of Full-time Voluntary Service.* Report to the Commission of the European Communities – Task Force Human Resources, Education, Training & Youth. Brussels: European Commission.

Stringham, J. (2003) *Some Ideas for a Humanitarian Help Corps.* Brussels: AVSO.

Zimmer, A. and Priller, E. (eds.) (2004) *Future of Civil Society, Making Central European Non-profit Organisations Work.* Wiesbaden: Verlag für Sozialwissenschaften.

3. More than a numbers game: a UK perspective on youth volunteering and active citizenship

Kate Stanley

Introduction

"Everybody can be great because anybody can serve." (Martin Luther King Jr)

There is a growing interest across Europe in the possibilities of public policy intervention in youth volunteering. In the UK, the government wants to promote youth volunteering and to stimulate civil renewal. The Home Secretary (Blunkett 2003) has argued that: "civil renewal must form the centrepiece of the government's reform agenda in the coming years". Both he and the Chancellor regularly link a civil renewal agenda with engaging young people in voluntary activity. In 2004 the Chancellor said: "the advantages [of volunteering] for young people are clear, [it helps people] to ... become more active citizens". A commission has also been set up by leading politicians to develop a national framework of volunteering for young people and "to examine ... whether we can, through making it a national priority, engage a new generation of young people in serving their communities" (Brown 2004).

The aim of this chapter is to examine this supposed relationship between youth volunteering and active citizenship and to suggest how effective and progressive public policy on youth volunteering might be developed with a focus on the UK. Firstly, I outline what I mean by active citizenship and civil renewal, and suggest civil renewal could be a strong motivating idea to guide the future development of youth volunteering. I then consider some examples of volunteering programmes and their links with civil renewal which reveals a paucity of evidence on their impact. Finally, I consider the implications of this analysis for research and for public policy.

Active citizenship and civil renewal

In this field, language frequently serves to obstruct rather than facilitate understanding. Civil renewal, civic service, active citizenship, even volunteering, are all expressions fraught with difficulty. Civil renewal, for example, is a complex term invoked to cover a range of events and experiences. If we could describe what it means, we may be able to achieve it. The UK Home Secretary (Blunkett 2003b) uses it interchangeably with active citizenship to describe government actions which enable people to act themselves:

> Civil renewal is about educating, empowering and supporting citizens to be active in their communities, socially and politically ... Civil renewal and active citizenship is about creating the conditions for people to take control of their own lives, with the state acting as enabler, a supporter and a facilitator.

It is, however, outside the scope of this chapter to fully interrogate the concept of civil renewal. Instead I follow Nash (2002) and take the concept of civil renewal to be an articulation of achieving civic engagement, where civic engagement means participation by citizens in the public realm. Civic engagement, as it is generally understood, comprises at least three forms of engagement. These are: informal social engagement with family, friends, neighbours and colleagues; participation in voluntary and community organisations, including self-help groups, charities, sports teams, clubs and churches; and participation in governing and running public bodies and government services. This chapter looks at the role youth volunteering action might play in promoting all these types of lasting civic engagement.

It is desirable to bring about increased levels of civic engagement. Civic engagement benefits both those who get engaged and the community as a whole. Robert Putnam (2000) and others have shown that people who are socially and politically active are healthier, happier and more prosperous; they find it easier to find a job and have a larger pool of friends and acquaintances to call on when things go wrong. At the same time, active communities are also safer, more attractive communities, able to pull in public services, and fight for their needs and advance their interests in other ways. It is important to note that levels of civic engagement are reported to be lower amongst more disadvantaged groups. For example, poor people report being much more interested in social issues than their middle class counterparts but less empowered to change things. The Prime Minister's Strategy Unit has reported that while 35% of middle class people believe they can influence local affairs, the figure falls to 20% for the least well off. This means the more disadvantaged in society have potentially most to gain from opportunities for genuine civic engagement.

I use "youth action" and "voluntary activity" as umbrella terms to describe all kinds of voluntary engagement characterised by being open to all, unpaid, undertaken of a person's own free will, educational (in the sense of providing non-formal learning) and of social value.[1] Whilst there is recognition of the link between youth action policy and civic engagement within the UK Government, often youth action is presented as an intrinsic good, something that should be promoted for its own sake. This is what leads to targets focused simply on increasing the numbers of volunteers or the number of hours they spend volunteering. Youth action can indeed deliver benefits to both the participant and the beneficiary of the action and this may be a reason for public policy intervention specifically to increase the level of youth action.

I would argue, however, that public policy should be both more focused and more ambitious in what it seeks to achieve by promoting youth action rather than simply seeking to increase the numbers of volunteers. This is because youth action has the potential to generate lifelong habits of civic engagement by virtue of its basic characteristics. Effective public policy needs a motivating idea. That is, it is important to be clear what objective we want public policy interventions to achieve. The objec-

---

1. Following the definitions adopted by the Council of Europe and the European Commission.

tive of promoting lasting habits of civic engagement is a desirable objective for public policy and can justify interventions to promote youth action.

Of course, promoting civic engagement is just one of a number of possible motivating ideas for public policy intervention to boost youth action. Other valid objectives might be enhancing life chances or improving public services. Clearly, though, there is a need to prioritise, and promoting civic engagement and achieving the goal of civil renewal is a strong contender for the priority objective. This is partly because youth action has already been shown to have potential to deliver in this area. And it is partly because although increased levels of civic engagement are desirable, there are very few public policy levers available to bring this about, so we have to maximise the use of those that do appear to be promising.

So, there is a common sense link between youth action and civil renewal, and public policy should make civil renewal an explicit objective of interventions to enhance youth action. The challenge now is to understand how youth action might best maximise its impact on civil renewal objectives by assessing the evidence to date.

Current policy and practice in the UK

I will now sketch out what we know about the links between youth action and civil renewal based on evidence from some of the most prominent and better evaluated forms of youth action in the UK.

One of the strongest trends in UK youth action in recent years is the rise of youth advocacy and projects led by young people. This trend has emerged from a growing appreciation that young people have a right to be listened to and taken seriously and to shape their own activities. A longitudinal study (Roker and Eden 2003) of 22 youth action groups found evidence of the ability of such programmes to influence levels of civic engagement and sense of civic responsibility. It found that as a result of their participation young people felt they could try and bring about change in society and their participation had impacted on their sense of who they were and their understanding of political and social issues. Interestingly though many young people felt significant change could be achieved locally, they felt national change would be much harder to achieve. A second important finding was that most young people did not see the activities they were involved in as "political" and viewed the world of party politics very negatively. None the less, they did feel young people should exercise their vote.

Another strong trend is the rise in the numbers of people taking "gap years". In 2002, 160 000 people in the UK took gap years. Most gap years involve spending time away from home and have an average cost of almost € 4 000. They can include formal and informal forms of voluntary action, but do not necessarily include any, and many gap years are primarily about leisure. There is much to be gained from overseas travel. However, it has been argued (Simpson 2003) that gap years tend simply to reinforce travellers' expectations of a place and fail to take proper account of the interests of the host community.

The UK Government has mainly focused its own efforts on the creation of two programmes: Millennium Volunteers and Young Volunteer Challenge. Millennium Volunteers (MV) is an award scheme established in 2000 for young people aged 16 to 24. The programme was designed to promote a commitment to 200 hours of voluntary action within one year. An award of excellence is given to those completing a 200-hour placement which is delivered through non-profit organisations or a self-designed project. Recognition is also given for service of 100 hours. By 2004, 130 000 young people had joined MV.

The evaluation (Institute for Volunteering Research (IVR) 2002) of MV found it had been largely successful in delivering experiences that reflected what young people wanted and that delivered benefits to both volunteers and the communities in which they volunteered. The evaluation found that 84% of volunteers agreed MV had increased their confidence and 65% believed it had increased their employability. Crucially for engendering civic engagement, 80% reported they were more aware of the needs of others and 68% agreed they had become more committed to volunteering, owing to their involvement in MV.

MV aims to be inclusive of everyone but particularly those with no previous experience of volunteering and those vulnerable to social exclusion and has had some success here. It attracted people from a variety of ethnic backgrounds and was very successful in attracting young people who were unemployed and nearly half had no previous experience of volunteering. However, it was suggested that the one-year timescale is insufficiently flexible to allow people to fit their hours around other commitments. This lack of flexibility may have a disproportionate effect on groups from "marginalised communities" and students. Another evaluation suggested the drive to meet scheme targets means that harder-to-reach groups who are less likely to become volunteers, or who may need greater support to volunteer, are neglected (Volunteer Development England and Youth Action Network 2003).

The distortions created by the focus on numerical targets making the programme less attractive to some groups must be tackled if we want youth action to become the norm for the broadest possible range of young people. MV provides a good basis for the future development of youth action programmes and suggests the potential of youth action programmes to generate lasting civic engagement although longitudinal research is needed to fully understand the extent of this.

Young Volunteer Challenge (YVC) is a government-designed and funded pilot programme offering opportunities for 18 and 19 year olds from low-income backgrounds to undertake voluntary work on community projects in nine areas. The programme aims to test the effect of financial incentives on young people's participation in youth action. Young people who have received particular means-tested benefits are eligible to participate. YVC is a full-time experience which lasts up to nine months. Participants receive a weekly allowance of approximately € 60 a week and a lump sum end-of-experience award of almost € 1 000.

Ongoing monitoring evidence indicates that the weekly stipend is proving a greater incentive and facilitator of participation in this programme than the lump sum payment at the end. Evidence from AmeriCorps in the US concurs in suggesting that the lump sum end-of-service payment does not incentivise people to stay in the programme if they do not think it worthwhile. The project has experienced difficulties in attracting young people to participate (partly due to the affect of the stipend on benefit entitlement) and to stay engaged with the programme. It is hoped the full evaluation of YVC will provide insights on the best way to develop youth action targeted at disadvantaged groups. Many other programmes exist but have strikingly weak evidence of their impact on civil renewal goals.

The AmeriCorps programme in the US is important to mention briefly here as it is often held up, not least by the UK Chancellor, as the gold standard for what we should be striving to achieve in the UK. AmeriCorps gives financial assistance to nearly 75 000 school – leavers each year for service with 2 100 non-profit and faith-based organisations and public agencies. The programme provides accommodation, a weekly stipend and an educational award in exchange for a year of full-time service in activities such as youth mentoring, running after school programmes and cleaning up parks. The goals of AmeriCorps include renewing "the ethic of civic responsibility".

A study of AmeriCorps participants indicated that, after their period of service, volunteers were significantly more likely to become involved in local community groups or to attend public meetings. A change in volunteers' expressed personal and social values was also identified. The programme has been found both to increase individual opportunity and to serve community needs (Simon and Wang 2000). Members who were part of programmes with clearly visible results were found to be most positively affected in terms of a sense of ongoing civic responsibility (Aguire International 2001). Whilst these findings are encouraging, the methodologies used to conduct evaluations of AmeriCorps were insufficiently robust to place too much store by them, for example, no efforts have been made to establish the counterfactual (such as a control group).

These examples have shown that whilst the connections are sometimes made between youth action programmes and lasting civic engagement and there is some evidence to support this intuitive link, the empirical evidence is grossly underdeveloped. The significant limitations of this evidence warn us that we cannot simply assume that voluntary action programmes will deliver lasting civic engagement. This means we need to develop a policy framework which explicitly prioritises its achievement.

These examples show that a host of different policy objectives lie behind different programmes, although in some cases these objectives are not clearly articulated. It is essential to have a clear understanding of the different goals programmes would pursue. Once the goals are established, the best structures for the achievement of these goals can be identified. Too often thinking in this area is not rigorous enough; as Lind (2003) has said, "service" is often "a solution without a problem". Only if we have a firm grasp of our goals and the models that might best meet these goals, can we have an informed discussion about the options available to us. Any one programme may aim to achieve one or more objectives. These objectives could be grouped together according to whether they aim to achieve personal, community or instrumental objectives.

Personal objectives often focus on enhancing the life chances of the individual undertaking the action and promoting equality of opportunity. The objectives may include building character and a sense of identity, providing experience of work, broadening horizons, building networks, easing transitions to adulthood or enhancing skills and experience. It is crucial personal benefits are delivered to ensure people sign up to programmes. These benefits will also make it more likely that people will develop an ongoing habit of civic engagement.

Community objectives come the closest to a direct focus on civil renewal. These might include encouraging the practice of volunteering as a form of civic engagement, promoting international understanding, building local or national identity, developing skills, knowledge and values for active citizenship or giving young people the opportunity to exercise choice and make decisions.

Instrumental objectives focus on the delivery of practical change. For example, through the provision of volunteers to enhance the capacity of the voluntary or public sector, improving the condition of those who are helped by volunteers or improving the quality and efficiency of public services through the use of volunteers. These objectives can deliver personal and community benefits at the same time although these will not be the primary drivers.

It should be clear that whilst there may be overlap between these sets of objectives, not all practices and programmes promote all these ends, or at least not to the same degree. So a programme like Young Volunteer Challenge does little to build shared identities. Some argue that compulsory national service does not do much to encourage volunteering. Domestic programmes do not do much to help international understanding.

I have suggested that youth action should be designed to deliver lasting civic engagement but found scant evidence that current practice – whilst showing considerable potential – is delivering on this objective. I will now turn to look at what public policy can do to help meet this challenge.

Implications for research and public policy

There are six key policy questions which must be addressed if youth action policy is going to match up to the challenge of delivering lasting civic engagement and reflect the need to shift thinking away from simple numbers and towards different types of experiences and groups. These questions relate to image and language, what young people want, targets, building on existing programmes, who to engage, and delivery.

Image and language

It has been argued that the concept and term "volunteering" have acted as obstacles to progressive policy development which seeks to bring about civil renewal (Nash 2002). This is partly because they are regarded by some as representing control of the volunteer over others through a one-way process (Brav et al. 2002). This notion is supported by the fact that in the UK those who participate in volunteer programmes tend to be more highly educated and have a higher income than average, with those from the highest socioeconomic groups almost twice as likely to take part in formal voluntary activity as those from the lowest (Smith 1997).

It is also partly down to evidence that the term "volunteering" causes some groups to disassociate themselves from voluntary activities which they might otherwise engage in. For example, Little (cited in Kearney 2003) suggests: "the v-word ... with its inevitable blue-rinse connotations of middle-aged, middle class women helping those less fortunate, alienat[es] young people and ethnic minorities". This notion was supported by Gaskin (1998) reporting a survey in which two thirds of young people interviewed said "volunteering" was not something people in their age group would do. Amongst other barriers to their participation peer pressure was cited and two thirds of those interviewed said volunteering would be "uncool". To address this image problem programmes need a brand that young people can identify with and aspire to, this makes their involvement in brand design and development essential.

If we want to make the widest possible range of opportunities available to the widest range of young people, we need to employ a concept which is sufficiently loosely defined and is not off putting to young people.

What young people want

The evidence also shows that many young people do believe in the value of voluntary work for both society and themselves, and in one survey 94% said they saw volunteering as a great way to gain experience (Gaskin 1998). Young people believe that youth action should be based on the principle of something for something.

Gaskin (1998) has identified a number of characteristics young people are looking for from voluntary opportunities:
- Flexibility – in working time, choice and spontaneity;
- Legitimacy – to combat peer pressure and negative associations;
- Ease of access – more information on where, how and when;
- Experience – stimulating opportunities and skills development;
- Incentives – tangible outcomes, references, certificates of achievement;
- Variety – types of opportunities available;
- Organisation – efficient but informal;
- Laughs – to incentivise continuing the activity.

As well as meeting young people's requirements, we also need to take account of the fact that some forms of voluntary activity are likely to do very little toward making a lasting influence on people's civic engagement, while others might be more likely to make people think about the politics of their world or immediate community. But it is important to note there is no obvious contradiction between what young people want and the civil renewal agenda. However, there are indications that what young people want may not match the kind of programmes which would deliver other goals such as increasing their employability, for example. This makes it all the more compelling that we consult young people in the development of all plans for youth action programmes.

However, at present we do not have a sufficient level of empirical evidence on which forms of voluntary action are most likely to lead to ongoing civic involvement. We also need to know if this civic involvement, or the voluntary action itself, boosts the life chances of those doing it through the personal benefits gained. So, in the short term, we should focus on the quality of voluntary opportunities as an aid to promoting further and continuing civic engagement as well as encouraging more people to engage. In the long term, government needs to contribute to building the evidence base on the civic impact of certain forms of volunteering. Once we have established a decent evidence base, more ambitious programmes can be developed.

Building on existing programmes

Given the knowledge, skills and experience embedded in existing youth action programmes, it is crucial to ensure that all future developments build on existing programmes. This means improving our ability to measure the impact of programmes on their increasingly sophisticated objectives. It will be important for policy makers to emphasise that the aim is to target scarce resources where they can have the greatest impact in terms of civil renewal.

Who to engage

The objectives a youth action programme is seeking to achieve are crucial to decisions about who the programme seeks to engage. Given that the most disadvantaged groups tend to be the least civically engaged (Fahmy 2003) and that participation can deliver personal benefits as well as greater civic engagement (IVR 2002), there is clear merit in targeting opportunities towards disadvantaged young people. Furthermore, experience tells us that programmes that do not specifically target disadvantaged groups tend to be unsuccessful in attracting them.

If we are going to successfully engage young people from disadvantaged groups, it is crucial to think about the cost of participation to young people. People often talk about payments for youth action as rewards. However, many young people will only be able to participate in a programme if they receive some form of financial payment (the Young Volunteer Challenge pilot recognised this although it has run into barriers with the interaction of payments and the benefit system). Payments can be as much about facilitating access to a programme, as they are about rewarding participation. As the evidence from Millennium Volunteers shows, it is also important to take into account the additional resources that can be required by delivery organisations to attract and retain participants from more socially excluded and marginalised groups.

There is a need to target those young people who are least likely to engage in civil society but targeted programmes run the risk of becoming stigmatised as for "poor people" (Open Agenda 2003). Clearly, this is undesirable in a programme designed to promote civic engagement. This is why it might be wiser to develop universally accessible programmes which take particular measures to ensure that people from a diverse range of backgrounds can participate. There may be additional advantages to such programmes. For example, programmes that bring people from different socioeconomic classes together may help to build social networks across, as well as within, social groups.

Targets: outputs or outcomes

The UK Government set a target of increasing the number of people volunteering by one million by 2004. The target reflects the current policy focus on numbers of volunteers. I have been arguing that the question to start with is not do we have enough numbers of volunteers, rather it is why do we want people to engage in youth action? Once we have our big idea – and we have argued it might be achieving civil renewal – we can then move on to the how we do it and how to measure if we have done it.

There is a role for targets. It is well known that what gets done is what gets measured and numbers are important. However, poor quality youth action experiences could be counterproductive. There is some evidence to suggest that those young people who volunteer are often dissatisfied with their experience. In one IVR survey (Smith 1997), seven out of ten of all volunteers reported dissatisfaction with the way their voluntary work was organised, with younger volunteers most likely to be critical of their experiences.

This suggests targets need to be about more than sheer numbers of programme participants. Targets for the number of volunteers (i.e. outputs) might be supplemented by measures of change in quality of life or community impact, such as trust, young people's political involvement, youth crime or safety on streets (i.e. outcomes, see Ellis 2000). The Home Office target to increase community participation by 5% by 2006 is a step toward this. To assess success by these measures would mean building-in the ability to address these issues in the design of programmes (Open Agenda 2003). It is not easy to develop measures, assess community impact or quality of life, but it is necessary.

Delivery

A national policy framework is needed to provide the strategic direction for the development of youth action. The necessary impetus could be delivered through existing bodies and partnership working. The first task is to identify the systemic barriers to youth action and propose remedies. For example, barriers exist in the tax and benefit system and barriers – sometimes put up by professionals – exist to developing opportunities for youth action within public services. There is also a continuing need for a clear legal framework around the status of voluntary action and different forms of payment. This removal of barriers will demand effective cross-departmental co-operation in government.

The second task is to identify funding sources for youth action programmes and manage that financial support. The role of the private sector in funding youth action also deserves full exploration and it may be possible to work in partnership with businesses that could either provide financing or donate goods in kind. There may be lessons to be learnt here from the American scheme, Business Strengthening America, which aims to use the business community as "a booster rocket" to efforts by government and voluntary and community organisations to inspire Americans to serve in their communities.

The third task is to identify infrastructure development and support needs in the voluntary and community sector. The key will be to improve the coverage, quality and sustainability of its infrastructure to enable the transferability of practice, including that which effectively links youth action and civil renewal objectives. It is also necessary to set out the common elements of youth action programmes, for example, setting standards in relation to monitoring and outcome-based evaluation and training. There is also a need for a systematic review of all evidence available on the relationship between voluntary action and ongoing civic engagement.

The fourth task is to identify gaps in current provision and suggest programmes that might fill them. This would include the development and funding of pilot programmes designed to deliver civic engagement through youth action. However, the decisions about how youth action should be delivered on the ground should be down to local partnerships to ensure community ownership and young people's input into programmes.

Conclusion

In this chapter I have argued that there is a need for a more focused and ambitious approach to public policy intervention in youth action programmes. Such an approach must begin with clarity about the purpose of youth action. We have argued that the motivating idea behind public policy intervention in youth action could be the achievement of civil renewal. In particular, we recommend the focus be placed on bringing about long lasting habits of civic engagement, including amongst the most disadvantaged young people.

There is, however, a lack of robust evidence to show exactly how youth action should be developed in the future and this evidence base clearly needs to be built. What we do know is that there is significant potential for youth action to bring about lasting habits of civic engagement and the time has come to get a better understanding of how we might exploit this potential.

References

Abt Associates Inc (2001) *Serving Country and Community: A Study of Service in AmeriCorps.* Cambridge MA: Corporation for National and Community Service.

Aguirre International (2001) *Serving Country and Community: A Study of Service in AmeriCorps. A Profile of AmeriCorps Members at Baseline.* Washington DC: Corporation for National Service and Community.

Blunkett, D. (2003a) *A New Agenda for Civil Renewal?* London: Institute for Public Policy Research (IPPR).

Blunkett, D. (2003b) *Civil Renewal: A New Agenda CSV Edith Kahn Memorial Lecture.*

Brav, J., Moore, A. and Sheraden, M. (2002) *Limitations on Civic Service: Critical Perspectives.* Working Paper 02-12, Washington: Global Service Institute.

Brown, G. (2004) *Speech at the NCVO annual conference 17th February 2004.* Available at: www.ncvol.org.uk (accessed 18 October 2004).

Dionne, E., Drogosz, K. and Litan R. (ed.) (2003) *United We Serve: National Service and the Future of Citizenship.* Washington: Brookings.

Ellis, A. (2000) *Measuring the Impacts of Volunteering.* A Total Audit Discussion Paper. London: Institute for Volunteering Research.

Fahmy, E. (2003) Civic Capacity, Social *Exclusion and Political Participation in Britain: Evidence from the 1999 Poverty and Social Exclusion Survey.* Paper presented at the Political Studies Association Annual Conference, University of Leicester, 15-17 April 2003. Leicester: University of Leicester.

Gaskin, K. (1998) "Vanishing Volunteers: Are Young People Losing Interest in Volunteering?" *Voluntary Action,* 1, 1.

Institute for Volunteering Research (2002) *UK -wide Evaluation of the Millennium Volunteers Programme.* London: Institute for Volunteering Research.

Kearney, J. (2003) *Re-thinking Volunteering for a Contemporary Society, Proceedings of the IPPR conference Re-thinking Volunteering.* London: IPPR.

Lind, M. (2003) "A Solution in Search of a Problem", in Dionne, E., Drogosz, K. and Litan, R. (eds.), op. cit.

Nash, V. (2002) "Laying the Ground: Civic Renewal and Volunteering". In Paxton, W. and Nash, V. (eds.) (2002) *Any Volunteers for the Good Society?* London: IPPR.

Open Agenda (2003) What Next in Youth Volunteering? Report of Open Agenda Event, St George's House, Windsor Castle, 11-12 June 2002. Windsdor: Open Agenda.

Prime, D., Zimmeck, M. and Zurawan, A. (2002) *Active Communities: Initial Findings from the 2001 Home Office Citizenship Survey.* London: Home Office.

Putnam, R. (2000) *Bowling Alone: The Collapse and Revival of American Community.* New York: Simon and Schuster.

Roker, D. and Eden, K. (2003) *A Longitudinal Study of Young People's Involvement in Social Action.* Brighton: Trust for the Study of Adolescents.

Simon, C. and Wang, C. (2000) *Impact of AmeriCorps on Members' Political and Social Efficacy, Social Trust, Institutional Confidence, and Values in Idaho, Montana, Oregon, and Washington.* Portland, Oregon: Northwest Regional Educational Laboratory.

Simpson, K. (2003) Personal communication based on an unpublished Ph.D. thesis. Newcastle: University of Newcastle.

Smith, D. (1997) *The 1997 National Survey of Volunteering.* London: Institute for Volunteering Research.

Volunteer Development England and Youth Action Network (2003) *The Ups and Downs of Millennium Volunteering. Putting Principles into Practice: An Evaluation of the Millennium Volunteers Programme in England by Participating Organisations.* Available at: http://www.vole.org.uk/downloads/millennium_report2003.pdf (accessed 18 October 2004).

A UK perspective on active citizenship

Part 3

**Barriers to participation
in voluntary activities**

1. Public-private obstacles to voluntary service and citizenship

Brian Gran

Introduction

What are trans-european obstacles to voluntary activities for young people? To foster young people's active citizenship and solidarity, private and public-private structures and practices must be considered in establishing national and transnational policies of voluntary service. Young people face considerable obstacles to participating in voluntary services. These obstacles are found in public and private sectors of social life; sometimes these barriers are formed by public-private collaborations. This chapter presents categories of private and public-private barriers to voluntary service participation by young people. It then examines survey data and political and socioeconomic data to place these categories in a European context. An overarching objective of this chapter is to contribute to debates on barriers to voluntary service activities and how to remove or alleviate their consequences. This chapter seeks to contribute to discussions of how voluntary service activities can foster active citizenship and solidarity of young people in Europe.

This chapter first presents an overview of what is meant by public and private, then a discussion of what is public and private when considering voluntary service activities. It then presents three categories of private and public-private barriers to voluntary service participation. This chapter concludes with a brief discussion of how these barriers may be overcome or mitigated for purposes of employing voluntary service activities to foster active citizenship and solidarity of young people in Europe.

What is public and private?

This research focuses on private and public-private barriers to voluntary activities for young people. Before examining these obstacles, it is essential to discuss what is meant by public and private and to highlight their differences. Sometimes called "the grand dichotomy" (Weintraub and Kumar 1997), across many societies the terms public and private are used to designate boundaries and responsibilities. The private boundary, for instance, prevents outsiders from looking in on family life and sexual practices. With great variation, nevertheless across many societies public responsibilities are held by government, such as sewage treatment, and private responsibilities are held by individuals, such as personal hygiene. The objective of this section is to offer an overview of conceptions of public and private as they relate to obstacles to voluntary activities for young people.

Common notions of what is public and private are presented by Nancy Fraser (1999: 28). "Public", for example, can mean (1) state-related, (2) accessible to everyone, (3) of concern to everyone, and (4) pertaining to a common good or shared interest. Each of these corresponds to a contrasting sense of "private". In addition, there are two other senses of "private" hovering just below the surface here: (5) pertaining to private property in a market economy and (6) pertaining to intimate domestic or personal life, including sexual life.

According to Fraser, public describes two societal components: government and matters that involve everyone. We often use public to describe work or responsibilities of government, such as a public pension programme or the military. Public is also used to describe a matter of broad interest. Examples are elections to public office or a public park. Often a public responsibility is of public interest, such as elected office. In democracies, nearly everyone, except young people and some other explicitly proscribed groups, can pursue elected offices. In turn, elections to that office and how work in the office is performed is typically of interest to all residents.

Fraser's definition of private suggests responsibilities and walls not related to government. Private describes a matter not involving everyone. Few people are eligible to vote or run for office in non-government institutions. For instance, in some economies, only shareholders are eligible to elect corporate leaders. In turn, not everyone is permitted to become a corporate director. Electoral processes in companies vary by legislation applying to the company. Other non-government institutions, such as churches and charities, often share similar characteristics. Despite possibly being of interest to everyone in a community, leadership selection of a private organisation is not public, but limited and sometimes exclusive. Yet the idea of private as non-government does not necessarily mean it is private in Fraser's other sense of private, which is not of interest to everyone.

As Fraser notes, private often denotes private property relations in a market economy. The market place in capitalist-oriented economies is idealised as a place where individuals can exchange goods and services without government interference (Smith 1776, Carruthers 1999). Private life is an area where individuals can decide with whom or how to live, including sexual practices and sharing property. Of course, in most societies, neither the market economy nor domestic life is without public interference. Governments often regulate market economies and household relations.

It is not clear where voluntary organisations fit in the framework identified by Fraser. While not state-related, many voluntary organisations are open to new members and, because their activities are often influential beyond their membership, they are of concern to many people, including government leaders. In some nation states, voluntary organisations sponsor programmes essential to government functioning, but rely on non-government support of members and contributors. It is difficult to characterise voluntary organisations as public or private.

Aristotle's ideas may be instructive for thinking about what is public and private and the location of voluntary organisations in the public-private framework. Aristotle's conception is not based on a dichotomy, but is cumulative. In Aristotle's model, a state is based on a group of villages. A village is made up of households; when households can fulfill more than their own basic needs, they unite to form a village. A male citizen, his wife, their children, and a servant together form a household. In Aristotle's conception, the male citizen governs the household. He governs his wife through constitutional rule and he royally governs his children. The father should rule his children as a loving parent, and his children should submit to his royal rule because they love and respect him. While it is not clear where a voluntary organisation would fit into Aristotle's conception, it would probably exist in the area where households create a village or where villages form a state. In his conception, only a male citizen would participate in affairs arising between households and the village and the state they form. As a result, in Aristotle's conception, only male citizens would participate in voluntary activities; the wife, children, and servant would not.

Voluntary organisations more clearly fit into Habermas' (1991) conception of a public sphere, the state, and the economy. His interest is in the public sphere, a location where people become socially integrated and where they can critically communicate in rational ways about their state and economy. People become part of the public sphere through communication, not by constitutional, royal rule, or ownership. In Habermas' conception, all individuals can enter the public sphere to exchange ideas and control the state and economy. It is not clear in Habermas' conception whether communication is expected to be used in the private sphere, which for Habermas is the household.

As this section has demonstrated, what is public and private is not easily distinguished. Aristotle described relationships between state, village, and household. Male household leaders negotiated these relationships, as well as relationships within the household. Roles of other household members, including wife, child, and slave, were conceptually limited to intra-household relationships. The male household leader participated in public and private sectors, while participation of women, children, and slaves were limited to the private sector. Habermas is concerned that state and economic marketplace will overwhelm the public sphere, which is a site of social integration that can encourage individuals to participate in controlling authority of the state and economic marketplace. In his later work, Habermas goes further to express concern that the state and economic marketplace will intervene in and to some degree control the private sphere. Habermas conceives that everyone will participate in the public sphere, but as his critics note (Benhabib 1999:92), he fails to consider barriers and abilities to participation. These barriers may be erected in the state and economic marketplaces as well as within the household (Gobetti 1997:105).

What is public and private for policies of voluntary service activities?

Voluntary activities may be undertaken as part of a relationship to a non-governmental organisation, a charity, a social movement, or less formally with like-minded individuals interested in pursuing similar activities. These activities may belong in Habermas' public sphere because they can integrate people. Most people would probably designate these activities and their relationships as private. Lines separating government and voluntary service activities, however, are fuzzy. Considering Fraser's (1999) conception of public and private, voluntary service activities are not explicitly tied to government and the relationships are exclusive in that they are not open to everyone. In some countries, on the other hand, people perceive strong ties between government and voluntary service agencies (Chaney and Fevre 2001) and these activities receive government support.

Voluntary activities belong in Fraser's (1989) social sphere as well. The immediate goal of this chapter is not to integrate a potential volunteer, but to communicate and critically discuss voluntary activities as a means of promoting active European citizenship and solidarity among younger people. Voluntary activities are not performed, of course, in a vacuum. Instead, understandings of voluntary activities are influenced by government and non-government actors and institutions. Perceptions of voluntary activities are affected by work in Fraser's social sphere. Attitudes toward government and social sphere actors can affect an individual's decision to participate in volunteer activities.

Barriers to voluntary service participation

This chapter presents and discusses three types of private and public-private barriers young people may face when pursuing voluntary service activities across European boundaries: obligations, information, and opportunities. These three types are not hard and fast; they are meant to serve as guidelines to thinking about barriers young people may encounter in participating in voluntary services in other European countries. Formal and informal obligations may hinder, even prevent, a young person from participating in voluntary service activities. These obligations can limit information the young individual receives about opportunities to participate in volunteer service activities. Available information may be limited by opportunities an individual enjoys. Some individuals may enjoy opportunities to participate, while others do not or think they do not. This section presents conceptualisations of each type, then offers information about how the barrier may influence young people's participation in voluntary service activities and the degree to which these barriers exist.

Obligations

Young people may face formal and informal obligations that influence their decisions on whether and how to perform voluntary service activities in other European countries. Coleman (1990) emphasises the leverage a group can bring on an individual member to ensure compliant behaviour. Group membership may be based in Habermas' public sphere or Aristotle's household. In the public sphere, these obligations may be to non-market institutions like religious organisations or market-related institutions such as trade unions.

While it is likely that individuals have varying depths of convictions, it is probable that many religious institutions mandate formal fulfillment of religious practices. Adherents to some faiths are expected to practice their faiths in explicit ways, often daily. They may require access to religious facilities and interaction with religious authorities. Adherents may have dietary needs they must fulfill to maintain their religious convictions. Some religious practices require adherents to undergo fasts or to avoid work in general. A young person may reasonably question whether he or she can fulfill faith obligations away from his or her home community.

Within Europe, approximately 271 million people adhere to Roman Catholicism, 166 million to Orthodox beliefs, 80 million to Protestant beliefs, 32 million to Muslim beliefs, and about 3 million to Jewish beliefs (Barrett, Kurian and Johnson 2001). Although Europe is known for its great religious heterogeneity, this heterogeneity is not evenly distributed.

Table 1: Religious adherents (percentage of population)

Country	Catholic	Jew	Muslim	Orthodox	Protestant	% of 18-25 year olds who say that "religion" is "very important"
Austria	75.5	0.1	2.2	1.9	5	13.7
Belgium	80.9	0.2	3.6	0.5	1.3	6.9
Bulgaria	1.1	0.1	11.9	71.6	1.2	
Cyprus	1.6	0	1	87.4	1.4	
Czech Republic	40.4	0.1	0	0.6	3.1	
Denmark	0.6	0.1	1.3	0	87.7	1.9
Estonia	0.4	0.2	0.3	16.5	17.2	
Finland	0.1	0	0.3	1.1	89.6	14.5
France	82.3	1	7.1	1.1	1.5	7.4
Germany	34.9	0.1	4.4	0.8	37	4.1
Greece	0.6	0.1	3.3	93	0.2	
Hungary	63.1	0.5	0.6	0.9	25.5	
Ireland	84.7	0.1	0.2	0	4.4	20.7
Italy	97.2	0.1	1.2	0.2	1	24.7
Latvia	20.8	0.6	0.4	23.6	23.8	
Lithuania	84.6	0.2	0.2	3.1	1.2	
Luxembourg	94.4	0.2	1	0.3	1.7	
Malta	94.5	0	0.5	0	0.6	
Netherlands	34.5	0.2	3.8	0.1	27	9.3
Poland	92.2	0	0	2.7	0.5	
Portugal	90.8	0	0.2	0	1.4	7.9
Romania	14.5	0	1.3	85.1	10.7	
Slovakia	67.9	0.1	0	0.4	11.1	
Slovenia	83.5	0	0.1	0.6	1.6	
Spain	96.1	0	0.5	0	0.3	9.9
Sweden	2	0.2	2.3	1.4	94.5	6.4
Turkey	0.1	0	97.2	0.3	0.1	
UK	9.6	0.5	2	0.6	53.3	6

An individual living in Austria who adheres to Muslim beliefs, for instance, may hesitate to participate in voluntary service activities in another European country because of concerns of religious practices. The number of mosques, for instance, varies across European countries.

Table 2: Number of adherents and mosques

Country	Muslim adherents	Number of mosques
Austria	120 000	87 (1999; Islamic voice)
France	4 200 000	1554 (2004; Islamonline.net)
Hungary	Few	None

A religious obligation can restrict an individual from building relationships outside his or her own country, hindering the process of becoming an active European citizen. Although it may be a less formal obligation, responsibilities toward children, parents, and other family members, including siblings and grandparents, may be significant obstacles to a young person's participation in voluntary service activities in another country. Aristotle characterised the relationship between parents and children as a royal rule, in which children and parents govern each other out of love and respect. Familial relationships may discourage young people from pursuing voluntary service activities. Formal and informal responsibilities can run the gamut from physical and social care to financial support.

Public–private obstacles

Table 3: Family ties and responsibilities

Country	Average age at which women become biological parents (UNECE 2000)[a]	Proportion of 20-24 year olds who live with parents	Proportion of 18-25 year olds who say that "family" is "very important" (IARD:Appendix 1)
Austria	27	65	78.5
Belgium	26.4	68	70.8
Bulgaria	23.5		
Cyprus	26.1		
Czech Republic	25		
Denmark	27.4		80.2
Estonia	24.1		
Finland	27.6	29	65.6
France	28.7	52	73.8
Germany	28	55	47.2
Greece	27.3	72	
Hungary	25		
Ireland	27.4	64	90.2
Italy	28.5	87	82.1
Latvia	24.5		
Lithuania	24		
Luxembourg	28.5	69	
Malta			
Netherlands	29.1	47	64.6
Poland	24		
Portugal	26.8	82	59.5
Romania	24		
Slovakia	23.1		
Slovenia	26.5		
Spain	29	89	74.1
Sweden	28		82.7
Turkey			
UK	27	47	86.6

a. Luxembourg Income Study (LIS) microdatabase, harmonisation of original surveys conducted by the LIS, Luxembourg, periodic updating. NB IARD cites Eurostat Labour Force Survey, 1998, 2000.

These data suggest different aspects of family ties may enter into a young person's decision to participate in voluntary service activities. While we note variation in the age at which a woman typically becomes a mother, the average age is older than 23 years. In some countries many young people live with their parents, with more than half of countries' youth living with parents in 10 of the 13 examined countries. Indeed, in all but one of the 13 examined countries, approximately 60% or more young people state their family is very important. Examining data from the Luxembourg Income Study (LIS) on households headed by young people between the ages of 16 and 26, these households typically provide small amounts of their disposable incomes to family members outside their households. In some countries, however, LIS evidence indicates that young people between the ages of 16 and 26 contribute non-trivial amounts to other family members. Italian young people on average contribute 6% of disposable income to child support or alimony and another 6% to relatives with whom they do not live.

The "family" has an important role in policies established by some European national governments. We can characterise some governments as employing principles of social capitalism. According to Kees van Kersbergen (1995:190), through

European youth voluntary activities

social capitalism "[s]ocial rights are attached to family or status groups, and the state only provides the conditions under which the family and social groups can continue to function according to their natural and organic roles … The state assists those who fail to help themselves in the performance of their natural duty". Van Kersbergen states (1995:190), "The very idea of social capitalism assumes women to be only marginally present on the labour market and the family to be the prime provider of care". Governments of different countries, including Germany, Italy, and the Netherlands, develop social policies based on social capitalism principles. These policies affect relationships within Aristotle's household and outside in his community, village, and state. Social capitalism can establish responsibilities and expectations that will influence a young person's decision to participate in voluntary service activities. Social capitalism may particularly influence women's decisions to volunteer in other countries. These policies may affect people's abilities to become active European citizens and thwart solidarity.

Young people may face a variety of formal requirements and informal expectations to support family members. As indicated, these obligations may discourage young people from pursuing participation in voluntary service activities at the European level. These private and public-private barriers may disproportionately affect young people in some nation states more than others.

information

Beyond obligations, other memberships an individual has may affect his or her decision to participate in voluntary service activities in other European countries. As various experts have noted, including Bourdieu (1986), Coleman (1990), and Putnam (2000) among others, most individuals belong to groups through which resources are shared and even guarded from others. These resources not only are financial, they can be information about opportunities. These kinds of group membership can criss-cross Aristotle's conception of the relationship between state, village, community, and household. Membership in one community can restrict relationships with other communities and villages. Strong community relationships may weaken ties to national and transnational institutions. This project will describe two ways distribution of information among community members can affect an individual's decision to participate in voluntary service activities based in another European country.

The first is group closure. Group organisation and shared beliefs may work against reception of information from outside the group. A group may be organised in a way that, intentionally or not, may isolate group members from outside information. A system of shared beliefs of this group, for instance, could work against receiving and accepting outside information. Norms shared by group members may discourage separation of young people from their own group. Granovetter (1973) finds that weak ties, through which an individual has infrequent and casual contact with another, produce more information. Strong ties are made when individuals frequently see each other over a long period. New information is less likely to enter into relationships based on strong ties than weak ties. For individuals who are members of strong groups, access to information may be restricted because of group closure. A relationship based on a weak tie suggests the other individual has ties to others. These relationships will produce new information that strong ties will not.

The second is unequal access. Rather than closure, a group may not have access to information. Some groups may not be in the position to receive information about voluntary service opportunities. Often tied to opportunities based in human capital and socioeconomic structures (see below), members of some groups may not have access to information presented in "mainstream" media. Some groups may either avoid or do not have access to major newspapers, radio and television programmes, or Internet information delivery. Access to a television does not guarantee an individual will view a programme about European citizenship, but in Europe televisions are widely available and may be an important means of communicating information about voluntary service activities (IARD 2001:18). In Malta nearly 70% of people own a television; in Romania only 23.2% do. Internet usage widely varies, ranging from 3.7% in Turkey to 67.6% in Sweden. Experiences with voluntary service organisations in home countries (Bode 2003) may shape individuals' opinions of voluntary service activities. Moore and Whitt (2000) have demonstrated that gender breakdown among leaders of a non-profit organisation influence women's decisions to participate in non-profit activities. Individuals may conclude conflicts between voluntary service agencies at home (Stroschein 2002) will be found in other European countries. These conflicts may discourage a young person from making a commitment to a voluntary service agency in another European country. Access to information in general and to specific kinds of information will influence a young person's decision to participate in voluntary service activities.

Table 4: Information access

Country	Proportion of 15-24 year olds belonging to an association (IARD:Table 6)	Proportion of 18-25 year olds who have "a great deal" or "quite a lot" of confidence in Europe	Proportion of 15-24 year olds who agree with the statement: "foreigners living in [own country] have same rights as [nationality]" (IARD:Appendix 1)	Number of individuals owning a television out of 1000 (nationalmaster. com)	Proportion of Internet users
Austria	60		15.6	519.03	45
Belgium	47	70.9	19.3	458.73	36.5
Bulgaria				439.11	16.5
Cyprus					19.4
Czech Republic				332.3	26.2
Denmark	77	47.1	32.9	579.63	62.6
Estonia				429.51	30.5
Finland	67	63.3	33.9	616.47	51.8
France	49	74.6	24.4	578.26	28.2
Germany	58	49.1	13.9	623.79	39
Greece			17.8	238.14	13.1
Hungary				440	12
Ireland	61	72.4	17.4	463.79	33.4
Italy	54	78.5	20.5	522.42	32.1
Latvia				519.41	13.3
Lithuania				473.2	9.5
Luxembourg	66		17.4	627.53	22
Malta				699.26	14.7
Netherlands	77	60.9	36.1	501.53	60.3
Poland				337.88	7.8
Portugal	40	60.9	18.1	327.65	43.6
Romania				235.72	4.5
Slovakia				482.5	31
Slovenia				366.79	12.9
Spain	38	53.7	27.8	402.81	19.6
Sweden	82	64.3	58.3	518.12	67.6
Turkey					3.7
UK	50	50	25.2	507.53	57.2

Membership in some groups may work against interest in Europe and European citizenship. Group membership is not only limited to ethno-linguistic or religious background. Group membership may be based in legal or social categories, such as people with mental and physical disabilities.

Opportunities

Beyond group membership, some individuals may not enjoy opportunities to participate in voluntary activities. Three factors may work against an individual's decision to seize an opportunity of voluntary service. The first factor is whether the individual can economically afford to participate in the voluntary service activities. This question can involve a multitude of factors, including whether a young person has obligations to his or her family. Other affordability factors include whether the person has sufficient income to participate in voluntary service activities: does an

Table 5: Opportunities

Country	Gross domestic product per capita (CIA 2003)	Youth (15-24) unemployment rate (UNECE 2000)	Difference between men and women in employment (IARD: Appendix 1)	Aggregate of non-mother tongue skills (Europa)	Proportion who have visited foreign countries
Austria	27700	4.9	5.8	82	
Belgium	29000	15.2	6.6	114	
Bulgaria	6600	38.4 (2001)		51	17
Cyprus	10000	10.5		71	70
Czech Republic	15300	17		67	82
Denmark	29000	6.7	0.6	154	
Estonia	10900	23.8		63	63
Finland	26200	21.6	3.7	105	
France	25700	20.7	4.9	65	
Germany	26600	7.7	5.2	74	
Greece	19000	29.5	12	54	
Hungary	13300	12.1		36	46
Ireland	30500	6.4	6.4	39	
Italy	25000	29.7	10.1	56	
Latvia	8300	22.9		78	52
Lithuania	8400	28.8		67	40
Luxembourg	44000	6.4	4.1	244	
Malta	17000	15.4 (2001)		147	41
Netherlands	26900	6.6	2.8	159	
Poland	9500	35.2		46	48
Portugal	18000	8.6	7.7	47	
Romania	7400	18.6		61	20
Slovakia	12200	35.2		72	75
Slovenia	18100	16.6		117	86
Spain	20700	25.3	10.9	54	
Sweden	25400	11.9	3.3	126	
Turkey	7000	13.2		43	2
UK	25300	11.8	5.2	34	

individual need to accept a paid job in the short term? Does an individual consider the EVS compensation scheme sufficient?

A second factor is other opportunity costs, besides income, that can affect an individual's decision to participate in voluntary service activities. What factors will an individual consider in making a decision to participate in voluntary activities? How will the decision to accept an opportunity to participate in voluntary activities affect an individual's short- and long-term circumstances? Considering availability of work suggests that these opportunities vary across countries. In some countries, a substantial gap exists between men and women in employment. A young person may obtain information indicating that the European country where he or she will participate in voluntary activities does not welcome him or her (Batliwala 2002: 393, 395). Opportunity costs may be greater than predicted benefits arising from voluntary service participation. In addition to foregoing work income, an individual may be concerned that he or she will lose formal educational and career opportunities while participating in voluntary service activities.

A third factor is whether the young person believes he or she is prepared to participate: do his or her educational background and other experiences prepare him or her to live and work in another country? For instance, does he or she possess (or believe he or she possesses) language skills needed to participate in voluntary service activities outside their own country? Despite impressive language abilities, Eurobarometer and other agencies report secondary-language skills as significant concerns to young people (INRA 2001).

Some individuals may mentally place these factors into an equation in which they try to determine whether "benefits" from participating in voluntary service activities outweigh their "costs". Benefits, of course, are not limited to enhancing paycheques or cosmopolitan pedigrees. They will include new experiences, opportunities for immersion in a second or third language, as well as participating in new group memberships. These new group memberships may bring new benefits of relationships and opportunities into a participant's life. Costs to a participant not only include foregoing a larger pay cheque and time off-track from formal educational structures, they can include moving away from group memberships and not fulfilling obligations. As mentioned above, a young person may have faith-based concerns. Beyond religious beliefs and practices, individuals may anticipate and experience antagonism because their group membership differs from natives of the receiving country in other ways, such as language, ethnic background, and nationality. While it is hoped and anticipated that voluntary service activities will help overcome these antagonisms, it is reasonable that a young person may hesitate to rise to a transeuropean challenge.

Nevertheless, it is reasonable to suspect that many young people will not work through a fully-informed calculus of benefits and costs to participating in voluntary service activities. Not only is it unlikely that an individual would consider every relevant benefit and cost, it is highly improbable an individual could obtain the necessary information. An individual will probably look to experiences of his or her peers, including group members, and information they find at school, on television, or through the Internet. Traveling outside one's home country may strongly influence the decision to participate in another European country. Data suggest that many young people have traveled to other countries (INRA 2001). These experiences will alert a young person to potential benefits from living elsewhere and that he or she has similar interests and concerns as young people living in other European countries.

Conclusion

This chapter has briefly presented three private and public-private types of barriers to voluntary service activities young people may encounter: obligations, information, and opportunities. Because these barriers are, in many ways, located outside government's purview, they may be more difficult to overcome. Some obstacles, for instance obligations, will be difficult to surmount. Passage of time and demographic change will reduce imagined boundaries separating European citizens, but as we know, these boundaries are often more durable than physical ones.

Information and opportunity obstacles may be easier to change, but will probably be expensive. Distributing information in a useful way to a particular group is one step. Another difficult but necessary step is devising distinctive opportunities for the needs of diverse young people, whether those differences are ethno-religious or socioeconomic.

It is not ironic that participation in voluntary service activities is an important step to overcoming these obstacles. Through co-operation in voluntary service activities across European borders, social participation will likely increase, along with promoting educational experiences, learning about different cultural perspectives and values, and exchanging information about opportunities. First-hand experiences in other European countries will hopefully result in less prejudice and more integration. Voluntary service activities will enhance European citizenship and promote solidarity.

Batliwala, S. (2002) "Grassroots Movements as Transnational Actors". *Voluntas*, 13 (4), pp. 393-409.

Barrett, D., Kurian, G. and Johnson, T. (2001) *World Christian Encyclopedia.* New York: Oxford University Press.

Benhabib, S. (1999) "Models of Public Space". In Calhoun, C. and Burger, T. (eds.) *Habermas and the Public Sphere,* pp. 73-98 Cambridge, MA: MIT Press.

Bode, I. (2003) "A New Agenda for European Charity". *Voluntas*, 14 (2), pp. 205-225.

Bourdieu, P. (1986) "Forms of Capital". In Richardson, J. (ed.) *Handbook of Theory and Research for the Sociology of Education,* pp. 241-258. New York: Greenwood Press.

Calhoun, C. (1992) "Introduction". In Calhoun, C. and Burger, T. (eds.), op. cit., pp. 1-48.

Carruthers, B. (1999) *City of Capital.* Princeton, NJ: Princeton University Press.

Chambers, S. and Kymlicka, W. (2002) *Alternative Conceptions of Civil Society.* Princeton, NJ: Princeton University Press.

Chaney, P. and Fevre, R. (2001) Inclusive Governance and 'Minority' Groups. *Voluntas,* 12 (2), pp. 131-156.

CIA. Available at: www.cia.gov/cia/publications/factbook/gros/ee.html.

Coleman, J. (1990) *Foundations of Social Theory.* New York: Belknap Press.

Council of Europe and European Commission (2004) *Pathways Towards Validation and Recognition of Education, Training and Learning in the Youth Field, Working Paper.* Strasbourg and Brussels: Council of Europe and European Commission. Available at: http://www.youth-knowledge.net/system/galleries/download/research-_reports/2004_ validation_and_recognition.pdf

Dekker, P. and Uslaner, E. (2001) *Social Capital and Participation in Everyday Life.* London: Routledge.

INRA (2001): *Young Europeans in 2001:* Eurobarometer Special Report 151, Brussels: European Commission, Directorate General for Education and Training.

Fraser, N. (1989) *Unruly Practices.* Minneapolis: University of Minnesota Press.

Fraser, N. (1999) "Rethinking the Public Sphere". In Calhoun, C. and Burger, T. (eds.) op. cit. pp. 109-142. Cambridge, MA: MIT press

Gobetti, D. (1997) The Grand Dichotomy "Humankind as a System". In Weintraub, J. and Kumar, K. (eds.) *Public and Private in Thought and Practice,* pp. 103-132. Chicago: University of Chicago Press.

Granovetter, M. (1973) "The Strength of Weak Ties". *American Journal of Sociology,* 78 (6), pp. 1360-1380.

Habermas, J. (1991) *The Structural Transformation of the Public Sphere.* Cambridge, MA: MIT Press.

IARD (2001), *Study on the State of Young People and Youth Policy in Europe final report for the Commission of the European Communities,* Directorate General for Education and Culture.

Luxembourg Income Study (LIS) *Microdatabase.* Luxembourg: LIS. Available at: http://www.lisproject.org (accessed 2 August 2005).

Moore, G. and Whitt, A. (2000) "Gender and Networks in a Local Voluntary-Sector Elite". *Voluntas,* 11 (4), pp. 309-328.

Putnam, R. (2000) *Bowling Alone.* New York: Simon and Schuster.

Smith, A. (1776) *Wealth of Nations.* New York: Prometheus Books.

Stroschein, S. (2002) "NGO Strategies for Hungarian and Roma Minorities in Central Europe". *Voluntas,* 13 (1), pp. 1-26.

United Nations Economic Commission for Europe (UNECE) (2000). Geneva: UNECE. Available at: http:// www.unece.org (accessed 2 August 2005).

War Kersbergen, K. (1995) *Social Capitalism A Study of Christian Democracy and the Welfare State.* London: Routledge.

Weintraub, J. and Kumar, K. (1997) *Public and Private in Thought and Practice: The Grand Dichotomy.* Chicago: University of Chicago Press.

Yeung, A. (2004) "The Octagon Model of Volunteer Motivation". *Voluntas,* 15 (1), pp. 21-46.

2. Challenges to the development of voluntary service by young people in Poland

Anna Musiala

Introduction

It is no exaggeration to affirm that volunteers are one of the most valuable assets of any country. There is ample emergent evidence that volunteering builds social and human capital, enhances social inclusion, provides a source of reconciliation and reconstruction in divided societies, and a means of lifelong learning. It constitutes an enormous reservoir of skills, energy and local knowledge, an important wealth of human experience and social ties, and beyond these qualitative examples, volunteering makes fundamental contributions in economic terms (Lorenz 1994:141). Despite this evidence, it is unusual for governments to recognise volunteering as a strategic resource that can be positively influenced by public policy. If volunteerism is to cement societies together, if it is to be an "engine of renewal", it needs to figure more prominently in public policy and gain more recognition as a valuable form of activity (McKinstry and Lindsnaes 1993:187).

It can be stated that the legal situation of young volunteers is quite precarious, as most countries do not have, or only rarely have, laws regulating the status of volunteerism, and sometimes only covering certain aspects. At international level some states refer to the European Convention on the Promotion of Transnational Long-term Voluntary Service for Young People of the Council of Europe (Council of Europe 2000). At the European level a very limited number of States refer to the European Parliament and Council (2001) Recommendation of 10 July 2001 on mobility within the European Union for students, persons, undergoing training, volunteers, teachers and trainers which contains measures that specifically concern volunteers. At national level states rarely have a specific legal basis for voluntary activities of young people. Generally volunteering is based on individual agreements and contracts, written and even oral, and is therefore subjected to general provisions of law and jurisprudence. That is why young people who want to engage in voluntary activities meet a number of difficulties. These difficulties usually concern: social protection, taxation of pocket money, and refusal of visa and residence permits. They represent real obstacles to the exercise of voluntary activities of young people and limit the access to them for significant numbers of young Europeans.

I would like to indicate those obstacles which may discourage young Polish people from taking part in voluntary activities both in Poland and abroad. I want to concentrate especially on the legal aspects of voluntary work as my own research concerns the legal status of people working without being paid for it. My intention is not only to show the problems but also to propose the possible solutions to them. I suggest that without defining clear and precise regulations concerning the general procedures, and especially the legal consequences of voluntary work abroad, it will be impossible to facilitate voluntary activities (Halba 2003). My country, Poland, provides a very good example of these issues.

The context

Poland has undergone dramatic political and economical changes over the last fifteen years. The government continues to liberalise its trade, foreign exchange and investment polices. There can be also observed widespread administrative and social reforms, including health care, social security and the educational system. Political freedom permits us now to establish parties and associations, vote in elections, open personal bank accounts and surf the Internet. Poland is becoming a consumer-oriented society with all the good and bad consequences of that change. A beneficial result of that change is the appearance of non-governmental organisations that use volunteers. More than half of all NGOs (55%) do not employ full-time paid personnel and 47% work with volunteers. There are estimated to be around 1.6 million volunteers in total, who invest on average eighteen hours per month. The majority of volunteers are employed (61%), school pupils (42%) or students (40%) (Ochman and Jordan 1993:6).

The Polish term *wolontariusz* (volunteer) has been used historically to describe either a person who has an unpaid apprenticeship or someone who offers to join the army. For a long time we have been interested in the broader meaning of the term and its social context, which is well known in countries with a long tradition of volunteerism, but was new for us in Poland. Before the Law on Public Benefit Activity and Volunteerism[1] there was no legal definition of voluntary activity. By volunteering we understood activities which were unpaid, conscious, based on free will for the benefit of others. Everyone might become a volunteer, in every field of social life, wherever there was a need, but not every volunteer could perform every type of work. The term "volunteer" was firstly used for people who carried out humanitarian aid in third countries after 1989. Now we have in our system of law a definition of volunteer. However, we must remember that in Polish the term "voluntary activities" defines broadly all types of voluntary engagement without remuneration.

The final adoption of the Law on Public Benefit Activity and Volunteerism followed some six years of discussion and preparation of drafts by NGOs and different governments. The International Year of Volunteers in 2001 served to highlight the need for political recognition of volunteers and its social importance. The Minister of Labour submitted the draft law to the government on 5 December 2001 (International Volunteer Day). After a series of amendments this law came into force on 29 June 2003. The new law does not change existing laws on associations and foundations. None the less, it is very important for the future development of the third sector as it defines the criteria for public benefit status of Polish NGOs. The law also provides a definition of NGO and procedural framework for co-operation between local governments and NGOs.

1. Law on Public Benefit Activity and Volunteerism, dated 24 of April 2003 – volunteer service act.

A "volunteer" is defined as a person who voluntarily and with no remuneration provides services based on regulations specified in the law. The law ensures the protection of volunteers working with accredited organisations regarding health and social security. Volunteers are entitled to receive reimbursement of expenditure for costs like travel and training, as well as a daily allowance exempt from taxes. The law contains provisions for international voluntary services programmes sending Poles abroad and receiving foreign volunteers from other countries. Volunteers are also entitled to benefits and reimbursements of the costs "generally acknowledged for the situation" (for example, board and lodging).

The law represents an important change for volunteers working in Poland with accredited organisations. However, we must realise that the provisions of the law are not sufficient for people working as volunteers. And there are many problems as a result of a very modest and inaccurate legal regulation. I would like to concentrate on four of these problematical issues from the Polish point of view:

- the lack of synchronisation (specific legal connection) between EVS and Polish law (the lack of proper (convenient) standards as well as of provisions on social protection);

- the problem of replacing full-time workers with volunteers;

- work which is necessary in vocational training (apprenticeship) is performed in Poland without any remuneration, even without reimbursement of costs and these people learning defined skills are called volunteers;

- the lack of clear structures concerning voluntary organisations and also the lack of information about voluntary activities.

The European Voluntary Service programme and the law in Poland

The Law on Public Benefit Activity and Volunteerism has helped to regulate some of the basic and most difficult issues.[1] This law (as can be observed) has encouraged even more people to participate in the voluntary actions. Now the volunteers know their legal situation and all legal consequences of their work. In the past they were very often discouraged from taking part in voluntary work just because they did not know their legal status. However, there are still many doubts concerning voluntary work in Poland. A very problematic issue concerns the term of "volunteer", which is not officially recognised. This lack of recognition means that volunteers have to accept financial disadvantages compared to other low-income groups such as students, unemployed people or pensioners because there is no institutionalised framework for volunteers and as a result they do not get any reductions, for example, tickets for public transport or cultural events.

It must be also remembered that the Law on Public Benefit Activity and Volunteerism does not refer to voluntary work in the frame of EVS. Therefore, I can point out some problematical issues concerning European Voluntary Service in the context Polish law (Sieveking 2001:176). There are many volunteers who could possibly take part in EVS but the lack of legal regulations makes them sceptical and dis-

1. Musiala 2003 – the legal situation of volunteers in Poland has been analysed with an indication that the Polish non-governmental sector needs some clear regulations concerning its activity (especially volunteers' work). The book was written at the beginning of the year 2003, just before the Law on Public Benefit Activity and Volunteerism came into force.

∧ Challenges in Poland

couraged. Also the National Agency in Warsaw sometimes encounters problems concerning legal position which results in uneasiness in their undertakings.

There are few general regulations concerning EVS in the Polish legal system.[1] Poland is not ready to deal with a lot of fundamental issues invoked by volunteers' undertakings, such as:

- the issue of social insurance; can the period of the voluntary work (which is unpaid) be treated like a period of normal work for which we get paid? It as regards both future pension and the unemployment allowance is a crucial problem (Supiot 2001:82);
- should the unemployed be deprived of their rights to the unemployment allowance if they want to participate in EVS? (Sieveking 2001:172)

European law does not tackle the above questions and the Polish law does not solve the problems either. So what are we to do then? When people willing to do the voluntary work abroad encounter such problems and nobody can help them, they simply resign.

A very common issue that appears when dealing with voluntary activities concerns military service. There is no regulation in the Polish legal system for people who have just finished school and who want to participate in EVS. There is, however, a regulation that they should perform military service. Is it possible to postpone this duty for one year in order to participate in EVS?

Moreover, young people with an unemployed or student status may lose their health insurance, if they go abroad for a long period. If an unemployed young person chooses to volunteer abroad, he/she loses access to benefits and needs to register again after his/her return. Concerning family allowances, volunteers going abroad longer than for three months also lose their right to receive family allowances. To restart the payment, a new application must be submitted to a parent's employer when the volunteer has returned. Young people, whose parents are divorced, are entitled to a special allowance until they have finished studying. In the case of volunteering abroad, they lose the allowance. Young people entitled to receive an orphan's pension until the start of their studies also lose the benefits if they go abroad as a volunteer for three months or more. Basic criteria for the end of payments are the fact that volunteerism is not recognised on a par with formal education and that young people often leave the country to perform this activity.

These examples give an idea of the restrictions on organisations and volunteers. They do not encourage participation in the EVS programme. Official recognition would create good conditions for young transnational mobility. More young people would be willing to engage in European citizenship if legal obstacles were removed.

Displacement and substitution

There is an understandable concern that the growth of the voluntary sector and temporary employment schemes will be used to substitute for properly paid permanent employment. As a result there has been a strong resistance in some Polish areas of highest unemployment to the involvement of voluntary organisations. In Poland it is less well understood that voluntary service is not a remedy for unemployment. What is more, it must be remembered that volunteering should never replace paid work but should be seen as a natural adjunct to the well-being of the

1. For an overview see http://www.youth.org.pl

community. Therefore, legislation should protect the rights and responsibilities of both paid employees and volunteers. Voluntary service can provide an important and worthwhile solution to the problem of unemployment but it should not be used by governments as a means of manipulating employment statistics and creating a "second labour market" with second-class jobs for second-class citizens. Neither should it be regarded as a cheap way for society to delegate public responsibilities to non-governmental organisations handling voluntary service. It is true that voluntary service schemes are generally less costly, leading some to feel they could be alternatives to more costly retraining schemes, but this reasoning is false. Voluntary service has its own value for young people and society and has always been regarded not only as an activity of public benefit and service rendered to society but also as an alternative means of access to working life, enabling young people to develop new skills that will help them gain a foothold in society and find a job. It forms an integral part of the concept and structures of adult education, implying active involvement in a long and wide-ranging process of learning all facets of life – it is not just a continuation of vocational training. It is a social learning process in the broadest sense, which cannot be achieved without educational support at the group or individual level. I am afraid that if Polish people do not realise the sense of voluntary activities, then very soon the Polish voluntary service will resemble certain alternative forms of national service designed for conscientious objectors, the unemployed and social welfare beneficiaries, as far as the organisation of the work and the form of payment goes (Street 1994:21). However, these types of service will be rarely voluntary and are often imposed or demanded by the authorities. It is for this reason that voluntary service worthy of the name must stem from a carefully considered personal decision.

Clearly there is a need for the Polish legal system to distinguish a volunteer from a worker or an employee by stressing the educational character of transnational voluntary service. The European Court of Justice has defined the concepts of employees and workers.[1] The court stated that an employee is any person getting a salary or wages in exchange for full or part-time work. This definition is explicitly only used in the realm of economic life. A volunteer is not active in economic life but participates in projects of mobility in the realm of youth or adult education. Money is not given to the volunteer for their work, but to provide for basic living. This allows them to contribute to the common good and learn for their own social and personal maturity.

---> ## Confusion in terminology and status

In Poland a person who has finished medical school and who wants to become a heart specialist must perform a period of additional training which lasts about four years. As a result of a lack of places in hospitals for everybody wishing to do this, some of these future doctors perform this period of special training without payment. In Poland they are called volunteers. The same issue affects people who have finished in faculty of law and want to be, for examples a judge. In this situation they work in a court of justice performing the necessary special training, but they do not receive any money. We also call them volunteers. Is this is typical only for Poland or maybe in other countries we can also find such practices?

1. European Court of Justice: decision in the case of D.M. Levin from 23 March 1982 – 53/81.

Structures and information

A crucial problem for further development of voluntary service is the lack of co-oper-ation between Polish associations in order to tackle common issues. One example of where good co-operation exists is the "Centrum Wolontariatu" in Warsaw, which acts as a co-ordination organisation for a network of 16 regional centres and organ-isations working with EVS. The idea of a common platform for voluntary youth organisations is not discussed. Polish people do not know the structure of Polish voluntary organisations, what kind of problems they deal with and how they fulfill their tasks.

Conclusion

From the research I have carried out, there is a need to create the special status of volunteer, because of the unusual nature of voluntary service, which tends not to fall within the framework of existing practices or legislation on, for example, youth mobility, education, the labour market, and social protection. The specific charac-teristics of voluntary service could, for instance, be recognised by:

- issuing volunteers with student visas and regarding them as non-wage earners, without any formal connections with the labour market and therefore not requiring a work permit. This approach might be considered if the definition of voluntary service placed emphasis on its educational value rather than its activity function;

- requiring the organisations to guarantee a status and a voluntary service con-tract providing for free board and lodging, appropriate health, accident insur-ance, pocket money, preparation, support and post-service evaluation.

These proposals would represent some starting points for clarifying the status of a volunteer (particularly in Poland) and for ensuring an appropriate framework for their support and for sustaining their involvement.

References

Allot, M. and Robb, M. (1998) *Understanding Health and Social Care.* London: Sage.

Beigbeder, Y. (1991) *The Role and Status of International Humanitarian Volunteers and Organizations.* The Haque: Martinus Nijhoff Publishers.

Council of Europe (2000) *European Convention on the Promotion of a Transnational Long-term Voluntary Service for Young People.* ETS No. 175. Strasbourg: Council of Europe.

European Parliament/European Council (2001) *Recommendation of 10 July 2001 on Mobility within the Community for Students, Persons Undergoing Training, Volunteers, Teachers and Trainers (2001/613/CE).* Strasbourg and Brussels: European Parliament/European Council.

Halba, B. (2003) *Bénévolat et volontariat en France et dans le monde.* Paris : La documentation Française.

Lorenz, W. (1994) *Social Work in Changing Europe.* New York: Walter de Gruyter.

McKinstry, M. and Lindsnaes, B. (1993) *The Role of Voluntary Organisations in Emerging Democracies. Experience and Strategies in Eastern and Central Europe and in South Africa.* Copenhagen: The Danish Centre for Human Rights.

Musiala, A. (2003) "The Legal Aspects of Voluntary Work". Ph.D. dissertation. Warsaw University.

O'Higgins, N. (1997) *The Challenge of Youth Unemployment.* Geneva: ILO.

Ochman, M. and Jordan, P. (1993) *Volunteers: A Valuable Resource.* Baltimore: Johns Hopkins University.

Sieveking, K. (2001) *European Voluntary Service for Young People. Questions of Status and Problems of Legal Policy.* Berlin: Walter de Gruyter.

Street, L. (1994) *Volunteering for Work Experience.* Ottawa: Volunteer Ontario.

Supiot, A. (2001) *Beyond Employment. Changes in Work and the Future of Labour law in Europe.* Oxford: Oxford University Press.

Part 4

Learning, evaluation and recognition

1. Learning and recognition of voluntary activities

Agnieszka Moskwiak

Introduction

At the beginning of the 1980s sociologists observed that a developing economy did not improve the situation on the labour market. There was a growing unemployment rate among young people, who after finishing school remained outside the labour markets. Great numbers of them did not have sufficient levels of educational attainment, skills and experience to get a job and start an adult life. There have, as a result, been some actions taken by the European Commission in order to support young people and their transition from school to the labour market.

In this chapter I will focus on the European Voluntary Service (EVS), a programme established by the European Commission in 1995, which aimed to create a space for young people to gain educational and professional experience. Based on my own research I will try to answer if and what Polish volunteers learn from voluntary activities and how it influences their educational and professional choices. In the second part of this chapter I will present Polish pathways to recognition of experiences gained during non-formal education.

From education to work?

In the opinion of the Italian sociologist Ferraroti (1977:39):

> youth is a social invention of industrial society and at the same time its most obvious failure …. In traditional societies, youth as a separate and specific social group simply did not exist. One would pass directly from infancy to adulthood and responsibility and full-time work. Schooling was but a passing phase … training was done directly on the job.

Traditional pathways of transition no longer exist. Education does not lead directly to employment. The education system is not flexible enough and lags behind fast changing technology and requirements of the modern labour markets. The university degree is not sufficient to get a job and start an adult life. Young people feel lost in this situation and have no knowledge of where to improve their skills and gain professional experience. They do not know what kind of experience provides the best pathways to work.

The European Commission has undertaken some initiatives, focused on improving the occupational and social position of young people. Among them there are programmes like Socrates and Erasmus, which enhance university students' exchange, Leonardo Da Vinci for young workers and last but not least European Voluntary Service for young people. The programmes together create European educational space.

On basis of Decision No. 1031/2000/EC of the European Parliament and the European Council on 13 April 2000 the European Commission implemented the Youth Community Action programme (European Union 2000). It was aimed at young people aged 15-25. This programme was, however, a continuation of the already existing programmes Youth for Europe and European Voluntary Service. Decision 1031/2000/EC made the programme structure more clear and comprehensible for the users and also added new programmes such as Youth Initiatives and Support Measures.

The European Voluntary Service programme

European Voluntary Service (EVS) was established in 1996 when a pilot action was made and 200 young people participated in voluntary activities abroad. Since then European Voluntary Service has been gaining greater importance as a source of educational and professional experience for young people and a means of involvement of young people from more disadvantaged backgrounds. What was important is the fact that EVS lay in the non-formal education arena. This is so important because EVS aims to engage participants who are early school-leavers or are outside the formal education system.

The main objective of the European Voluntary Service programme is to reinforce social and occupational inclusion of young people and help local communities by introducing good practices involving young volunteers who work for between six and twelve months. During their period of voluntary services volunteers get new social and professional experiences, improve their knowledge and develop personal skills.

Voluntary activities are not only a way of using spare time but also a source of new professional experiences. That is why it should be recognised as a part of professional experience gained in a non-formal way. The definition of volunteering changes its meaning from help others to helping others, help yourself. Young people are more and more aware of this fact, so that each year the number of young people in Poland involved in voluntary activities increases. Also the numbers of young people who participate in European Voluntary Service increase constantly. Data presented below show the engagement of people in voluntary activities in Poland. Comparing 2001 and 2003 we see an almost threefold percentage increase of volunteers under 25 years of age (table 1), and table 2 presents the number of EVS participants in Poland.

Table 1: Engagement in voluntary activities in Poland

Age	Volunteers		
	2001	2002	2003
Under 25	8.10%	11.90%	22.50%
26-35	7.80%	9.60%	19.40%
36-46	10.40%	13.60%	18.60%
46-55	14.50%	13.60%	20.50%
Over 55	10.10%	7.10%	8.30%

Source: Polish volunteerism and philanthropy research – KLON/JAWOR 2005.

European youth voluntary activities

Table 2: Number of European Voluntary Service participants in Poland

	Total 2000	Total 2001	Total 2002
Applications submitted	51	211	378
Financed projects	49	159	285
Number of volunteers	49	159	285

Source: Polish National Agency of the Youth Programme internal report, 2002.

The data presented above show that in Poland there is a growing engagement of young people in voluntary activities, both in home and foreign volunteering programmes. It was these data that inspired me to conduct research related to the European Voluntary Service.

Empirical research

The aim of the research was to assess educational and occupational benefits gained by young people involved in EVS. In particular, the specific objectives of the research project were to understand:

- The motivation of young people participating in European Voluntary Service;

- Whether young participants are aware of benefits they can obtain during the service;

- Whether participants apply in order to get particular skills and knowledge or is it only a desire for "foreign adventure";

- Whether volunteers participate in EVS in order to improve their job opportunities.

My empirical research is focused on young people who participated in long-term European Voluntary Service between 2000 and 2002. In the first part of the research I focused on the motivation of young people to participate in EVS and what people learn during their periods of voluntary service. The second part is an attempt to assess whether the experience gained during voluntary service can be recognised in Poland and what should be done in order to increase the recognition of these experiences. The research was conducted at the beginning of 2004.

Methodology

The methodology included a questionnaire sent via post and e-mail to Polish EVS volunteers who completed their service in years between 2000 and 2002. I decided to send questionnaires only to volunteers who provided an e-mail or a postal address. Volunteers were chosen from the database of volunteers from the Polish National Agency of the Youth Programme. I chose a group of 241 volunteers who fulfilled the sampling criteria: 150 with an e-mail address and 91 with a postal address. On 16 January 2004 I sent questionnaires to volunteers. Some 68 completed questionnaires were returned, a response rate of 30%. This response was relatively high for a random sample (Sztabinski 1997), but was nevertheless supplemented through further communication with respondents (for example, some missing dates, unclear answers). The data presented below show only some selective conclusions from my research.

Learning and recognition

Demographic structure of respondents – Sex, age, level of education

A majority of participants in European Voluntary Service are females in all countries of the programme. Equality policy has been introduced, however, to increase the number of male participants. Some national agencies of the EU Youth programme have introduced a points system when assessing applications, in order to encourage sending and hosting organisations to accept also male volunteers on projects. Among Polish participants in EVS, 84.3% are women and 15.7% are men, and the average age of respondents in my research was 25 years (see table 3). The average age of European volunteers is much lower, at 20-21 years old.

Table 3: Age of the respondents

Years	%
29	2.90%
28	8.80%
27	11.70%
26	14.70%
25	32.30%
24	14.70%
23	2.90%
22	8.80%
21	2.90%

Source: Own research.

Young people from the former EU (the fifteen countries before enlargement in May 2004) usually take up their service after they finish high school. In contrast, Polish young people mostly decide to become involved in voluntary service (EVS) after they enrol at university (table 4). The reason for this difference lies in the fact that, in the majority of the countries, students simply have to sign up to universities on the basis of prior qualifications (e.g. France, Italy). In Poland the majority of higher education institutions require entrance examinations. A one-year break makes it almost impossible to pass these exams. Recent research conducted by the Polish Evaluation Society on Polish participants in the European Voluntary Service programme does suggest, however, that the age of volunteers in Poland is decreasing and more people around the age of 20 or 21 are now deciding to become volunteers.

Table 4: Level of education of respondents

High school students	2.90%
Recently graduated high school students	14.70%
University students	64.70%
University graduates	17.70%

Source: Own research.

Motivation to do voluntary work and participants' perspectives on what has been learned

Previous experience in voluntary work

One of the main questions to consider in relation to EVS participants is if they have ever participated in voluntary activities before. What is so significant about Polish volunteers is the fact that most of them (45.9%) have never been volunteers before. Some 44.1% of EVS volunteers, however, had participated in some kind of volunteer work: 86.6% of them worked with children, 20% were engaged in development of NGOs, 13.3% worked for NGOs, which manage volunteers on different projects, and 13.3% helped in an NGO office.

Motivation to go on EVS

When we take into consideration the motivation to go on EVS we have to ask also why volunteers chose certain areas of activity for their project. This refers to interests and the expectations of the volunteers towards project content. Table 5 presents what is important for volunteers when they choose projects within EVS. It can also give answers to what they expect to learn during EVS. For the majority of young people taking up service the most important things are: relation to their interests (47%), country (47%) which usually is connected with a desire to learn the language (47%) and the possibility of acquiring new skills and knowledge (47%). The least important reason is any connection of the project with previous volunteer and work experience (5.8%).

Table 5: What was important for you when choosing project subject?

1	It had to correspond to my interests	47.00%
2	It had to be placed in a certain country	47.00%
3	It had to give me a chance to get new skills and knowledge	47.00%
4	It had to give me a chance to learn a language	47.00%
5	It had to give me a chance to use my knowledge and skills from school, university	23.50%
6	There were places available	20.50%
7	It had to correspondent to my education	17.60%
8	I wanted to know a new area	14.70%
9	The subject had to concern certain areas	11.70%
10	The project should be with other foreign volunteers	11.70%
11	Other – I don't know: 2 – I knew the hosting organisation before: 3 – Someone told me it was interesting: 1	8.80%
12	It had to corresponded to my previous work experience	5.80%
13	It had to correspondent to my previous volunteer experience	5.80%

Source: Own research.

Volunteers were asked to write five reasons for their decision to participate in EVS, in order from the most important reason (1) to the least important (5) one. Table 6 illustrates that, first and foremost, volunteers wanted to get to know new cultures and people. Some 14% of all responses identified this reason. The second most chosen reason was to learn or improve foreign languages (12.8%).

I was also interested to see if volunteers choose EVS because they think it will improve their chances to get a better job in the future. Some 4.8% of volunteers stated that EVS offers occupational experience and the same proportion felt that it helped to improve their future job prospects. The table also shows that most volunteers choose participation in EVS because they want to know about other people and new cultures – such as their history, politics, education, mentality and customs. As Kristensen (1999) has suggested, intercultural competencies are part of what are now being referred to as "international key qualifications".

Table 6: Motivation to go on EVS

	Why did you decide to participate in EVS?	Ranking (number of choices)					%
		1	2	3	4	5	
1	I wanted to know other people, a new culture	6	16	8	14	2	14.0
2	I wanted to learn a language	8	6	12	10	6	12.8
3	I wanted to get new skills and knowledge	2	8	4	12	8	10.3
4	I wanted to help other people	4	10	8	2	6	9.1
5	It was an adventure	6	0	10	4	8	8.5
6	I wanted to make a break in my schooling to think about what I wanted to do in the future	6	6	2	0	8	6.7
7	Because I wanted to be independent	2	2	6	6	0	4.8
8	EVS gives a chance to get occupational experience	6	2	2	0	6	4.8
9	EVS experience helps to get a better job in the future	8	0	4	2	2	4.8
10	I wanted more experience in this area	2	4	2	2	2	3.6
11	I wanted to know better myself	2	0	4	4	2	3.6
12	I was unemployed	4	0	0	0	4	2.4
13	The EVS project was adequate for my education area	2	0	0	2	4	2.4
14	One of my friends was a EVS volunteer	2	2	0	0	2	1.8
15	Employers prefer people with volunteer experiences	0	0	2	0	4	1.8
16	I wanted to check if the subject interested me	0	0	4	0	2	1.8
17	I wanted to go abroad before I continue my education	6	0	0	0	0	1.8
18	Other – I knew the hosting organisation before – I couldn't have found an interesting job in Poland	4	0	2	0	0	1.8
19	EVS gives a chance to develop knowledge and skills gained in school, at the university	0	0	0	4	0	1.8
20	I have just finished school/university and I didn't know	0	0	0	2	2	1.2

Source: Own research.

It seems that young people are aware that participation in EVS increases job opportunities; however, they volunteer because they want to experience living in a different culture, with young people from all over Europe. Only 1.2% chose EVS because they did not have any idea about what to do after finishing school.

Skills required by projects and learned through participation

I also asked volunteers if their projects required any specific skills or knowledge (table 7). Some 67.6% of the respondents said that their project did not require any skills; 32.4% stated that they were asked for previous experience. They mentioned various skills and, importantly, also characteristics such as openness, tolerance and courage. Some 36.4% of hosting projects required fluent knowledge of a language.

Table 7: Skills required by EVS hosting project

1	Fluent knowledge of a language	36.4
2	Character traits: tolerance, openness, courage	36.4
3	Previous experience in work with children/youth	36.4
4	Computer processing	27.3
5	Artistic creativity	9.1
6	Knowledge of subject area	9.1
7	Organisational skills	9.1
8	Driving licence	9.1

Source: Own research.

The vast majority (76.5%) of volunteers, when asked if they got new skills and knowledge during their projects, said that they had (see table 8). The most obvious outcome arising from participation in European Voluntary Service, to which 46.1% made reference, was knowledge of a language. This was followed by "interpersonal skills" (30%). Some 23% of the volunteers also said that they had acquired some organisational skills during their projects, and another very important outcome was the capacity to live in a different culture (19.2%).

Some 11.5% of volunteers indicated that an outcome of their EVS experience was the broadening of their horizons and developing values such as tolerance, openness and respect. Volunteers also indicated that they had acquired a better understanding of certain subjects like youth, and issues relating to disabilities, and ecology.

Table 8: Skills and knowledge gained during EVS

1	Language skills	46.1%
2	Interpersonal skills	30%
3	Organisational skills	23%
4	Better understanding of certain subjects: youth, issues relating to disabilities and ecology	23%
5	Ability to live in a different culture	19.2%
6	Technical skills	15.3%
7	Better knowledge about youth programmes	15.3%
8	Some values: openness, tolerance, respect	11.5%
9	Artistic skills	7.7%
10	Ability to work with "disadvantaged" youth	7.7%
11	Cooking skills	7.7%
12	Sporting skills	3.8%

Source: Own research.

Learning and recognition

Overall evaluation of EVS influence

Participation in EVS most influenced the personal development of the volunteers. We can assume, however, that personal development influences educational and occupational choices. Volunteers are more open and equipped for new experiences; sometimes they decide to study subjects they would never have chosen before or they become convinced that occupational choices they made were right. Over 50% of the volunteers stated that EVS had had an influence on educational choices and over 60% stated that their participation also influenced their occupational choice. Over 50% of volunteers answered that participation in EVS had had an influence on getting a job. In contrast, however, 32% of volunteers stated that their EVS experience had had no influence on increasing their employability.

Table 9: Influence on different areas of life

Influence on	Significant influence	Big influence	Average influence	Small influence	No influence
Educational choice	23.50%	29.00%	12.00%	0%	35.00%
Occupational choice	23.50%	44.00%	12.00%	0%	21.00%
Getting job	26.40%	24.00%	12.00%	5.90%	32.00%
Personal development	70.50%	21.00%	2.90%	2.90%	2.90%

Source: Own research.

Summary of research findings

The aim of my research was to find answers to some core issues relating to the influence of EVS on volunteers and their educational and occupational choices. Polish volunteers, the research suggests, are aware of the benefits they can get by participating in EVS, but this consciousness comes after the experience of EVS, rarely prior to involvement. Most prospective volunteers want to get some new intercultural experience, and to learn or improve a language. At the start, they do not associate EVS with professional experience. After the service is completed, however, volunteers discover that it has a great influence on their personality and as a consequence on their choices concerning adult life.

EVS is an important experience in the voluntary curriculum. In Poland, however, it is not recognised enough by the employers. In the second part of this chapter I will try to highlight some core issues concerning recognition and validation of experiences gained during non-formal education.

Recognition of voluntary experience

Research conducted on Polish volunteers shows that a lot of Polish EVS participants expect that experience gained whilst volunteering will help them not only to develop their knowledge, skills and personality, but will also be a trump card which will enrich their curricula vitae compared with those who do not take up opportunities for volunteering.

The European Union and governments of the EU countries make efforts to increase recognition of experiences gained during volunteering activities. My research affirms that voluntary activities are still not recognised by Polish employers who

European youth voluntary activities

still view them as an interesting break in people's careers, but they do not know how it could be useful in work.

The main problem is that volunteering itself is not recognised in certain countries where programmes for volunteers have existed for a short time only. In post-soviet countries, for example Poland, Czech Republic, Slovakia and Hungary, volunteering still has very bad connotations, for it recalls the communist ideology where "each citizen should be involved in community improvement and should do something beneficial for society". As a result, at the beginning of the 1990s, when the fall of the Iron Curtain took place, and even with the appearance of new non-governmental organisations, not many people were keen on volunteering because of these foundations and associations. KLON/JAWOR's statistics (KLON/JAWOR 2005) mentioned at the beginning of this chapter indicate that even in 2001 not many people were involved in voluntary activities, for example only 8.1% in 2001 of people under 25 years of age. In Poland, according to some research, the word "volunteer" is not recognised by many people.

We should, however, also take into consideration that the voluntary sector in central and eastern Europe has an alternative, longer story. Before the development of civil society post-1989 an earlier "civil society" had proved its ability to organise itself under extremely difficult circumstances in central and eastern Europe. Even though there was initially no legal framework for NGO activities, it has been suggested (Les 1994) that this sector was already remarkably developed, though words such as "volunteering" and "non-governmental" organisation did not exist at that time.

Since the beginning of the 1990s considerable work has been done to overcome the negative connotations associated with voluntary activities. People were no longer forced to work for the common good, and were given the choice to participate in the activities of the NGO sector. The way to increase recognition of the volunteer sector is to inform people about voluntary activities, and where they can be done. Newspapers and magazines have a very important role to play as they are the most widespread source of information, including for young people.

One of the aims should also be to increase the recognition of voluntary programmes among young people who are "actors" in the voluntary scene. There are still a lot of young people, especially from less privileged backgrounds, who do not know that they can volunteer or that there are programmes for volunteering that may help them to gain experience. There should be more open information access, by means of different institutions of public life, such as NGOs and government institutions. There should be a greater engagement of the state in the promotion of voluntary activities. Poland has not had a youth policy for many years, but in 2003 the Polish Youth Strategy for the years 2003-12 was adopted by the Ministry of National Education and Sport. The second strategic objective is creating chances for the development of self-detemined activity and initiative on the part of young people. This could clearly be achieved in part through the development of youth voluntary service, either at a national or international level. In 2003 the ministry and the National Agency of the Youth Programme started popularising international forms of youth voluntary service, for example the EU Youth programme. In 2004 a database on youth voluntary service was created. Within this structure there is Eurodesk Polska, and the next step will be in 2004-05, building a national system of youth information compatible with Eurodesk. These actions should increase access for young people to information and recognition of the experiences gained during periods of voluntary service.

Learning and recognition

Furthermore there is no good system of certification of skills gained whilst volunteering. NGOs did not have to certificate engaged volunteers before 2003. To change this situation the Law on Public Benefit Activity and Volunteerism in Poland was adopted in April 2003 (and came into force on 29 June 2003). This law provides a framework for the activity of the third sector and for its volunteers. NGOs are obliged to issue a written volunteer agreement when the period of voluntary work exceeds thirty days. In addition they have to provide safe and hygienic work conditions, cover travel expenses incurred by volunteers in connection with their service, and cover training costs. These solutions are still not complied with by many organisations, which find them bureaucratic and time consuming.

The Polish Government also adopted the programme "First Job" which was created for young graduates. Voluntary service was included in this programme as a valuable source of work experience and to combat social exclusion.

----> Conclusion

Much has been done to increase recognition of voluntary service in Poland. However, there are still challenges to be faced and some solutions missing. Voluntary activities still have not been treated as a "period of employment" for the purposes of receiving state welfare payments. There is no distinction between short-term and long-term voluntary activities. Solutions in these areas would encourage employers to treat voluntary experiences as equal to work experiences. As I noted at the start of this chapter, employers often still do not understand what it means to work as a volunteer and that volunteers are often engaged in activities which require a very good knowledge of those areas of "work".

Recognition and validation of experiences gained during non-formal education (for example, European Voluntary Service) is still not appreciated enough in Poland. However, the Polish National Agency of the Youth Programme and some NGO umbrella organisations are working to promote and enhance the recognition of this area of learning. On 8 December 2004 the first Polish conference on non-formal learning took place, which brought together stakeholders such as politicians, youth workers, youth leaders and others who are interested in the recognition of non-formal education.

References

Association of Voluntary Service Organisation (AVSO) (2000) *Voluntar-e-news*, 2 (June).

Association of Voluntary Service Organisation (AVSO) (2001) *Voluntar-e-news*, 1 (January).

Association of Voluntary Service Organisation (AVSO) (2001) *Voluntar-e-news*, 3 (August).

Association of Voluntary Service Organisation (AVSO) (2002) *Voluntar-e-news*, 2 (July).

Association of Voluntary Service Organisation (AVSO) (2003) *Voluntar-e-news*, 1 (January).

Bonkost, K. (2002) Od marzen do zawodu. In Podczaska, (ed.) *Hanna Nauczycielstwa Polskiego. Osrodek Uslug Pedagogicznych i Socjalnych*. Tomal, Warsaw: Zwiazek.

Czerniawska, O. (2000) "Przygotowanie do wolontariatu jako zapomniany obszar w polskiej oswiacie doroslych". *Edukacja Doroslych*, 1, pp. 9-16.

Danilowicz, P. et al. (1992) *Podrecznik socjologicznych badan ankietowych*. Warsaw: Polska Akademia Nauk, Instytut Filozofii i Socjologii.

European Centre for the Development of Vocational Training (1995) *Structures of the Education and Initial Training Systems in the European Union, EURYDICE and CEDEFOP*. Luxembourg: Office for Official Publications of the European Communities.

European Commission (Directorate-General XXII, Education, Training, and Youth) (1999) *European Voluntary Service for Young People*. Luxembourg: Office for Official Publications of the European Communities.

European Commission (Directorate-General for Education and Culture) (2001) *Europe and Youth: A New Impetus*. Brussels: Office for Official Publications of the European Communities.

European Union (2000) "Decision No. 1031/2000/Ec of the European Parliament and of the Council of 13 April 2000 establishing the 'Youth' Community action programme". *Official Journal*. Luxembourg: Office for Official Publications of the European Communities. Available at: http://europa.eu.int/eurlex/pri/en/oj/dat/2000/l_117/l_11720000518en00010010.pdf (accessed: 2 August 2005).

Fabisiak, J. (ed.) (2002) *Mlodziezowy wolontariat*. Warsaw: Fundacja "Swiat na Tak".

Ferraroti, F. (1977) *Youth and Work. The Incidence of the Economic Situation on the Access of Young People to Education, Culture and Work*. Regional youth meetings, report, recommendations and documents of a European regional meeting. Venice: (n.p.).

Gruszczynski, L. (2002) *Elementy metod i technik badan socjologicznych*. Tychy: Wyzsza Szkola Zarzadzania i Nauk Spolecznych w Tychach.

Komenda Choragwi Ziemi Lubuskiej Zwiazku Harcerstwa Polskiego (2001) *Jestem ... mysle ... dzialam ... (czyli: Jak przygotowac mlodziez do wejscia na rynek pracy?)*. Zielona Góra: Komenda Choragwi Ziemi Lubuskiej Zwiazku Harcerstwa Polskiego.

Komisja Europejska (2000) *Nowe impulsy dla mlodziezy europejskiej: Biala Ksiega Komisji Europejskiej.* Luxembourg: Office for Official Publications of the European Communities.

Kristensen, S. (1999) "Mobility as a Learning Process". *European Journal of Vocational Training,* 16, pp. 24-28.

Kristensen, S. (2001) "Learning by Leaving — Towards a Pedagogy for Transnational Mobility in the Context of Vocational Education and Training (VET)". *European Journal of Education,* 36 (4).

KLON/JAWOR (2005) *Polish Voluntary Sector.* Warsaw: KLON/JAWOR. Available at: http://www.ngo.pl/labeo (accessed 2 August 2005).

Les, E. (1994) *The Voluntary Sector in Post-communist East Central Europe.* Washington DC: Civicus.

Markiewicz, Z. and Sikora, P. (eds.) (2001) *Wolontariat: od samopomocy do samozatrudnienia.* Opole: Regionalny Osrodek Polityki Spolecznej w Opolu.

Orr, K. (2000) "From Education to Employment: The Experience of Young People in the European Union". In Groth, C. and Maenning, W. (eds.) *Zukunft schaffen: Strategien gegen Jugendarbeitslosigkeit.* Frankfurt: Peter Lang.

Parzecki, R. (2001) "Wybory zawodowo edukacyjne mlodziezy w stadium". *Edukacja,* 4, pp. 53-60.

Pietrowski, D. (2001) "Wolontariat w Polsce — nowe spojrzenie na prace". *Rocz. Nauk. Carit,* 5, pp. 31-38.

Przyszczypkowski, K. and Zandecki A. (eds.) (1996) *Edukacja i mlodziez wobec spoleczenstwa obywatelskiego.* Torun: Edytor.

Ramoff, A. et al. (1994) *Vocational Education and Training in Central and Eastern Europe.* Luxembourg: Office for Official Publications of the European Communities.

Sieveking, C. (2001) *European Voluntary Service for Young People: Questions of Status and Problems of Legal Policy.* Frankfurt: Peter Lang.

Soldra-Gwizdz, T. (ed.) (1997) *Mlodziez — wyksztalcenie, praca: dylematy w zmieniajacej sie rzeczywistosci spolecznej.* Opole: Panstwowy Instytut Naukowy, Instytut Slaski.

Sztabinski, F. (1997) *Ankieta pocztowa i wywiad kwestionariuszowy.* Warsaw: Wydawnictwo IFiS PAN.

2. Recreational Activity Study Book system in Finland: an example from experience

Lauri Savisaari

Introduction: learning in voluntary activities – Why recognition?

School is an important learning environment for young people. However, young people learn outside school, as well, especially from participation in voluntary and leisure activities which offer good places for learning. Young people learn many valuable life skills in voluntary and leisure activities, for example, co-operation and team skills, communication skills, goal-orientation and problem solving skills. These skills are also useful when a young person attends further education or starts working.

Learning in voluntary and leisure activities carries various names: it might be called "civic learning", "non-formal learning" or "informal learning". If a learning activity is defined to be "non-formal learning", the organising party should have a clear understanding of the learning that is supposed to take place in the activity. That implies at least some educational principles or an "educational programme" behind the activity. One cannot argue that a learning activity is "non-formal" without a clear, well-defined understanding of the learning that takes place in it. In addition, it is essential that both the learner and the educator are aware of the aims and methods of the supposed learning situation. Without these features, the learning is "informal" or "occasional" by nature. In this context, both non-formal and informal ways of learning things and acquiring competencies are dealt with in parallel. Most organisations that deal with young people do have a clear educational role and many even have their own educational programmes (for example, the scout movement).

Formal education and non-formal or informal learning (that takes place for example in voluntary and leisure activities) support and complement each other. In line with the principles and aims of lifelong learning, the learning environment of young people should be approached as an entity, the ingredients of which are a formal educational system, working life and free-time environments (such as home, leisure activities, family, peer groups). Integration of formal and non-formal learning implies actions and a change of traditional attitudes. The learning of young people in voluntary and leisure activities is usually observed from the point of view of formal education. When doing so, the essential concepts are a) identification, b) recognition, and c) validation of learning.

From the viewpoint of voluntary and leisure activities, it is important that the learning taking place in activities is recognised and appreciated in society. Thus, evaluation of non-formal or informal learning is also important. Through evaluation the learning environment produced by youth organisations can be further developed. Evaluation or measurement of informal learning is particularly complicated, though, since the learning outcomes are very difficult to place in a specific context, time or place. In addition, informal and non-formal learning includes also non-course-based activities like information, advice or guidance, which do not usually have an agreed curriculum.

Accreditation of non-formal learning in voluntary and leisure activities can also carry risks: if, for example, a formal educational institution automatically credits a certain activity, the voluntary nature of the learning activity could be endangered. In addition, the formal educational system is relatively equal (at least in the Nordic countries) in regard to place of residence, but opportunities to actively participate in voluntary and leisure activities vary a great deal, depending on which area or region of the country one happens to live in. Therefore, it is necessary to evaluate the learning experiences in voluntary and leisure activities always personally, and on a case by case basis and in regard to specific fields of formal education.

Towards better recognition: Recreational Activity Study Book

In Finland there has been a system called "Recreational Activity Study Book" since 1996. The system is developed by the Youth Academy, which is a co-operation organisation for major Finnish youth and sports NGOs. The Finnish Ministry of Education and Culture supports the study book system. The study book is a non-formal and informal learning CV for young people. They can collect entries from all learning experiences in voluntary and leisure activities. In October 2004 there were over 70 000 study book owners in Finland. The book serves young people as a tool for making all the experiences and learning – self-development, growth etc. – outside school visible. It is also an instrument for identifying and crediting non-formal learning when applying for a job or further education. The Youth Academy has a written agreement with 250 formal educational institutions on how to value and credit the entries in the book. The study book is a feasible way to document and recognise the non-formal and informal learning of young people. The entries in the book can be presented in Finnish, Swedish or English.

The Finnish study book system focuses strongly on the development of the individual learner – young people. Despite the fact that some pathways towards formal education have been created as a part of the study book system, the idea is to cherish the very voluntary nature of the learning taking place outside school. Therefore, there are neither any criteria for the measurement of learning outcomes or performance, nor any public examinations held to assess the competencies supposedly acquired.

The Recreational Activity Study Book system is feasible for the documentation – and recognition – of both qualifications and competencies acquired by participating in youth voluntary activities. More focus is, however, placed on the competencies. That has to do with the individual learner-centeredness of the study book system. In the study book, more emphasis is put on the development of each young person's personality rather than the actual qualifications of the skills required in particular job requirements. The underlying idea is that by participating in youth voluntary or recreational activities, young people do have a chance to acquire key competencies in regard to personal development, such as social, communicative skills.

Rationale

The reasons for the openness and "non-measurability" of the Finnish study book system are several. First of all, as Bentley (1998) argues subjective perceptions of learning outcomes or competencies acquired should not be of marginal validity, as they often are in systems depending on public examinations. He states that subjective perceptions are "central to the quality of learning, and the extent to which what has been learned will be retained and applied in other contexts" (Bentley 1998:147).

The second reason for the openness and flexibility of the study book system is the already mentioned appreciation of the voluntary nature of youth informal and non-formal learning. By formalising the system, the basic motivation for participation in youth activities, i.e. the joy of being, doing and learning together, would be endangered. The Youth Academy attempts to encourage the representatives of the formal education system to recognise and value the learning and competencies young people acquire outside school, as well as to co-operate more with organisations offering young people meaningful learning environments. But the issue is always approached from an individual learner's point of view, not the point of view of the formal educational system, for example.

The third reason for keeping the study book system informal and flexible is that by doing so, all young people can gain access to it and collect entries from various learning activities. The Recreational Activity Study Book is not only targeted to those young people who are active in one or another youth organisation. Competencies can be acquired and things can be learned in various situations and settings, even the non-organised ones. Therefore, even though the study book system is developed by the Youth Academy and its 12 member organisations (major Finnish youth and sports NGOs), it is open to all young people, and the content is designed in a way that all young people "fit" in to be able to make use of it.

Content

The study book itself is divided into nine categories, according to the nature of the learning activity. The categories are:

1. regular participation in leisure activities;

2. holding positions of trust and responsibility within NGOs;

3. activities as a leader, trainer or coach;

4. participation in a project;

5. courses;

6. international activities;

7. workshop activities (apprenticeship);

8. competitions; and

9. other activities.

By looking at the categories, one can see that there are environments of both non-formal and informal learning present. The most formalised form of learning is the category "courses" which means organised and often hierarchical educational programmes offered by various youth and sport NGOs and other learning providers. The eight other categories fall more or less under the umbrella of informal learning, in which the learning-by-doing approach is often the method for acquiring competencies and skills.

According to a survey carried out by the Youth Academy in spring 2003 (690 informants), the most popular category is "courses" (17.4 %). The categories "activities as a leader, trainer or coach", "holding positions of trust and responsibility" (see figure 1) and "regular participation in leisure activities" are also quite popular (12-13% each). The following figure illustrates a sample page from the Recreational Activity Study Book.

Figure 1: Sample page from the Recreational Activity Study Book

Type of activity: Holding positions of trust and responsibility within NGOs	
Organisation in which the activity took place _____	Time/dates of the activity _/_/___ - _/_/___ On average _____ hours per week/month
Position of the young person in the organisation _____	Successes and competencies acquired _____ _____ _____ _____ _____
Description of the activity _____ _____ _____	Place Date _____
Young person's self-assessment of the learning _____ _____ _____	Signature of the person responsible for the activity _____ Contact information of the signatory _____ Position of the signatory _____

The entries in the book are always written by an adult (= over 18 years of age) person who is either responsible or well aware of the particular activity. Young people themselves fill in the part "self-assessment of the learning". The idea is to focus more on what and how things have been learned rather than what has only been done. The person signing the entry adds his/her contact information, in case someone wants to check whether the young person actually has participated in the activity or not.

The educational institutions involved in the system have a written agreement with the Youth Academy on how and to what extent they value and credit the entries in the book. It is essential to bear in mind that accreditation and validation of the learning experiences documented in the study book are always individual and case sensitive. The system does not aim for direct accreditation in formal education in any way. It is of great importance that the voluntary nature of participating and learning in voluntary youth activities, whether organised or not, will not be endangered.

The Recreational Activity Study Book is distributed to young people mainly through youth and sports NGOs. Young people usually receive or purchase the study book when involved in the activities of a particular NGO, for example when attending courses, etc. Recently, more and more private companies have purchased a limited number of study books and given them to young people locally, either through schools or youth and sport organisations.

Critical reflections: strengths and weaknesses of the Recreational Activity Study Book

The Recreational Activity Study Book was originally developed by several experts from the member organisations the of Youth Academy. The need for such a product was of a rather instrumental nature in the first place: how could those young people that are very active in the voluntary work of specific NGOs gain and benefit from their experiences and learning? The main focus was on the benefits rather than on the development of individual young people. A hidden agenda was also present: the NGOs behind the Youth Academy felt the need for better recognition of their own activities and even existence.

The Recreational Activity Study Book was very effectively distributed to the young active members of the founding organisations in the first years (1996-98). The organisations were strongly committed to the promotion of the study book, but less focus was put on the actual use of the book. Therefore, a lot of the study books distributed in the first years were given to the "right" young people, but after that there were hardly enough support measures to encourage young people to go on using the book and collecting entries in it.

Having learned important lessons from the first years with the study book, the Youth Academy invested in supporting those young people that already had the book. The Youth Academy began to publish a magazine for the study book owners. The magazine came out twice a year, and it included articles about different kinds of organisations, voluntary activities, learning in leisure time, funding own projects, using the study book in formal education and job recruiting, etc. The magazine was sent to those study book owners who had registered with the Youth Academy.

At the same time, the Youth Academy began to do biannual surveys on how the study book was actually used and how the product could be developed. The main results from the surveys have been that, although some young people actually have used the book when applying to further education or a job, most of the study book users are somewhat passive in using the book. The most important function for the study book users seems to be that the book is a black-on-white documentary for themselves on what actually has been going on in their youth.

The educational institutions involved in the Recreational Activity Study Book system have not always found it easy to recognise and value previous learning experiences of young people. This has mostly to do with the fact that the book is structured according to the nature of voluntary free time activities rather than according to the curricula of different formal educational institutions. The book focuses on experiences of young people and the learning in those experiences rather than on the skills and competencies actually acquired. A more competence-based approach would suit the educational institutions better, and probably some young people as well. However, it has been a strong strategic – and even ideological – decision by the Youth Academy and its member organisations that the Recreational Activity Study Book has to be structured on the activities, not the competencies. This has to do with the more general question in youth work and youth policy about the extent to which youth work can focus on the employability as opposed to the citizenship of young people. The answer to that question has been – at least thus far – that youth work focuses on the development of the individual and their role in civil society, not merely on employability issues.

When writing this article, the Youth Academy is a national partner in a European project called "REFINE – Recognising Formal, Informal and Non-formal Education". The Youth Academy participates with the Recreational Activity Study Book. Being a partner in the REFINE project has made it possible to test the suitability of the book in formal vocational education. At the moment, 30 young students are using the study book in In Jyväskylä Vocational Institute, in which there is a project aiming at prevention of dropping out of vocational education. As a part of that project, the institute organises free time activities for the students. The students participating in those free time activities are testing the Recreational Activity Study Book and they are promised to get study credits from the entries in the study book at the end of the term. Results from this pilot project are expected in spring 2005. Preliminary feedback has sent the message that the study book probably needs some "calibration" to be done to it in order to be able to serve the needs of formal education curricula.

Conclusion: adaptation to the European mainstream?

The Recreational Activity Study Book system has raised positive interest at a European level – it is also mentioned as a good practice in the European White Paper on youth by the European Commission. The Finnish study book system could be one starting point in creating a European model for the recognition of youth non-formal and informal learning, bearing in mind the cultural and educational differences across European countries.

There are several other European processes regarding the recognition and validation of non-formal and informal learning. Most of the work in those processes is carried out by experts in the field of formal education. From the point of view of voluntary civic activities, this is a bit problematic, since the approach towards recognition is almost always focused on skills and competencies rather than rewarding activity as such. The Youth Academy has closely followed the ongoing processes and is considering their possible effects on the future of the Recreational Activity Study Book. It is inevitable that for example "Common European Principles for the Identification and Validation of Non-formal and Informal Learning" by the

European Commission have to be taken into account when further developing the study book. Luckily, in most of the European processes regarding the theme, youth organisations and youth voluntary free time activities have been – at least to some extent – treated and dealt with as important learning environments.

It is likely that, in the future, the Recreational Activity Study Book will be restructured to relect better the common European principles and standards. Even if this happens, we have to be careful not to sacrifice the most valuable asset of the Recreational Activity Study Book, namely the appreciation of voluntary activities and young people's engagement to participate voluntarily in different free time activities.

References

Bentley, T. (1998) *Learning beyond the Classroom: Education for a Changing World*. London and New York: Routledge.

Euler, D. (2001) "Ambitious Expectations and Social Key Competencies". *Lifelong Learning in Europe*, 4, pp. 197-204.

Katus, J. (2002) Literature review of two books by Veronica McGivney: *Informal Learning in the Community, a Trigger for Change and Development* (1999, Leicester: NIACE); and *Working with Excluded Groups. Guidelines on Good Practice for Providers and Policy-makers in Working with Groups Underrepresented in Adult Learning* (2000, Leicester: NIACE). *Lifelong Learning in Europe*, 2, pp. 124-125.

Sahlberg, P. (1999) *Building Bridges for Learning: the Recognition and Value of Non-formal Education in Youth Activity*. European Youth Forum in co-operation with the National Board of Education, Finland.

3. Using qualitative research methods for analysing the volunteers' experience

Kateryna Shalayeva

Introduction

This chapter is focused on certain types of qualitative research methods for the study of long and short-term evaluation of voluntary experiences of young people across Europe. It is different from a quantitative approach to studying voluntary activities as it can provide the source for verification and estimation of the impact of voluntary service on a volunteer, and the hosting and home community. This type of qualitative research represents the position of one type of feminist methodology that focuses on the real individual lived experiences as a way to developing a greater understanding of the topic of study. Consequntely, this chapter proposes this empirical method, which should assist in creating a more precise and complete pictures of the skills and competencies that young people learn by completing voluntary activities and how voluntary experiences can be transferred to the purposes of social development. By the term "voluntary experiences" we are referring to intercultural learning, job qualification, interpersonal skills, social identities, and other related characteristics gained through voluntary involvement.

This chapter describes methods of case study, personal development reporting, biography, and qualitative research of documents. Our description of the case study is oriented towards the exploration of the community impact of voluntary activities. Personal development reporting is used as a method of analysis of the personal voluntary experiences within volunteering and of its possible impact at later stages of life. We also emphasise in the chapter that biography methodology allows the study of the experiences of pre-volunteering. In particular, it gives an opportunity to focus on the specific life stories of minority and socially excluded groups as a way to include those groups in voluntary activities on the basis of better understanding of their needs. The last method to which we give consideration is qualitative research of documents. This concerns the analysis of photos, drawings, and notes produced during voluntary activities and in the period of their rethinking that serve to include non-verbalised practices and hidden impacts in the process of social research on volunteering. Other methods of a qualitative nature are possible in research of voluntary experiences but they are not a focus of this chapter.

Rationale for more creative methodologies

An actual need to develop the methodology of social research in volunteering was indicated in the "Analysis of the Replies of the Member States of the European Union and Acceding Countries to the Commission Questionnaire on Voluntary Activities of Young People". It states: "... much still needs to be done to improve the evaluation and monitoring of voluntary activities ..." (European Commission 2004:7). First of all the sources of social information on volunteering must be diversified and this brings qualitative methods into use. Diversification of methods that aims to collect social information will lead to inclusion and consideration of minority and previously excluded social experiences as well as to immersion and clarification of previously studied aspects of volunteering and discovery of new areas. This will consequently improve the understanding of voluntary activities in general as well as the quality of their provision.

The advantage of the qualitative approach developed in this chapter lies in its capacity to draw together information on feelings, beliefs and attitudes of an individual in contrast to the generalised and de-personalised statistical figures of quantitative research. As a result the researcher who has based her study on a qualitative method can make her research sensitive and adjust the focus of research to an actual situation. This allows for gathering information that is highly personalised. It tells us stories of individual lives and therefore adds a more subjective human dimension to existing "objective" social research.

The use of qualitative methods as a general approach to discovering social reality helps to find answers to the research questions already programmed in the research scheme and the new upcoming questions that appear through the process of research. Methods of a qualitative nature do not only answer the question "what", but they also answer the questions "how" and "why". Usually in quantitative methodology (typically conducted through questionnaires) the researcher defines the main subject of research before the empirical stage, so that the whole process of data finding refers to the chosen definitions. As a result, the picture of the social reality is determined from the very beginning by the standpoint of the researcher.

It is of course true that any research is influenced by the personal values of the scientist. In the use of qualitative methods the influence of a scientist appears even more clearly. In relation to this, the moderation of a process of social discoveries goes through encouragement and inclusion of personal descriptive opinions of respondents and an in-depth look into the field of research. For example, the initial research question in the study on the impact of voluntary experiences on young people would be "What is voluntary experience?" For the quality of the qualitative research it is important to know what respondents themselves consider as voluntary experiences, because on this specific basis they create descriptive pictures of being active within different social domains as volunteers and legitimise their experiences for themselves and other agents.

By knowing what respondents mean behind "voluntary experience" we can harmonise the social research through introducing the significant social meanings delivered by respondents into the process of research and its conclusions. Prior to evaluating the "voluntary experience" we have to know what the respondents who have such an experience mean by it. The inclusion of respondents' understanding of voluntary activities provides greater validity in social research. In contrast to quantitative methodology, when categories are often predetermined, the subject plays a stronger part in shaping subsequent classifications and analysis.

Having described the focus of qualitative research as the focus on individual experiences, choices and attitudes that represent a realist, feminist methodology, we now move on to analyse four of the above-mentioned methods of qualitative research that can facilitate the social study of voluntary experiences.

Methodological innovation

The first method to be addressed is a case study. Case study is a popular sociological method used broadly when there is a need to draw a general picture of a particular situation. In the field of voluntary experience it might be oriented to explore community impact. People as human beings live in the society. Society shapes our personality and every activity of an individual makes an influence on a society at a larger scale. Voluntary activities are meant for the purposes of society. Therefore it is very important to be able to make a clear estimation of the results and impacts of voluntary activities on community life. For the purpose of developing a deeper understanding of the society at trends and the place of voluntary activities in it, we need to create an extensive and detailed picture in which domains, by which tools and with which features voluntary activities bring changes into the society.

Human life is full of emotions and feelings that are addressed through qualitative methodology. Therefore qualitative case study assists both a scientist and a broader audience to realise, through both a process and the results, what specific changes and influences have been made through voluntary activities. Case study describes and delivers the conclusions in an easy, accessible language.

In the case study we may attract individual stories of volunteers, newspaper articles, feedback from the participants of related events, expert opinions, different published and unpublished materials about particular voluntary activities including background papers, reports and proceedings, transcripts of interviews with representatives of a target group, visual documents (photos, drawings, postcards, advertisements, logos, other promotional materials), and texts of mottos of related events. Everything that comes to the attention of a researcher is of potential interest for a colourful, detailed and explanatory case study – a story of the event (see Kirby and McKenna 1989, Eichler 1988). Our purpose is to highlight the specific points related to the research of voluntary experiences. Last, but not least, in the case study is the role of the researcher who shall be creative and sensitive towards discovering new and outstanding information.

As well as the case study method allowing the researcher to define the community impact of volunteering, the personal development report facilitates our knowledge of what an impact voluntary experience makes on an individual life of a volunteer. Personal development reports are created in two ways: short term and long term. Short-term personal development reports cover the period of volunteering and are conducted prior to, within and shortly after the term of volunteering. The aim of a short-term personal development report is to collect up-to-date information about current influences and changes that voluntary experience exercises on an individual life. Within short-term reports we are able to compare the values and life practices for a person before and shortly after a term of volunteering. By this we can analyse immediate impacts that voluntary activities produce on a volunteer.

At a later stage of life, a long-term personal development report might be drawn up. Within a certain period of time a volunteer returns in her memories to a past voluntary experience and gives an opinion on what was significant or insignificant in specific areas of voluntary experiences and how it has influenced her future social achievements. Personal development reports may be executed in written or oral forms, when a volunteer describes her life on paper or participates in a semi-structured interview.

For both short and long-term reports a list of recommended questions is desirable. In our research we are interested in what competencies and life chances a volunteer has acquired through their activism? How a new situation in life has influenced personal motivation and world orientation of a volunteer? The evaluation of the reports can follow any of the established methods of qualitative analysis.

In the social research of the last decade special attention has been paid to discovering the life experiences of minority and socially excluded groups. One method that in principle allows learning the social experiences of volunteering of minority and socially excluded groups is the biography method. This is oriented to researching a general life path of an individual with a special consideration given to the turning points of human biographies. Turning points of human biographies apply to certain events, conditions and people that played a crucial role in defining life strategies and determination of life achievements.

There is a condition of social development that every individual receives equal chances to enrich her personality and to harmonise relations with the social world. Therefore specific measures and social actions must be introduced in order to involve minority and socially excluded groups in societal interaction on an equal opportunity basis. In order to do so, we need information on how and why the groups have been named "minority" and "socially excluded", and have been shifted to the margin of society.

Using the biography method, two initial questions are raised: if a new experience gives a volunteer better social benefits in terms of recognition, employment and social choices; and if any impact has been made on the close social circle of a volunteer, like family and friends? The answers that we find will be our starting point for the building up of outreach strategies as a first step towards the re-inclusion of those groups, including their involvement as volunteers.

There is an elaborated set of requirements guiding the organisation of biography study for minority and socially excluded groups. General recommendations are drawn from my doctoral research (Shalayeva 2005). Biography study may be organised through an in-depth interview, in which semi-structured or non-structured interviewing are the most appropriate. A semi-structured interview is based on a list of pre-established guiding questions. These questions will scan the whole duration of life of a respondent and have a focus on specific periods, social institutions and organisations that produce an impact on the individual's life as well as considering the influence of significant others.

The role of the researcher in the interview requires special consideration, for there is always the possibility of direct or indirect influence on answers, which needs to be minimised. In the interview researchers regularly face circumstances in which respondents may be inclined to give "desirable" answers related to expectations and assumptions to do with the characteristics of the interviewer (such as gender, ethnicity, class, age, ability). For that reason similar gender and life experience can facilitate the establishing of a common language between the respondent and the interviewer and eliminate "desirable" answers. At the same time it also increases the probability of a more correct interpretation of the results by the researcher, which will, in turn, enhance social knowledge. The results of the biography studies are the optimum results for illustrating the changes that occurred as a result of social activism in the form of voluntary involvement.

The last method to be described in this chapter is the use of qualitative research of documents. This includes the analysis of photos, drawings, postcards, logos, advertisements, and other visual materials, where visual representation forms the basis of conclusions about the non-verbalised practices and hidden impacts of social interaction among individuals and their groups. Visual practices are significant in defining social relations and therefore need a place in the process of social research.

We shall consider a wide range of materials that tend to promote volunteering in different ways. All of them can become the focus for potential documentary research. The qualitative research of documents can be used to reflect on the meanings of signs and symbols introduced in the documents that are studied. What is of interest to us is the image drawn by volunteers as an expression of their emotions and opinions in relation to their volunteering involvement? The study of pictures and drawings that volunteers produce during their activism gives an indication of the individual voluntary experience and the impact of that voluntary activity on the community. Through studying visual objects we introduce another cognitive source into the research.

For potential documentary research of this nature we may look into the questions of popular and specific meanings that visual documents hold. It will provide evidence of the real interests of the individuals involved in voluntary activities. This knowledge can be specified according to the target groups, their backgrounds and their interests. This enables us to see what images are most relevant to which audiences so we may develop more efficient outreach strategies in the voluntary field. It is in particular relation to the voluntary experiences of disabled people that qualitative research of documents connects more closely to the experiences of cognitively excluded volunteers. It is this new language of signs and symbols that requires further study.

Volunteers can themselves, without any special procedures, estimate the results of their activities. These methods have already been used as a training tool and as a part of the evaluation of training events in a number of social programmes including volunteering. The future of this method as an evaluation, rather than a training or self-assessment, technique lies in strengthening its capacity for broader analysis and explanation – although there is already a body of literature on which to build (see Harding 1987, Mehan and Wood 1975).

Conclusions

Qualitative methods of social research, such as those mentioned in this chapter, open up new areas of research on social experiences that are important for developing a better understanding of social reality and for the development of efficient social policies, including deeper institutionalisation and wider social recognition of voluntary activities. Therefore we argue for the qualitative approach that allows for focusing on the specific nature of the studied subject and their life experiences, including volunteering.

This chapter has identified several reasons for the introduction of qualitative methods in research on volunteering. First, they have the potential for gathering more diverse data. Second, they promote the inclusion and consideration of minorities. Third, they offer more sensitive research instruments and correspondingly richer data. Fourth, they assist in the clarification of previously studied aspects of volunteering and the discovery of new issues. Finally, they add a human and personal dimension to the current framework of research. Overall, the results of qualitative studies contribute to the visibility and quality of voluntary activities.

References

European Commission (2004) "Analysis of the Replies of the Member States of the European Union and Acceding Countries to the Commission Questionnaire on Voluntary Activities of Young People". Commission Staff Working Paper SEC (2004) 628, p. 7, Brussels.

Braidotti, R. (1994) *Nomadic Subjects: Embodiment and Sexual Difference in Contemporary Feminist Theory*. New York: Columbia University Press.

Devault, M. "Talking and Listening from Women's Standpoint: Feminist Strategies for Interviewing and Analysis". *Social Problems*, Vol. 37 (1), pp. 96-116.

Eichler, M. (1988) *Non-sexist Research Methods: A Practical Guide*. London: Allen & Unwin.

Harding, S. (1987) *Feminism and Methodology. Women's Perspective: Social Science Issues*. Bloomington: Indiana University Press.

Mehan, H. and Wood, H. (1975) *The Reality of Ethnomethodology*. New York: Wiley and Sons.

Kirby, S. and McKenna, K. (1989) *Experience, Research and Social Change: Methods from the Margins*. Toronto: Garamond.

Shalayeva, K. (2005) *Social Mechanisms of Life Style Formation in the Context of Feminist Paradigm*. Kyiv: Kyiv University.

Qualitative research methods

Part 5

**Contemporary position
of the European Union
and the Council of Europe**

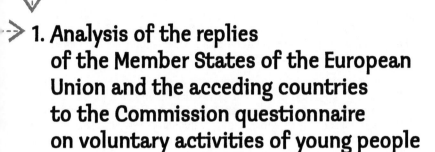

1. Analysis of the replies of the Member States of the European Union and the acceding countries to the Commission questionnaire on voluntary activities of young people

Commission staff working paper

introduction – Procedural and political background

The Commission White Paper "A new impetus for European Youth", adopted in November 2001,[1] identifies several priorities for action in the youth field amongst which participation, information, voluntary activities and a better knowledge and understanding of youth. In its Resolution of 27 June 2002 setting a new framework for co-operation in the youth field,[2] the Council called for an open method of co-ordination to be applied to the above priorities and gave mandate to the Commission to draft common objectives for those priorities on the basis of reports on the situation in all Member States.

In accordance with its mandate, and on the basis of questionnaires sent to the Member States and candidate countries, the Commission first drafted reports and proposed common objectives for participation by and information of young people. These common objectives were presented to the Council on 11 April 2003. In its Resolution of 25 November 2003,[3] the Council adopted those proposed common objectives.

Pursuant to this same mandate, and as it has done for participation and informa-tion, the Commission drew up questionnaires in consultation with the Member States and the European Youth Forum for the two following priorities, i.e. voluntary activities and a greater knowledge and understanding of youth. These question-naires were sent to the Member States, acceding countries and candidate coun-tries. Both questionnaires were drawn up using the same approach as for the questionnaires on participation and information, with the same general structure,

1. COM (2001) 681 final.

2. OJ C 168, 13 July 2002.

3. Council Resolution of 25 November 2003 on common objectives for participation and information for young people, OJ C295.

thereby first gathering basic information, then outlining the current policy with examples of best practice, and, finally, describing the expectations at European level. Countries were also asked to specify the channels used nationally for consulting young people.

While the way in which the questions were handled differed from one country to another depending on the national situation of youth policy and voluntary activities, the replies in terms of information supplied, ideas, proposals and examples of good practice put forward provided a fertile and interesting basis for reflection.

The purpose of this report is to present a synoptic analysis of the replies given by the Member States and the acceding countries to the questionnaire on voluntary activities of young people, which will serve as a basis for proposing common objectives in that area for adoption by the Council.

For the purpose of this analysis, the present report purports to describe, as a first step, the situation with regards to voluntary activities of young people such as acknowledged by the Member States and acceding countries. To this end this analysis report will first of all depict the data quality, the legal basis, the main actors, the finances as well as management, supervision, evaluation and monitoring. Then it will refer to specific information given by Member States and acceding countries on young people in voluntary activities and will treat voluntary service in particular.

After concluding on this first point, this analysis report will describe the challenges identified by the Member States and acceding countries for voluntary activities of young people, at national as well as at European level, giving examples of good practices for each of the identified challenges. Four challenges, covered each one by a chapter, have been identified about voluntary activities of young people:

• Development of voluntary activities

• Facilitating voluntary activities

• Promotion of voluntary activities

• Recognition of voluntary activities

Each of these chapters starts with an analysis of the situation in the Member States and acceding countries, outlines key-points and good practices and refers to the expectations in terms of European common objectives.

Consultation of young people and other actors for the purposes of the questionnaire

The Member States used various channels for consulting young people when preparing their replies to the questionnaires.

In some cases, this was done formally by addressing the questionnaire to various youth and voluntary organisations. In others, the authorities responsible for youth affairs set up specific national consultation bodies bringing together representatives of youth organisations with young people who were not members of an organisation.

Finally, in certain cases, specific consultation events were organised (conferences, seminars, discussion forums, etc.) bringing together representatives of various youth and voluntary organisations and young people who were not members of an organisation.

Often, specific Internet sites were set up to provide young people with information on the questionnaire, sometimes even with the questionnaire adapted to young people's "language", and to ask them, in particular those who were not members of an organisation, for their views.

Consultation did not only involve young people, but also, in many cases, other government departments, regional and local administrative bodies responsible for youth, researchers, experts on the ground and others working in the field (youth centres, town councils, youth services, national agencies for the Youth programme, associations engaged in voluntary activities etc.).

Some shared the answers to the questionnaires with the young people and their organisations, others did not.

Basic considerations

Due to the fact that there is a variety of traditions and practices of voluntary activities in the different states and in order to allow for clarity the following definitions are used in this context:

Voluntary activities: are all kinds of voluntary engagement. They are characterised by the following aspects: open to all, unpaid, undertaken by own free will, educational (non-formal learning aspect) and added social value.

Voluntary service: is part of voluntary activities and is characterised by the following additional aspects: fixed period; clear objectives, contents, tasks, structure and framework; appropriate support and legal and social protection.

Civic service: is a voluntary service managed by the state or on behalf of the state.

Civilian service: is an alternative to compulsory military service in some countries, but not voluntary.[1]

Analysis of the situation by the Member States and acceding countries

General information on voluntary activities of young people

I – Data quality

There are various approaches to gain knowledge on young people's voluntary activities in the different countries. All countries have a certain number of data, but their focus, their nature and the means and frequency of their collection differ largely, making it difficult to compare them. Also, their sources vary greatly. Sources mentioned are reports, surveys, studies, questionnaires, etc., collected by public authorities, NGOs, in particular youth and voluntary organisations, associations, universities, research institutes and young people themselves.

II – Legal basis

Concerning the legal basis of voluntary activities we have to distinguish between the European and the national level.

1. Sometimes the civilian service is also referred to as "community service".

At international level some states refer to the Convention on the Promotion of a Transnational Long-term Voluntary Service for Young People of the Council of Europe.[1]

At the European level a very limited number of states refer to the European Parliament and Council Recommendation of 10 July 2001 on mobility[2] within the Community for students, persons undergoing training, volunteers, teachers and trainers which contains measures that specifically concern volunteers. In a recent report[3] on the follow-up to this Recommendation the Commission concluded that a lot still needs to be done to implement the Recommendation in the Member States.

At national level states rarely have a specific legal basis for voluntary activities of young people. Those who have specific laws are mostly those which have a voluntary or civic service. Some regulate specific sectors of voluntary activities, as e.g. development co-operation, civil protection, social voluntary activities, etc... Others invoke a number of laws that resort to other domains but cover certain aspects of voluntary activities, as e.g. laws on associations, social care, child protection, safety and health, rescue services, etc.

Reference is often made to the fact that volunteering is based on individual agreements and contracts, written and even oral, and is therefore subject to general provisions of law and jurisprudence.

Most countries do not have a specific legal status for the protection of their volunteers. Some informed about initiatives to create a more stable legal basis for volunteering. Sometimes work related provisions also apply to volunteers. This is also the case concerning taxation, where quite a number of states treat volunteers like employees and consequently tax their pocket money. Some states have tax reductions or exemptions for volunteer organisations and for the reimbursement of costs of individual volunteers. However, these tax reductions and exemptions are sometimes bound to certain conditions, as e.g. their limitation to a certain amount of money, or the condition that a voluntary organisation is only reimbursed if it qualifies as a charity.[4]

Concluding it can be stated that the legal situation of young volunteers is quite precarious, as Member States and acceding countries do not have, or only rarely have, laws regulating their status, and sometimes only covering certain aspects.

III – Main actors

Actors in the field of voluntary activities of young people which were expressly mentioned are: national governments, regional and local authorities, international organisations, voluntary and youth organisations, Youth Councils, youth work organisations, the National Agencies of the YOUTH Programme, voluntary centres and agencies, associations and particular bodies, mostly set up by the state, like councils, committees or commissions on volunteering.

1. Council of Europe, ETS. No. 175, to be found on http://conventions.coe.int

2. Recommendation of the European Parliament and the Council of 10 July 2001 on mobility within the Community for students, persons undergoing training, volunteers, teachers and trainers (2001/613/CE).

3. Report from the Commission to the Council, the European Parliament, the European Economic and Social Committee and the Committee of the Regions: Report on the follow-up to the Recommendation of the European Parliament and the Council of 10 July 2001 on mobility within the Community of students, persons undergoing training, volunteers and teachers and trainers, COM(2004)21final of 23 January 2004.

4. See also study on "Legal Status of Volunteers – Country Reports" by the Association of Voluntary Service Organisations (AVSO) on http://www.avso.org

Other actors sometimes quoted were political parties, social partners, schools, colleges and universities, federations, the private economic sector, funds, foundations, churches and religious groups.

While the role of the public authorities is mainly funding, defining the conditions and limits, and in some cases certification, the role of the other actors lies rather on the operational side. Altogether there is a mix of tasks and responsibilities among all actors. As far as the role of youth and voluntary organisations is concerned, it can be said that they have a wide range of tasks that include co-ordination, recruitment, assignment and training of volunteers, contacts with public authorities and those benefiting from voluntary activities, development and innovation of projects, as well as fundraising and networking with other organisations.

The main actors of voluntary activities are therefore public authorities and NGOs. While the public authorities are mainly engaged in setting the conditions and limits for voluntary activities, NGOs are mostly in charge of organising them.

IV – Finances

As for the financial sources of voluntary activities, some states indicated public funding at all levels (local, regional, national), as well as private funding via foundations, sponsorship and donations, membership and other fees, etc. Some referred to the national lottery.

The amount of the money available for voluntary activities is difficult to identify, due to the various forms of funding and the widespread recipients. However, the need for more funding is widely recognised.

V – Management, supervision, evaluation and monitoring

Very few answers related to management and supervision structures. Those countries that replied referred mainly to controlling mechanisms in the context of funding.

Few confirmed having voluntary activities evaluated and monitored. Methods vary and include studies, surveys, questionnaires, but also follow-up, reporting and indicators, etc. In many cases evaluation and monitoring takes place within the voluntary organisations.

It can be stated that much still needs to be done to improve the evaluation and monitoring of voluntary activities in order to make their value and benefit more visible and to assure as well as increase the quality of voluntary activities.

Young people in voluntary activities

All states give young people the opportunity to carry out voluntary activities. However, the definitions, forms, possibilities and organisational approaches are many and diverse, sometimes even within one and the same state, which adds to the complexity of the issue.

The number of young people rendering voluntary activities is not always known and, where indicated, is not always calculated in the same way. It also refers to different age groups. However, it can be said that in all states young people commit themselves on a voluntary basis and seem to find it a valuable experience.

Some states pointed to the fact that all voluntary activities were open to young people. The following areas of voluntary activities in which young people engage themselves were frequently quoted: sports, environment, nature and animal protection, culture, social sector, school or university, youth organisations, scouts, neighbourhood help, religious service, fire-fighters, civil protection, development aid, political parties and trade unions.

The activities that young people undertake in these areas can be quite different, but sometimes comprise also, among others, organisational, management and administrative tasks. The areas, activities and tasks are often subject to change according to the growing age of the young volunteer (e.g. engagement in school matters to be replaced by university related activities).

The following reasons for young people to commit themselves to voluntary activities were mentioned, among others: defending a cause, being of use to others, meeting other people, using one's time and one's competencies and improve them, to bridge a waiting gap, enhance one's employability, training opportunities, fun, etc.

In all Member States and acceding countries young people are committed to voluntary activities. Even if their exact number is difficult to identify, there is information about the areas they engage in, about the tasks they take over and about their motivations.

Voluntary service

Only a minority of states has a civic service in place (Germany, France, Italy, Luxembourg and Czech Republic). All of these countries have legal provisions for it, or at least for some kinds of voluntary service. The forms, the age limits, the duration as well as the organisations allowed to organise voluntary service differ. Restrictions to state run service can be found as well as a strict limitation to NGO run service. Sometimes the areas in which the voluntary service can be carried out, are a priori defined.

A number of other countries are clearly not in favour of establishing such a civic service and prefer promoting voluntary activities or voluntary services through NGOs.

Quite a number of countries referred to the European Voluntary Service (EVS), which is Action 2 of the YOUTH Programme and which offers transnational voluntary service and aims at developing the solidarity of young people, thereby promoting their citizenship and supporting the mutual understanding of young people.[1]

As far as the relationship between military service and the various forms of voluntary service are concerned the picture is quite manifold and varied. Of those countries that have a military service in place most also offer the possibility to carry out a civilian service instead. In a few countries a tendency to progressively replace the military service by civic service can be observed.

Challenges identified by the Member States and acceding countries

Member States and acceding countries have highlighted the following challenges, entailing action not only at national but also at European level:

1. More information on the YOUTH Programme and EVS can be found on http://europa.eu.int/comm/youth

Development of voluntary activities of young people

The possibilities for young people to engage in voluntary activities vary considerably in the different countries. Even if a wide range of voluntary activities is available for young people, they are not always transparent and easily accessible and should be developed.

Key points:

- Voluntary activities of young people are an expression of active citizenship and solidarity and therefore need to be enhanced.

- The voluntary activities landscape in each Member State and in Europe is quite a patchwork.

- There is a need for more transparency of the existing possibilities.

- Voluntary activities should be developed, within and beyond the existing categories and scopes.

- Organisations play a key role in voluntary activities. In order to be able to carry out their role they need support.

- Training of volunteers and their managers and supervisors is important to improve the quality of voluntary activities.

- At European level the exchange of information, experience and best practices need to be enhanced.

- The European Voluntary Service (EVS) should be reinforced.

- A closer co-operation between civic services is desirable.

I – Analysis of the situation in the Member States and acceding countries

According to the replies to the questionnaire there is agreement that voluntary engagement of young people is an expression of active citizenship and solidarity and therefore needs to be enhanced. All replies underline the high value of voluntarism for society.

It can be stated that the situation of voluntary activities in Europe is quite complex. There is a wide range of activities, sometimes even within one and the same country.

Some countries have a voluntary service in place in addition to other possibilities of voluntarism, others consider setting one up. Those that already have a voluntary service sometimes know more than one form of it (e.g. Voluntary Ecological Year and Voluntary Social Year, Civic Service, European Voluntary Service, etc.). Organisers and domains of the voluntary services differ, as well as the duration and the responsibilities and tasks of the volunteers. The services can be carried out within or outside the country, either in another EU country, another European country or in a non-European third country.

Countries which base their approach on more informal voluntary activities, allow for long or short term activities; often both are possible in one and the same country. Sometimes the voluntary activities are organised, with clear structures and rules, sometimes they are occasional and flexible and self-organised.

This patchwork of possibilities add to a risk of lack of transparency which sometimes makes it difficult for young people to get the information they need about possibilities to volunteer. (See point "Promotion of voluntary activities" for more details.)

It is equally difficult for voluntary or youth organisations which wish to network to identify appropriate partners, inside and outside their home country. There is some networking going on, but there is an interest in more exchange, at all levels.

Almost all states seem to be ready to develop further voluntary activities, at least within the existing categories and scopes. Some are also considering to extend or are already extending them beyond the possibilities currently existing in their countries. Different kind of organisations play a major part in voluntary activities. In many countries they organise most of the voluntary activities. The support that they receive from the state mostly consists of financial support, sometimes of training, and in a very few cases of protective legal regulations. Sometimes support is given to the recruitment of volunteers. Another form of support is recognition, rarely formal recognition, but more often social recognition. The need for more funding of voluntary activities is widely recognised.

Many states underline the importance of fostering training of young volunteers and those managing and supervising them, with a view to capacity-building and in order to assure and improve the quality of voluntary activities and organisations, but also as a means of recognition.

II – Expectations in terms of European common objectives

There is broad agreement that exchange of information, experience and good practices on voluntary activities should be encouraged at European level. As far as an enhanced co-operation is concerned, some countries wish for a better co-ordination, others propose that the EU should facilitate networking.

Co-operation and networking were also the subjects of the first European Conference on Civic Service and Youth, which was organised by the Italian Presidency, with support of the European Commission, in Rome in November 2003. This conference aimed at allowing an exchange of views, activities and national practices on the civic service of young people. Another aim of the conference was to identify ways of a closer co-operation between civic services at European level, including the European Voluntary Service (EVS).

In the conclusions[1] of the president of the conference[2] it is suggested to further discuss, follow up and monitor the co-operation among civic services in the framework of the open method of co-ordination in the youth field. A reinforced participation of young people in these activities with a view to strengthening their citizenship and solidarity is proposed as well as the reinforcement of the transnational co-operation. It is also suggested to enhance the exchange of young volunteers in a

1. The full text of the Conclusions of the conference can be found on http://europa.eu.int/comm/youth

2. The conference was chaired by the Italian Minister responsible for the contacts with the Parliament, Mr Carlo Giovanardi.

number of domains, to recognise their civic service experience and to exchange information and good practices on a systematic and regular basis.[1]

In their replies to the Commission questionnaire on voluntary activities many countries comment on the YOUTH Programme, and in particular on the European Voluntary Service (EVS). They underline the importance of the YOUTH Programme and of the EVS and draw attention to the fact that it is often only in this framework that young people can carry out a voluntary service in another than their own country. A number of proposals point towards the reinforcement of this service, also with a view to extending it. Many wish for more funding for the EVS.

There is a demand for a greater flexibility of volunteering opportunities in the framework of the EVS, for easier and shorter procedures and for reinforcement of the tutor concept. Some countries wish to expand the possibility of a short-term EVS, others want it to be more accessible, but also more varied and enlarged in scope. There is a proposal that the EVS as such should be reinforced and developed by national experiences and should allow for the combination of national and EVS projects.

Most Member States refer to the draft Constitution of the Convention on the future of Europe[2] a Voluntary Corps of Young People is suggested and show a certain openness for considerations about possible links with the EVS at the appropriate time and by appropriate means, if it is ensured that the specific nature of the EVS and in particular its prevailing non-formal learning aspect will be kept.

III – Good practices

Of the various examples of good practices in the field, the following could be singled out:

- In Flanders a high number of young people are involved in youth work on a voluntary basis. An example is the scout movement where each local scout group is supported at least by 10-20 young volunteers and where voluntary activities follow the approach: "by young people for young people".

- In Hungary voluntary activities are developed at local level by students in the Debrecen Volunteers Team. The students use the knowledge from their university studies for programmes useful for their local community in the environmental, social and educational field.

- Italy has set up a civic service that is constantly developing further. It started originally as alternative to the military service, and was later opened also for young women and now evolving to a full voluntary service for all young people. Italy is also playing an active role in the co-operation with the civic services of other countries.

---

1. In view of an enhanced co-operation among the Member States, acceding countries and the European Commission a joint meeting of all agencies involved in the YOUTH Programme and all national voluntary civic service bodies is envisaged for spring 2004.

2. Draft treaty establishing a Constitution for Europe: draft articles on external action in the Constitutional Treaty, CONV 685/03 of 23 April 2003.

> Analysis of replies of EU Member States

- Lithuania has recently established a national voluntary service, the "Youth Social Year", based on German experience, and initiated and implemented by the youth organisation A.C. Patria and its partner organisations. The target group are young people between the ages of 15 and 23.

- Luxembourg developed in co-operation with the Red Cross for Youth a specific training for young volunteers who wish to carry out a voluntary activity for the benefit of other young people in so-called Youth Houses.

- In the Netherlands the project "The neighbourhood for all ages" ("De Buurt voor alle leeftidjen") was geared towards a greater social cohesion and solidarity. The idea is to develop voluntary activities further, in the sense of inciting voluntary activities at local level, e.g. by young people engaging for senior citizens, and thereby bringing together people living in the same community.

- Poland is developing voluntary activities of young people in the framework of its new Youth Strategy. It is a political objective of this Strategy which also refers to instruments and tools, like a database for voluntary activities.

- Scotland is in the process of taking a more strategic approach to the voluntary engagement of young people. Further to the evaluation of the Scottish Executive Millenium Volunteers Programme it is planning to develop a scheme, provisionally called "Scotscorps" that will encourage young people, including those from disadvantaged backgrounds, to volunteer full time during a gap year. Accreditation is also being considered. Even, if this new scheme is still in the preparatory phase, it seems to be a good example for developing young people's voluntary activities.

Facilitating voluntary activities of young people

Member States and acceding countries acknowledge in their replies that young people who wish to engage in voluntary activities often meet a number of difficulties which represent real obstacles to their exercise of voluntary activities and sometimes limit their access to these activities. The nature of these obstacles as well as approaches to overcome them are outlined in the following paragraphs.

Key points: The main obstacles to the voluntary activities of young people are still of legal, administrative, fiscal and social nature (e.g. exclusion of certain groups of young people, lack of language skills, and lack of training).

- When carrying out their voluntary service in another country young people often do not receive the visas and residence permits they need.

- Another obstacle is the lack of funds.

- Exchange of information, experience and good practice at European level between all relevant actors can help remove the obstacles.

- Legal means and instruments could be considered at national and European level.

- Member States should start implementing first the recommendation on mobility that they approved at European level in 2001.

I – Analysis of the situation in the Member States and acceding countries

There are numerous obstacles to voluntary activities of young people. Member States and acceding countries refer to the following obstacles:

Legal obstacles to the voluntary activities of young people are e.g. the lack of a specific statute for volunteers, which leads to problems in terms of recognition, of social protection, of taxation ... The lack of minimum standards as well as of provisions on social protection is certainly a major issue for young volunteers.

The lack of rules and instruments recognising voluntary activities in the framework of formal education, e.g. in high schools or at university, by enterprises and employers or by society in general is another factor for young people being reluctant to participate in voluntary activities.

The treatment of volunteers as employees leads to the taxation of their pocket money. Only a few countries have tax reductions or exemptions for volunteers and voluntary organisations. Where they exist, they are sometimes limited to certain amounts or to the reimbursement of costs only, or they are only accessible for certain kinds of voluntary activities (e.g. those that qualify as charities).

Another important obstacle mentioned quite frequently is the lack of funds for voluntary services or activities. A lack of funds often leads to long waiting periods for young volunteers incompatible with their expectations or does not allow all young people interested in volunteering to indeed carry out a voluntary activity.

Administrative obstacles are e.g. long and tedious procedures for the individual volunteer, certain requirements imposed to voluntary organisations, the lack of appropriate housing, the lack of language courses for those who wish to carry out voluntary activities abroad and the lack of training. As far as voluntary activities in third countries or of third country nationals in EU countries is concerned, the refusal of visas and residence permits creates a major problem for young volunteers.

In order to overcome these obstacles countries have different approaches. Very few countries have adopted laws, and those that have, have done so in the context of voluntary service, or regulating only certain aspects relating to volunteering.

There are examples of countries where minimum standards or codes of good practice exist. In most cases they are rather set up by voluntary organisations than by public authorities. One possible approach could be to progressively replace control-based by trust-based approaches, which would be characterized by more confidence in the individual volunteer and less controls. Such a system can only function if responsibility is assumed on the side of the volunteer but also of the body organising the voluntary activity.

Some countries mentioned that, in order to overcome the obstacles, they had signed or were in the process of signing the Council of Europe's Convention on the Promotion of a Transnational Long-Term Voluntary Service for Young People.[1]

II – Expectations in terms of European common objectives

As far as the role of the EU in removing obstacles to voluntary activities is concerned, Member States and acceding countries propose a regular exchange of information, experience and good practices in order to enhance the removal of obstacles.

Some countries see a role for the EU in removing obstacles to cross-border voluntary activities, others call for classifying volunteers as a specific category at EU level, which sets them apart from employees. One Member State proposed that the EU should incite Member States to ensure health insurance and social protection in general for volunteers. In this context it should be mentioned that volunteers are subject to Community rules on free movement of people and should in principle be covered by Directive 90/364 of 28 June 1990 on the right of residence (OJ L 180 of 13.7.1990). This directive provides that EU nationals who do not enjoy the right of residence under any other provisions of Community law shall be granted the right of residence in other Member States provided they are covered by sickness insurance in respect of all risks in the host Member State and have sufficient resources to avoid becoming a burden on the social assistance system of the host Member State during their period of residence.

Volunteers under the European Voluntary Service[2] scheme enjoy full insurance coverage under a group insurance scheme, receive full board, lodging and allowances as well as travel costs.

This is a demand of a few countries, and by a number of NGOs and other organisations in charge of voluntary activities, for laying down the rights and obligations of volunteers at EU level. Some countries express it as "setting out common rules or standards" or propose that the EU should set minimum standards.

The Commission is ready to consider if legal means and instruments could help reach the aim of making it easier for young people to carry out voluntary activities. In the context of facilitating voluntary activities, reference should again be made to the European Parliament and Council Recommendation of 10 July 2001 on Mobility[3] within the Community for Students, Persons undergoing Training, Volunteers, Teachers and Trainers. By this recommendation measures which specifically concern volunteers were adopted.

In a recent report on the follow-up to the recommendation on mobility the Commission found that there are still big gaps in the transposition of the recommendation in the Member States.[4] The first step of actions to be implemented at European level by Member States should be those actions recommended and accepted by Member States.

1. Convention of the Council of Europe of 11 May 2000 on the Promotion of a Transnational Long-Term Voluntary service for Young People; http://conventions.coe.int/Treaty/en/Treaties/html/175.htm

2. The full text of the Conclusions of the conference can be found on http://europa.eu.int/comm/youth

3. The conference was chaired by the Italian Minister responsible for the contacts with the Parliament, Mr Carlo Giovanardi.

4. In view of an enhanced co-operation among the Member States, acceding countries and the European Commission a joint meeting of all agencies involved in the YOUTH Programme and all national voluntary civic service bodies is envisaged for spring 2004.

Of the various examples of good practices in the field, the following could be singled out:

- Finland recognises young people's efforts in voluntary activities by the International Award for Young People. Young people participating in this scheme acquire certificates for their achievements. These certificates exist at various levels.

- In Germany the project – within the Voluntary Social Training Year – "Environment and Cleanliness in the city quarter of Boy/Welheim" (Bottrop) aimed at motivating young people with less opportunities to engage in environmental protection and cleaning up their local community in Boy/Welheim in the Ruhr area. The young people were involved in the planning and carrying out of the project. Their voluntary engagement for their area was recognised by a social event with the participation of high-ranking politicians.

- In the United Kingdom (UK) the Year Out Group, an association of independent UK-registered organisations of various sizes, has developed a Code of Practice that provides guidelines in standards for services for its members to follow. The member organisations involved have adopted the Code of Practice as their operational standard. Operational standards have equally been created to assist in monitoring placements and measuring satisfaction.

- In Wallonia a Higher Council for Voluntary Activities was recently put in place ("Conseil supérieur du Volontariat") as a measure of recognition of the voluntary sector. This Council brings together the social partners and aims at supporting voluntary activities.

Promotion of voluntary activities of young people

Even if all Member States and acceding countries agree that voluntary activities of young people should be promoted, the engagement in actually promoting them has to be reinforced, as well as the means vary from one country to the other. The aims of promoting voluntary activities among young people are quite manifold and include amongst others which are outlined below, the inclusion of young people with less opportunities in voluntary activities as well as networking of voluntary organisations.

Key points:

- Member States and acceding countries agree that voluntary activities of young people should be promoted.

- A number of Member States feel that they could do more to promote the voluntary activities of young people.

- Promotion is up to now mainly done by voluntary organisations themselves.

> Analysis of replies of EU Member States

187

- The means of promotion are quite varied. However, word of mouth still seems to be an important means of information and promotion.

- Young people with fewer opportunities need to be addressed by promotional measures particularly.

- Networking of voluntary organisations at all levels and co-operation between all relevant actors are judged as important.

- At European level, it would be useful to contribute to the promotion of voluntary activities for young people.

I – Analysis of the situation of Member States and acceding countries

There seems to be widespread agreement about the aims of promoting voluntary activities as means of reinforcing the solidarity of young people and their engagement as citizens. The aim of promoting voluntary activities is in fact manifold and should inform young people about possibilities to volunteer, provide advice and support, raise young people's awareness about volunteering, increase the number of young volunteers.

However, the degree of state involvement in promotion measures varies considerably. While some are quite active, others leave promotion measures to voluntary organisations themselves and limit their support to financial support of these organisations.

In general the actors promoting young people's voluntary activities are mainly the voluntary organisations themselves, but also young people, public authorities, youth organisations and centres, schools, churches, religious groups, etc. Places where information about volunteering is distributed are libraries, job offices, universities, etc. The means of promotion are quite varied and cover media, websites, action and information days, public awareness campaigns, subsidies, leaflets, booklets, newsletters, gatherings, forums, seminars, etc., even if a very important means of promotion is still the word of mouth.

Among the public authorities some ministries in charge of youth affairs play an active role in voluntary activities of young people.

Quite a number of states referred to the YOUTH Programme as promoter of voluntary activities. Many states underline the importance of promoting voluntary activities in particular among young people with fewer opportunities. The reasons these states mention are the low involvement of these young people in voluntary activities, giving those who have failed or done less well in formal education a "second educational chance", and offering them opportunities of mobility they might not have otherwise. However, indication was made that language might be a barrier for these young people in international voluntary activities and that promotion measures should take this aspect into account.

In general, networking of voluntary organisations was judged important and some networks already exist. However the need to encourage an enhanced co-operation between all relevant actors in the field of voluntary activities in view to exchanging information, experience and good practice would be beneficial to the promotion of voluntary activities among young people.

It should also be mentioned that some states referred to the International Year of the Volunteer, proclaimed by the UN in 2001, as having boosted promotion activities about volunteering.

II – Expectations in terms of European common objectives

Many states wish for the promotion of voluntary activities of young people at the European level by appropriate information actions. Some countries underline in particular the awareness-raising aspect in this context. There are proposals for actions around the European Volunteer Day or in the framework of the European Youth Week. Another proposal is to create a European Youth Voluntary Service Day. Some countries would like to see voluntary activities promoted in the framework of the life-long learning strategy. Another proposal, either creating a European voluntary activities portal or promoting voluntary activities via a youth portal, has already been taken on board in the framework of the development of the European Youth Portal.

Majority of Member States and acceding countries could also agree on European objectives for increasing at national level information on volunteering, enhancing co-operation of all actors and for developing approaches focused on some target groups for which it is more difficult to participate in voluntary activities.

III – Good practices

Of the various examples of good practices in the field, the following could be singled out:

– The Czech Republic developed a peer training programme entitled "One-to-One" that promotes voluntary activities among young people by peer support from young volunteers. This programme is carried out in 15 regions of the Czech Republic.

– In Denmark the Danish Youth Council (DUF) has developed materials on volunteering that help youth organisations to inform young people about voluntary activities.

– In Greece the ONG "Bridges of Friendship – Institute of Social Solidarity" organises an annual national exhibition on volunteerism. This exhibition gives about 100 NGOs, including those giving young people the opportunity to carry out voluntary activities, the possibility to promote their activities, to recruit volunteers and donors, to raise public awareness and to network.

– In Latvia the bringing together of young local volunteers with young international volunteers in voluntary camps helps promoting voluntary activities at local and international level.

– Malta has a specific broadcasting station, "Education Channel 22", that promotes voluntary activities free of charge.

– Northern Ireland offers a free telephone number that links members of the public to their local Volunteer Bureau from anywhere in the country. It gives everyone free access to local volunteering opportunities free of charge.

– In Portugal a website has been created for young people interested in volunteering, www.voluntariadojovem.pt. Promotion is done by mailing-lists and sometimes by media campaigns.

- Slovakia states that the organisation of a big public event, the visit of the Pope in Slovakia, gave rise to voluntary engagement, knowledge about it and its acknowledgement.

- Sweden's National Forum started an Internet platform for voluntary activities at local level, in a part of Stockholm named Volontärbyrån, which informs about possibilities for volunteering in this area. Most of the users of the website are young people. The Ministry of Justice recently decided to support an extension of this activity at national level.

Recognition of voluntary activities of young people

Young people's commitment to voluntary activities is often not or not properly recognised and validated. Formal and social recognition is about acknowledging the young people's voluntary engagement for society, their educational experience as well as their social, cultural and personal competencies, professional skills and employability that derive from the voluntary activities. Another important issue in this context is who should recognise the voluntary experience of young people.

Key points:

- Formal and social recognition of the voluntary engagement of young people is important.

- Some forms of recognition exist but are not sufficient.

- What needs to be recognised are the personal, cultural and social competencies and professional skills acquired through voluntary activities as well as the added value of voluntary activities for society.

- Recognition of young people's voluntary activities needs to be ensured by public authorities, the private economic sector and civil society.

I – Analysis of the situation in the Member States and acceding countries

In their replies the Member States and acceding countries inform the Commission that young people confirmed in the consultations on the questionnaire that voluntary activities are a rewarding experience for them and that recognition of these activities is important to them.

There is agreement that measures need to be taken to properly acknowledge and validate the personal competencies, professional skills and the added value that evolve from the voluntary engagement of young people. The measures to be developed should be appropriate to the nature of the voluntary activity carried out.

If recognition takes place, it is often of social nature and takes only place within the organisation in which the young volunteer is engaged. It then takes the form of celebrations, small gifts, thanking letters, memberships of honour, higher ranks within the organisations, etc.

At a more visible level, social recognition is sometimes given either by organisations, umbrella organisations or public authorities through awards, cards that offer reductions, access to sports events, concerts, travels, etc.

Formal recognition is mentioned rather rarely and takes the form of references, testimonials and certificates, or advantages in formal education. As far as certificates are concerned, they are very rare, often limited to voluntary service and issued only upon request either by the voluntary organisation, or by public authorities. Another example for a certificate is a regional "passport of voluntary activities" which is mentioned by one country.

Advantages in formal education are that the recognition of the time spent with voluntary activities as waiting period for studies or diplomas. Sometimes this time counts as practical experience within a formal study.

Advantages in the labour market are sometimes granted because employers more and more recognise the value of voluntary commitment of young people, their experiences gained abroad or in diverse social environments. Nowadays it is largely undisputed that intercultural and social key competencies are an integral part of learning and employability.

The issuing of a certificate at the end of the European Voluntary Service is recognised as a useful first step for recognition of European voluntary activities. The EVS certificate consists of two parts, one confirming the participation, and the other one describing the voluntary activity carried out as well as the learning experience acquired.

Other forms of recognition quoted are monetary recognition understood as reimbursement of costs, insurances and financial support of projects, as well as training. Member States and acceding countries agree largely that the current validation and recognition of young people's voluntary activities is not sufficient and needs to be enhanced and propose to strengthen the formal recognition, by e.g. certificates, training, advantages in formal education and in employment, etc. This implies a stronger involvement of other stakeholders, in particular in the field of education and training, but also of social partners in order to develop appropriate strategies and tools at national level. As means of social recognition they propose a National Volunteer's Day, a National Volunteers Action Week, awards to groups of volunteers, awareness-raising campaigns, etc.

II – Expectations in terms of European common objectives

Most countries also wish for an enhanced formal and social recognition of voluntary activities at the European level. Member States and acceding countries also expect to link strategies for a better recognition of non-formal learning and informal learning experience in the youth field at national level to the initiatives and development at European level. As means of formal recognition they propose to make use of ongoing processes or existing means in the education field, as e.g. the Europass, and as means of social recognition they suggest to reinforce actions on European Volunteer's Day, in the framework of the European Youth Week, etc.

The common European principles on validation and recognition of non-formal and informal learning, which are currently in preparation aiming at ensuring greater comparability between approaches in different countries and at different levels could be used as a way of recognising voluntary activities of young people.

Another means of recognition that is currently being developed and that integrates some specific certification instruments, such as the European CV format, is the Europass. It could be used to develop other instruments within its framework with a view to improving the transparency of qualifications and competencies acquired in voluntary activities.

Of the various examples of good practices in the field, the following could be singled out:

–   Austria organises a yearly election of the "Volunteer of the Year", which has advanced to a fixed event in the agenda of policy-makers and media. A call for proposals and a festive event guarantee for visibility. Each year a focus is put on a particular theme. In 2002 it was "Volunteers Against the Floods" and in 2003 engagement for citizens with disabilities.

–   The German speaking community of Belgium celebrates each year the Day of the Voluntary Activity, which was developed from the Day of the Social Voluntary Activity and which allows for social recognition and appreciation of those carrying out voluntary activities.

–   Cyprus honours its volunteers on 5 December, the International Volunteer's Day, with a dinner with the President and the First Lady at the Presidential Palace. At this occasion the volunteers receive diplomas and commemorative presents.

–   In France the departmental Council for Youth in the Territory of Belfort has developed a passport of voluntary activities ("passeport du bénévole") which will serve as basis for a future "passport of engagement". This document will allow to trace back the voluntary pathway of young people and allow for recognising their personal experience and professional skills. In order for this passport to be developed in the entire region it will be adapted to the specific needs at local level.

–   Ireland's annual Foróige Citizenship Award forms part of its Citizenship Programme. This is an out-of-school education programme which aims to involve young people in the protection and development of the environment in their own community areas.

–   Spain offers the Voluntary Work Award, which is promoted by several enterprises from the private economic sector in co-operation between the Platform for Promoting Voluntary Activities and the Ministry for Labour and Social Affairs. The prize offers recognition by a financial contribution to the voluntary organisation at which the volunteer who received the award is engaged.

–   In Slovenia the project NEFIKS aims at recognising young people's non-formal learning experience through voluntary activities. This project is carried out by the Youth Guild ("Mladinski ceh") with financial support of the Youth Office of Slovenia.

–   Wales holds a National Volunteering Week each year that highlights achievements of volunteers and encourages others to engage in voluntary activities, and is thus an example for recognition and promotion.

Co-operation at European level

The open method of co-ordination, as set out in the Council Resolution of 27 June 2002 regarding the framework for European co-operation in the youth field,[1] provides for common objectives to be defined and followed-up.

This procedure was already applied to the two first priorities of the White Paper on youth, participation and information, for which the Council adopted common objectives on the basis of the Commission's proposal.[2]

The priority of voluntary activities follows the same procedure. In the questionnaire, the Commission therefore asked the Member States and acceding countries to propose common objectives and to specify their expectations to the European level.

Based on the answers of the Member States and acceding countries which are presented in this analysis report the Commission proposes common objectives for voluntary activities of young people. The common goal is to develop, facilitate, recognise and promote the voluntary activities of young people with a view to enhancing their active citizenship and solidarity.

The Commission informed the European Youth Forum of its analysis of the Member States' and acceding countries' replies and consulted it on the common objectives that it intended to propose, based on this analysis report.

1. See footnote 2, p. 175.
2. See page 14 of this analysis report for references.

2. Resolution on common objectives for voluntary activities of young people

Council of the European Union

The Council of the European Union and the representatives of the governments of the member states, meeting within the Council

Whereas:

- The Commission White Paper entitled "A new impetus for European youth" presented on 21 November 2001 sets out a new framework for European co-operation in the youth field;

- In its Resolution of 14 February 2002[1] the Council recognised the added value of voluntary activity for young people in the context of the development of community action on youth and adopted the UN strategic objectives.[2]

- In its Resolution of 27 June 2002[3] the Council adopted the open method of co-ordination as a new framework for co-operation in the youth field and endorsed four priorities, i.e. participation, information, voluntary activities and a greater understanding and better knowledge of youth;

- In its Resolution of 25 November 2003[4] the Council adopted common objectives for the first two priorities, i.e. participation by and information for young people;

- In its Communication of 30 April 2004[5] the Commission proposed common objectives for voluntary activities of young people, based on the replies of the Member States to a Commission questionnaire and after consulting young people;

1. OJ C 50 of 23.02.2002, p. 3.
2. Strategic objectives of the UN:
    – The accessibility and promotion of information provision on voluntary activity, with a view to reinforcing a positive image;
    – Recognition and support for voluntary activity, *inter alia*, by authorities at all levels, public opinion, media, commerce, employers and civil society;
    – Support for voluntary activity through incentives and the training of volunteers, their mentors and their associations;
    – Networking between all parties involved, with special attention to the perspective of young people themselves;
    – Quality care with regard to youth voluntary activity, including health and safety aspects.
3. OJ C 168 of 13.07.2002, p. 2.
4. OJ C 295 of 5.12.2003, p. 6.
5. Doc. 9182/04 (COM(2004) 337 final).

- The Council of 28 May 2004 confirmed the importance of the priority of voluntary activities of young people;
- The European Voluntary Service (EVS) is an Action of the YOUTH Programme and a quality model for transnational voluntary service that allows young people to engage in volunteering in a variety of areas, thereby promoting their solidarity, active citizenship and mutual understanding;
- Reference is made to the definitions used by the Commission in its Communication of 30 April 2004 on common objectives for voluntary activities of young people, in particular regarding voluntary activities and voluntary service.

Consider

- Voluntary activities represent important opportunities for non-formal learning. They are an important means for the self-development of young people and their engagement as active citizens. Voluntary activities also contribute to enhancing solidarity, social cohesion and community development.
- Voluntary activities need to be clearly distinguished from employment and should by no means replace employment.
- The development of attractive and stimulating voluntary activities needs to be encouraged, in order for young people to be involved in voluntary work;
- Transnational co-operation in the framework of voluntary activities should be encouraged with a view to promoting a European dimension in this field.
- Voluntary activities present opportunities for the development and the structuring of civil society.
- All forms of discrimination and stereotyping should be combatted and equality should be promoted in the field of voluntary activity.

Agree the following common objectives for voluntary activities of young people:

With a view to enhancing active citizenship and solidarity of young people, voluntary activities should be developed, facilitated, promoted and recognised at all levels:

I) Encourage the development of voluntary activities of young people with the aim of enhancing awareness of the existing possibilities, enlarging their scope and improving their quality.

II) Make it easier for young people to carry out voluntary activities by removing existing obstacles.

III) Promote voluntary activities with a view to reinforcing young people's solidarity and engagement as responsible citizens.

IV) Recognise voluntary activities of young people with a view to acknowledging the value of their personal skills thus acquired and their engagement for society and the role that voluntary activities play in terms of facilitating the transition from education to work and adult life.

A non-exhaustive list of the possible lines of action for the above common objectives is set out in the annex hereto;

Recall that implementation must be flexible, incremental and appropriate for the youth field and must respect the competences of the Member States and the principle of subsidiarity;

Invite the member states to

- specify implementing and follow-up measures, in the light of their particular circumstances and their national priorities with regard to those common objectives;

- submit reports on the national contributions to the implementation of the priority of voluntary activities, by the end of 2006;

- consult and encourage the participation of young people, and their associations, young volunteers and volunteer organisations, as well as national and regional youth councils – if appropriate – for the elaboration of those reports;

Note that the Commission intends to

- prepare, on the basis of the above reports on national contributions to the implementation of the common objectives, a progress report for submission to the Council in order to encourage mutual exchange of information and good practice concerning voluntary activities of young people, after consultation of the European Youth Forum, while not excluding other forms of consultation;

- propose, if appropriate, amendments to the common objectives for voluntary activities of young people;

- suitably inform the European Parliament, the Economic and Social Committee and the Committee of the Regions;

Invite the Commission to

- convene, when appropriate, representatives of the national administrations in charge of youth in order to promote the exchange of information on the progress made and on best practices;

Take note of the following procedure

The Council and the Representatives of the Governments of the Member States, meeting within the Council will take the necessary initiatives within the framework of the common objectives, in order to facilitate their implementation. They will adapt, and when appropriate, amend the common objectives on the basis of the progress report and the amended drafts submitted by the Commission.

ANNEX: Measures for achieving the common objectives for voluntary activities of young people

In the light of the actual circumstances and the priorities of each Member State, the following non-exhaustive list of lines of action may be pursued:

a) Encourage the development of voluntary activities for young people with the aim of enhancing awareness of the existing opportunities, enlarging their scope and improving their quality.

At national, regional and local level

(i)   In view of creating a clear and visible picture of voluntary activities available for young people identify existing models of voluntary activities (e.g. voluntary service, occasional voluntary engagement, etc.) and voluntary organisations.

(ii)   Enhance existing voluntary activities of young people by:

– developing the different categories of these activities, and in particular broaden their range of possibilities,

– supporting activities of particular interest to young people,

– supporting civil society organisations active in voluntary engagement of young people,

– reinforcing voluntary services where they already exist and, where appropriate, encouraging the creation of new ones.

(iii)   With a view to improving the quality of voluntary activities and their organisational framework foster training opportunities for young volunteers and those co-ordinating and managing such activities.

At European level

(iv)   Encourage:

– a better co-ordination of the transnational co-operation of civic services, where they exist,

– an enhanced exchange of young volunteers in various domains;

– an enhanced exchange of information on national voluntary programmes and their European dimension.

(v)   Develop and promote the European Voluntary Service (EVS) further within the framework of the current Youth Programme.

(vi)   Take into consideration the feasibility of extending the European Voluntary Service (EVS) to a wider range of actions with a view to giving young people the possibility to participate in actions of solidarity of the European Union.

b) Make it easier for young people to carry out voluntary activities by removing existing obstacles, whilst respecting immigration controls, visa and entry requirements of Member States.

At all levels

(i)   Take the measures considered appropriate to remove the legal and administrative obstacles to the mobility of persons undertaking a voluntary activity, as set out in the Recommendation of the European Parliament and the Council on Mobility.

(ii)   Reinforce co-operation between the relevant authorities in order to facilitate the issuing of visas and residence permits to young volunteers when and where appropriate.

(iii)   Enhance the exchange of information, experience and good practice of all relevant actors in the field of voluntary activities of young people with the aim of removing all kinds of obstacles and developing simplified procedures.

(iv)   Consider which legal means and instruments can be implemented to make it easier for young people to carry out voluntary activities and for organisations to develop quality activities.

c) Promote voluntary activities with a view to reinforcing young people's solidarity and engagement as responsible citizens whilst combating all forms of discrimination and stereotyping and promoting equality

At national, regional and local level

(i)   Disseminate information on volunteering at all appropriate levels, with the aim of raising young people's awareness about volunteering, informing them about concrete possibilities to volunteer, providing advice and support and promoting a positive image of volunteering.

(ii)   Encourage an enhanced co-operation between all relevant actors (young people, youth and voluntary organisations, public authorities, private economic sector, schools, etc.) on the promotion of voluntary activities, by exchanging information, experience and good practice.

(iii)   Analyse more carefully the phenomena that lead to the exclusion of certain groups of young people from voluntary activities and develop approaches focused on encouraging them to participate in voluntary activities, particularly for young people with fewer opportunities.

At European level

(iv)   Launch appropriate information actions with a view to promoting voluntary activities of young people as well as the values of voluntarism.

d) Recognise voluntary activities of young people with a view to acknowledging the value of their personal skills and their engagement for society and the role that voluntary activities play in terms of facilitating the transition from education to work and adult life.

At national, regional and local level

(i)   Acknowledge young people's voluntary engagement, acquired individual skills, knowledge and competencies, by developing measures that lead to an enhanced recognition of voluntary activities at all levels, by various actors, e.g. public and private employers, social partners, civil society and young people themselves, and in the appropriate form.

(ii)   Acknowledge the added social value that the voluntary sector offers to society by developing actions that lead to an enhanced recognition by society of voluntary activities such as promotion activities.

At European level

(ii)   Ensure a better recognition of voluntary experience of young people in the framework of ongoing processes and by existing means in other policy fields, as e.g. the open method of co-ordination in the education field, the lifelong learning strategy, the development of Europass, the social dialogue, etc.

3. Recommendation No. R (94) 4 of the Committee of Ministers to member states on the promotion of a voluntary service

Council of Europe

The Committee of Ministers, under the terms of Article 15.*b* of the Statute of the Council of Europe,

Considering that the aim of the Council of Europe is to achieve a greater unity between its members;

Having regard to the relevant conclusions (Recommendation 20.b.iii) of the Conference of European Ministers responsible for Youth (Vienna, 13-15 April 1993);

Considering that voluntary service is an important part of governmental policies affecting young people and constitutes for young people an opportunity for learning and solidarity as well as a service to society;

Aware of the difficulties of young volunteers from central and eastern Europe when they want to perform voluntary service abroad;

Considering that, if the voluntary service, carried out abroad or with other young Europeans, contributes to civic education, to intercultural exchanges and to the acquisition of a European consciousness, it is necessary to promote youth mobility, especially for the youth of central and eastern Europe, by reducing obstacles to this mobility;

Considering that voluntary service should be open to all young people independently of their financial resources,

a) Recommends that the governments of the member states:

- define voluntary service at national level, emphasising its educational aspects and its importance for society;
- seek, within the framework of their respective legal provisions in vigour for foreigners, possibilities to establish voluntary service at national and European level, clarifying the role of this service and establishing rules regarding its conditions of exercise;

- develop and promote voluntary service, under all its forms, at national and European level;
- and to achieve this:

i. reduce the obstacles to free circulation of young volunteers, especially those from central and eastern European countries;

ii. provide appropriate financial support, within the framework of their respective legal provisions and policies, to the organisations or groups of young volunteers who do not have proper resources to achieve their aims, individually or in groups, in order that the promotion and expansion of voluntary service may concern all European countries;

iii. encourage increased co-operation between the European Union and the Council of Europe, in order to create an appropriate political, legal and financial framework of support for voluntary service in all European countries;

b) Instructs the Secretary General to transmit the text of this recommendation to the governments of the non-member states which are parties to the European Cultural Convention.

European youth voluntary activities

4. European Convention on the Promotion of a Transnational Long-term Voluntary Service for Young People

Council of Europe

Preamble

The member States of the Council of Europe and the other States Parties to the European Cultural Convention, signatory hereto,

Considering that the aim of the Council of Europe is to achieve greater unity between its members;

Considering that promoting transnational long-term voluntary service is an important part of governmental policy in respect of young people;

Acknowledging more particularly the need to develop and promote transnational long-term voluntary service, in all its forms, at European level;

Considering that transnational voluntary service, carried out abroad with other young people, contributes to civic education, intercultural projects and the acquisition of a European consciousness;

Believing that transnational long-term voluntary service, while providing non-formal education for volunteers and for the people with whom they collaborate, constitutes an opportunity for young people to learn and promote solidarity, as well as to serve society;

Aware of the difficulties of young volunteers wishing to perform voluntary service abroad;

Stressing the importance of equal opportunities for young people and considering that transnational long-term voluntary service should be open to all young people notwithstanding their financial resources;

Considering that public authorities can contribute to ensuring and supervising the implementation of the above principles within the framework of their national legislation and according to the rules in their respective countries,

Have agreed as follows:

Chapter I – General provisions

Article 1 – Object and purposes of the voluntary service

- Voluntary service shall pursue an educational aim and contain elements of intercultural learning; it shall be carried out by volunteers under the responsibility of organisations as defined in Article 2, paragraph 2, of this Convention.
- Voluntary service must be based on a non-remunerated activity and a free personal decision of the volunteer.
- Transnational long-term voluntary service does not replace the compulsory national service, where this exists, and cannot replace remunerated employment.

Article 2 – Definitions

For the purposes of this Convention:

- "The volunteer" means a person legally residing in one Party who is legally present in the territory of another Party for a continuous period of time, not less than three months and not longer than twelve months, to perform full-time voluntary service activities. The volunteer may either belong to or co-operate with the sending or receiving organisations mentioned in Article 2, paragraph 2.
- "Sending or receiving organisations" means:
  - non-profit-making and non-governmental organisations undertaking voluntary service for the benefit of society, and contributing to the development of democracy and solidarity; or
  - youth organisations, that is, non-governmental organisations run for and by young people; or
  - local public authorities; or
  - any other organisation wishing to develop specific voluntary projects which will be approved by the co-ordinating bodies defined in Article 4.
- "Transnational long-term voluntary service" means an activity voluntarily undertaken abroad, without any remuneration for the volunteer, providing a mutual non-formal education process for the volunteer and for the people with whom he or she collaborates.
- "Co-ordinating body" means any authority appointed by a Party in accordance with the provisions of Article 4 of this Convention.

Article 3 – Undertakings of the Parties

- The Parties undertake to afford each other the widest possible measure of co-operation in respect of transnational long-term voluntary service, in accordance with the provisions of this Convention.
- The Parties further undertake to promote the development of a common concept of transnational long-term voluntary service.
- The provisions of this Convention shall not affect more favourable provisions within national legislation concerning the status or the legal regime of voluntary service.

Article 4 – Co-ordinating bodies

- The Parties shall designate the co-ordinating bodies which shall be entrusted with the tasks described in this Convention.

- Each Party shall, at the time of signature or when depositing its instruments of ratification, acceptance, approval or accession, communicate to the Secretary General of the Council of Europe the name and address of the co-ordinating body designated in pursuance of paragraph 1 of this article.
- Each co-ordinating body, or body appointed by the latter, shall grant recognition to sending and receiving organisations within their country, in compliance with the provisions of this Convention.
- Each co-ordinating body, or body appointed by the latter, is entrusted with approving the activities of transnational long-term voluntary service to be carried out on its territory, thirty days prior to the beginning of service, certifying that they are in accordance with the provisions of national legislation and Article 6 of this Convention.
- For the purpose of implementation of this Convention, each co-ordinating body or body appointed by the latter shall exchange information concerning protection against the risks referred to in Article 11, and shall use its best endeavours to ensure appropriate supervision and evaluation of the activities of transnational long-term voluntary service.
- Each co-ordinating body, or body appointed by the latter, shall use its best endeavours to facilitate the settlement of any difficulty to which the implementation of the contract concluded in accordance with the provisions of Article 6 may give rise.

Chapter II — Transnational long-term voluntary service activities

Article 5 – Age limits
- Volunteers shall be over 18 and under 25 years of age at the beginning of service.
- Nevertheless, the Parties may conclude bilateral or multilateral agreements with one another derogating from the provisions of paragraph 1.

Article 6 – Contract
- All activity shall be subject to a contract and be performed in accordance with the legislation of the receiving State.
- A model contract is contained in Appendix I to the Convention; it is intended for guidance only and has no treaty value.
- A copy of the contract mentioned in paragraph 1 shall be deposited with the co-ordinating body of the receiving state or a body appointed by the former.
- The contract shall specify *inter alia* the conditions under which the volunteer is to carry out the activities of the receiving organisation.

Article 7 – Medical certificate

Each Party shall ensure that the sending organisation will provide a medical certificate issued by the public health authorities, established less than three months before the start of voluntary service, indicating the general state of health of the volunteer.

Article 8 – Training
- Each Party, through their co-ordinating bodies, shall ensure that the sending or the receiving organisation, or both, shall take the appropriate steps to provide

the volunteers, prior to their voluntary service activity, with appropriate preparation and training for the activity to be carried out by them.

- Volunteers shall, in particular, be informed of the fundamental legislative provisions, the social and economic structures of the receiving State, and receive an introduction to the language as well as to the culture and history of the receiving State.

Article 9 – Rights of volunteers

- Volunteers shall receive board and lodging from the receiving organisation.

- Volunteers shall be given adequate opportunity for relevant linguistic, intercultural and vocational development. They shall be accorded every facility as regards the arrangement of the activity to this end.

- Volunteers shall have at least one full free day per week, not less than one such free day in every month being at the choice of the volunteer.

- Volunteers shall receive a sufficient amount of pocket money, to be agreed upon between the sending and receiving organisations.

- These rights shall be granted within the framework of the legislation of the receiving State.

Article 10 – Financial rules and regulations

- Financial support for transnational long-term voluntary service activities may be provided for by:

  i. contributions from public local, regional, and national authorities, from international organisations and from the co-ordinating bodies appointed in accordance with the provisions of Article 4 of this Convention;

  ii. contributions from recognised non-profit making organisations;

  iii. contributions from private companies, in accordance with the provisions of paragraph 2;

  iv. personal contributions or others;

  v. any combination of the sources mentioned above.

- Contributions in accordance with the provisions of paragraph 1, contributions in kind or grant shall not oblige volunteers to undertake profit-making activities on behalf of a commercial enterprise or to make advertisements for it.

Article 11 – Protection against risks

- Health, accident as well as civil liability risks shall be covered either in accordance with national legislation or by bilateral or multilateral agreements in force or, failing that, by means of personal insurance subscribed and paid for by the volunteer concerned or on the volunteer's behalf.

- Each Party shall transmit, by a declaration addressed to the Secretary General of the Council of Europe, the means of cover of these risks. Any change in these means shall be notified to the Secretary General of the Council of Europe by the Parties.

- The level of benefits shall correspond to the standards laid down by the national legislation or the bilateral or multilateral agreements.

Article 12 – Certificates

- Each Party, through its co-ordinating bodies, shall ensure that during the period of voluntary activity, and at the end of the voluntary service programme, the receiving organisation will, upon request of the volunteer, provide a certificate of participation in accordance with the model provided in Appendix II to this Convention. Appendix II is intended for guidance only and has no treaty value.

Article 13 – Administrative formalities

- The candidates for voluntary service who shall address to the relevant authorities to obtain a temporary residence permit for the duration of their voluntary service shall present the contract signed by the three Parties and an identity document.
- Each Party shall endeavour, where possible, to reduce the administrative barriers restricting mobility of volunteers.

Chapter III – Multilateral consultations

Article 14 – Multilateral consultations

- The Parties shall, within five years from the entry into force of the Convention and every five years thereafter, or more frequently if a majority of the Parties should so request, hold multilateral consultations to examine the application of the Convention and the advisability of revising it or extending any of its provisions.
- Any Party may be represented at the multilateral consultations by one or more delegates. Each delegation shall have one vote. The Parties shall draw up the rules of procedure for the consultations.
- Any State referred to in Article 16, paragraph 1, or the European Community, which is not a Party to this Convention, may be represented at the multilateral consultations by an observer.
- After each consultation, the Parties shall submit to the Committee of Ministers of the Council of Europe a report on the consultation and on the application of the provisions of the Convention.

Chapter IV – Amendments

Article 15 – Amendments

- Any amendment to Articles 1 to 15 of this Convention proposed by a Party or the Committee of Ministers shall be communicated to the Secretary General of the Council of Europe and forwarded by him to the member States of the Council of Europe, to the other States Parties to the European Cultural Convention, to the European Community and to any State which has acceded to or has been invited to accede to the Convention in accordance with the provisions of Article 17.
- Any amendment proposed in accordance with the provisions of the preceding paragraph shall be examined at a multilateral consultation not less than two months after the date of forwarding by the Secretary General. The text shall be adopted by a two-thirds majority of the Parties.
- Any amendment adopted at a multilateral consultation shall be submitted to the Committee of Ministers for approval. After its approval, the text shall be forwarded to the Parties for acceptance.

- Any amendment shall enter into force on the first day of the month following the expiration of a period of three months after all the Parties have informed the Secretary General of their acceptance.

Chapter V – Final provisions

Article 16 – Signature and entry into force

- This Convention shall be open for signature by the member States of the Council of Europe and the other States party to the European Cultural Convention. Such States may express their consent to be bound by:

  i. signature without reservation as to ratification, acceptance or approval;
  or

  ii. signature subject to ratification, acceptance or approval, followed by ratification, acceptance or approval.

- Instruments of ratification, acceptance or approval shall be deposited with the Secretary General of the Council of Europe.

- This Convention shall enter into force on the first day of the month following the expiration of a period of three months after the date on which five states, of which at least four are member States of the Council of Europe, have expressed their consent to be bound by the Convention, in accordance with the provisions of paragraph 1.

- In respect of any signatory state which subsequently expresses its consent to be bound by it, the Convention shall enter into force on the first day of the month following the expiration of a period of three months after the date of the expression of its consent to be bound by the Convention in accordance with the provisions of paragraph 1.

Article 17 – Accession

- After the entry into force of this Convention, the Committee of Ministers of the Council of Europe, after consulting the Parties to the Convention, may invite any State which is not referred to in Article 16, paragraph 1, as well as the European Community to accede to this Convention, by a decision taken by the majority provided for in Article 20.*d* of the Statute of the Council of Europe and by the unanimous vote of the representatives of the Contracting States entitled to sit on the Committee.

- In respect of any acceding State or of the European Community, in the event of its accession, the Convention shall enter into force on the first day of the month following the expiration of a period of three months after the date of deposit of the instrument of accession with the Secretary General of the Council of Europe.

Article 18 – Territorial application

- Any State or the European Community may, at the time of signature or when depositing its instrument of ratification, acceptance, approval or accession, specify the territory or territories to which this Convention shall apply.

- Any Party may, at any later date, by declaration addressed to the Secretary General of the Council of Europe, extend the application of this Convention to any other territory specified in the declaration. In respect of such territory, the Convention shall enter into force on the first day of the month following the expiration of a period of three months after the date of receipt of such declaration by the Secretary General.

- Any declaration made under the two preceding paragraphs may, in respect of any territory specified in such declaration, be withdrawn by a notification addressed to the Secretary General. The withdrawal shall become effective on the first day of the month following the expiration of a period of three months after the date of receipt of such notification by the Secretary General.

Article 19 – Relationship to other treaties and Community law

- The provisions of this Convention shall not affect the provisions of international treaties which are already in force or may come into force, under which more favourable rights are, or would be, accorded to volunteers.
- In their mutual relations, Parties which are members of the European Community shall apply Community rules and shall not therefore apply the rules arising from this Convention except in so far as there is no Community rule governing the particular subject concerned.
- The Parties may conclude bilateral or multilateral agreements with one another on the matters dealt with in this Convention, for the purpose of supplementing or strengthening its provisions or facilitating the application of the principles embodied in it.

Article 20 – Reservations

No reservation to this Convention may be made.

Article 21 – Denunciation

- Any Party may, at any time, denounce this Convention by means of a notification addressed to the Secretary General of the Council of Europe.
- Such denunciation shall become effective on the first day of the month following the expiration of a period of three months after the date of receipt of such notification by the Secretary General.

Article 22 – Notifications

The Secretary General of the Council of Europe shall notify the member States of the Council, the other States Parties to the European Cultural Convention, the European Community and any State which has acceded or has been invited to accede to this Convention of:

i. any signature;

ii. the deposit of any instrument of ratification, acceptance, approval or accession;

iii. any date of entry into force of this Convention, in accordance with Articles 16 and 17;

iv. any declaration made under Article 4, paragraph 2;

v. any declaration made under Article 11, paragraph 2;

vi. any other act, notification or communication relating to this Convention.

In witness where of the undersigned, being duly authorised thereto, have signed this Convention.

Done at Strasbourg, this 11th day of May 2000, in English and in French, both texts being equally authentic, in a single copy which shall be deposited in the archives of the Council of Europe. The Secretary General of the Council of Europe shall transmit certified copies to each member State of the Council of Europe, to the other States party to the European Cultural Convention, and to any non-member State or the European Community invited to accede to this Convention.

Appendix I: Contract

By this contract,

I. The sending organisation ...., authorised by the co-ordinating body ...., undertakes:

– to send Mr/Mrs/Ms .... to .... in order to participate in the following transnational long-term voluntary service activity: ....

The duration of this activity is from .... to ....

Mr/Mrs/Ms .... will have the following duties:

– ....

– ....

– ....

On the understanding that these activities will not replace remunerated employment, and that the transnational long-term voluntary service under no circumstances replaces compulsory national service;

– to ensure the following:

training courses:

....

....

language courses:

....

....

information on the receiving country:

....

....

medical certificate delivered on .... by ....

– to cover:

two-way travel expenses of Mr/Mrs/Ms .... from .... to ....

insurance expenses for Mr/Mrs/Ms ....[1] in the event that he or she does not have his or her own insurance policy.

This insurance covers the following risks:

....

....

1. This provision applies only if the receiving country does not foresee social coverage for the volunteer.

II. The receiving organisation ...., authorised by the co-ordinating body ....,
undertakes to:

– accomplish the administrative and other formalities (visa, residence permit, guarantee of resources in particular);

– ensure coverage of the following risks: ....;

– deliver a participation certificate;

– cover:

> – board and lodging for Mr/Mrs/Ms .... during the period from .... to ....;
>
> – pocket money of ..../per day/per week/per month;
>
> – participation in the following courses:
>
> > – ....
> >
> > – ....

The organisation guarantees that:

– the activity will not exceed .... hours per day and .... hours per week;

– Mr/Mrs/Ms .... shall have at least one day off per week;[1]

– Mr/Mrs/Ms .... shall not be impelled to undertake profit-making activities on behalf of a commercial enterprise nor to make advertisements for it.

III. Mr/Mrs/Ms ...., participating in the long-term voluntary service described above, declares that he/she is aware of his or her rights and of his or her duties and undertakes to comply with the obligations arising in connection with this activity, in particular to take out private personal insurance if this obligation cannot be met by the sending and/or receiving organisation.

Approved by the co-ordinating body of:

Sending State   Receiving State

The volunteer and the sending organisation   the receiving organisation

1. At least one day per month shall be at the choice of the volunteer.

Appendix II: Certificate

1. Family name

2. First name

3. Date of birth (day/month/year)

4. Place of birth

5. Resident in

6. Citizen of

7. Name and type of receiving organisation

8. Type of activity

9. Length of activity from .... to ....

10. Field of activity

11. Certificate(s) received during the programme as appended

12. Programme consisted of the following activities (please give detailed information)

13. Exceptions/journeys abroad

Date   Signature   Position   Stamp

Part 6

Conclusion

1. Youth policy directions for volunteering

Bryony Hoskins

Introduction

Rigorous and comparable research on youth voluntary activities across Europe is in the early stages of development. The seminar "How does voluntary engagement of young people enhance their active citizenship and solidarity?" and this follow-up publication of papers that were brought together in the context of the partnership between the European Commission and the Council of Europe gives an important impetus towards creating a better understanding of youth volunteering in Europe. Developing a deeper knowledge of the realities of youth voluntary activities, who are taking up these opportunities, the barriers to participation and their impact on civil society is central to building an evidence – based youth policy on voluntary activities and active citizenship. Without the evidence, policies on volunteering are developed on the basis of conviction that volunteering is beneficial for the individual and society and therefore policy is aimed at creating as many young volunteers as possible in order to produce good citizens and a functional civil society. This chapter does not refute this hypothesis but explores the complexities that the evidence provides towards creating an effective voluntary activities policy to enhance citizenship and what further research is needed to establish the relationship. It explores who is volunteering, the barriers to participation for young people with less opportunities and what policy steps can be taken to include them.

The impetus for a research seminar and publication on the topic of voluntary activities arose from the consultation process that is used to create European youth policy. In the case of the European Union it was the process of creating common objectives and for the Council of Europe the evaluation of existing policy tools in this area. These policy initiatives will be explained in detail in this chapter but can be summarised as follows:

Council of Europe

- Recommendation No. R (94) 4 on the promotion of a voluntary service;
- European Convention on the Promotion of a Transnational Long-term Voluntary Service for Young People (ETS No. 175, not yet ratified).

Policy question

Evaluate if there is enough interest and need for the convention to be ratified. What are the next steps using the recommendation?

European Union

- White Paper "A New Impetus for European Youth";
- Council resolution on common objectives for voluntary activities of young people;
- European Voluntary Service (EVS).

Policy question

How can member states implement the common objectives at national level?

The recommendations for policy made in this chapter will be advanced in relation to the implementation of the European Commission's common objectives on youth and the Council of Europe recommendation and convention. These policy initiatives are directed towards reducing barriers to participation in, particular aiming at groups of young people who are participating least and how to ensure the development of citizenship from participating in volunteering.

European policy initiatives

European Commission

The European Commission launched the European Voluntary Service (EVS) in 1996, which has become increasingly popular among young people reaching almost 4 000 young volunteers in 2005 and has been considered a quality model in transnational voluntary service. The Commission has noted, in its mid-term evaluation of the Youth programme, a positive impact of EVS on young people, organisations and national youth policy. As a result it has proposed the development and extension of EVS in the context of the "Youth in Action" programme (2007-13). Youth volunteering boosted at a more political level the consultation process with young people and the subsequent White Paper of the European Commission of November 2001 "A New Impetus for European Youth".

According to a resolution of the Council of Youth Ministers voluntary activities priorities are tackled by the open method of co-ordination, a method that is already applied in the education and employment field but was new to the youth field. This method aims for closer co-operation between the member states on different topics and involves several steps, from sending out a questionnaire from the European Commission to the member states, to an analysis of the member states' replies and a proposal of common objectives by the Commission, leading to a EU Council resolution on common objectives and reporting back by the member states on the implementation of these objectives. This procedure was launched for voluntary activities in 2003 and led to an analysis report of the member states' replies by the Commission and to a Commission proposal for common objectives (see chapters 1 and 2, Part 5). Based on the Commission proposal the Council of Youth Ministers adopted a resolution on common objectives for voluntary activities of young people on 15 November 2004. The current state of play is that member states are in the process of implementing the common objectives. By the end of 2006 they will report back on the progress made.

The common objectives, of which there are four on this topic, aim at developing voluntary activities of young people, removing obstacles to their voluntary activities, promoting those activities and recognising them. Aspects like transparency, increasing possibilities, improving quality, removing barriers to participation, promoting citizenship and solidarity and recognition are touched upon in the framework of the guidelines that aim at helping to implement the common objectives. This chapter will focus on policy proposals in the framework of two of these objectives:

2.2. Objective 2 – Making it easier for young people to carry out voluntary activities by removing existing obstacles.

2.3. Objective 3 – Promote voluntary activities with a view to reinforcing young people's solidarity and engagement as citizens.

The question which then arises is how to convert these objectives into policies at national level.

Council of Europe

The Council of Europe has rich and long-term experience with youth issues and with youth volunteering in particular. It has a number of existing tools for policy implementation of voluntary activities: a recommendation on the promotion of voluntary services and the European Convention on the Promotion of a Transnational Long-term Voluntary Service for Young People (as yet not ratified).

The recommendation asks national governments to create a definition of voluntary services that emphasises both educational aspects and the importance for society, and to promote voluntary services. It also recommends the removal of the difficulties for volunteering across national boundaries in Europe, in particular for central and Eastern European countries and the promotion of financial support for individuals or groups who wish to volunteer at the European level. Finally, it recommends encouraging increased co-operation between the European Union and the Council of Europe, in order to create an appropriate political, legal and financial framework of support for voluntary service in all European countries. The convention sets a legal framework for transnational volunteering, providing details of the roles and procedures of all actors involved in sending, hosting and participating in volunteer activities.

Building the picture in Europe

The typical image of a volunteer is not a young person at all but a white middle-aged woman doing good to the less fortunate (Stanley, in this book)

How do the European policies match the picture of volunteering in Europe?

Who are volunteers?

What the different chapters have shown is that the typical young volunteer across Europe is female (Moskwiak), relatively wealthy (Stanley), educated and more often has vocational training than formal academic qualifications (Machin) – but not young people who have dropped out of the education system all together (as Williamson suggests in the introduction). The proposed reason for this is that the educated and wealthy have better access to information (Gran) and better understanding of the skills that will be learnt and are more likely to have the language skills needed for international volunteering and the financial resources to take time away from paid work. The gender difference in terms of greater participation by young women has been attributed to women's traditional relationship to the labour market – namely, as marginal players with stereotypical roles that place less expectation on them to achieve paid or career jobs (Mínguez). Now that the benefits of volunteering on intercultural, citizenship, inclusion and key skills for the labour market have been highlighted, the need to include young male volunteers in equal measure has become an issue. In many European countries Youth national agencies have been finding ways to include more young men in EVS projects (Moskwiak). Data on participation by minorities are notable by their absence.

Regional differences

In the former communist countries/new member states of the European Union, volunteering has a historical link to communist ideology where citizens were expected to be involved in community improvements (Moskwiak) in "so-called" voluntary activities (Schröer), thus leading to a negative image of this activity. Although many people were involved in NGO activity in spite of the regimes present, this was not considered to be volunteering (Moskwiak). Thus involvement in volunteering was slow to restart in the new democracies of Europe. However, in the last couple of years volunteering by young people has increased as information about the different possibilities have developed in countries such as Poland, which are now oversubscribed for the EVS programme (Moskwiak).

Civil society as a whole and in particular volunteering grew rapidly during the 1990s in southern Europe, in particular Italy, Spain and France (Sudulich). These voluntary activities were no longer linked to the traditional organisers of volunteering, such as political institutions which people had lost trust and faith in, and there were fewer volunteers connected to religious and ideological work. Thus it was the informal and new forms of volunteering in which the numbers grew.

In contrast, in the UK participation in volunteering, in particular regular activities, has been decreasing. There is an absence of data on young people involved in voluntary activities in other northern European countries.

Policy measures

The European Commission and the Youth national agencies are implementing the strategy for inclusion of young people with fewer opportunities in the Youth programme. This has opened up the possibility for widening participation, notably through youth exchanges and youth initiatives and with EVS. In 2004 the European Commission introduced additional support and flexibility for organisations working with this target group using the EC – funded Salto Inclusion Resource Centre, to assume an important role in sharing good practice and providing training, information and tools for successful inclusion projects.

Policy implications

The greatest difficulty in seeking to identify trends across Europe is that the definitions of voluntary activities and young people are numerous and different. The quality of data collection in different countries has also varied (EC working paper on voluntary activities). In particular there is a lack of empirical data from northern Europe, on minority/migrant populations and participation levels of people with disabilities. With definitions now established (see section on definitions) and a standard 13-30 age band created for collecting data on young people, the research picture should improve. This is facilitated by the creation of the European Knowledge Centre for Youth Policy (www.youth-knowledge.net), a database that will collect data from across Europe on this topic and other youth policy priorities.

The standards and the collection of data will enable a better knowledge of volunteering across Europe. What is clear is that national policy makers need to fund the necessary research to fill the gaps of knowledge to ensure that the European Knowledge Centre for Youth Policy is fed with quality and up-to-date information on voluntary activities.

Barriers to participation

As the above picture has described, certain groups of young people are participating much more than others in volunteering. Objective number two of the common objectives and the Council of Europe recommendation both highlight the need to reduce obstacles to participation for those groups which are less involved in voluntary activities. The chapters in this book have highlighted a number of areas in which barriers exist for people with less opportunities, in particular those from backgrounds that are financially less well off and/or those who have to financially support a family themselves.

Young people with less opportunities

As we have read above, it is the wealthy and the educated who participate in voluntary activities and as for the reasons already stated volunteering is reasonably easy for this group to participate in. If, as the research suggests, there is a link between volunteering and the learning of civic engagement, then the fact that young people with less opportunities are being further excluded by not participating in these learning opportunities is a cause for concern. And conversely, if voluntary activities are successfully targeted at these young people with less opportunities, it will facilitate their inclusion in civil society. Therefore, there is a clear youth policy direction that needs to be taken towards targeting participation in volunteering. This has to be conducted with sensitivity because, as Stanley has highlighted, the targeting of young people with less opportunities can stigmatise those involved. What she proposed instead was a scheme that was made accessible to all so that people can work together from diverse backgrounds and therefore develop wider social networks. This approach has also proved to be successful in EVS, which is open to all young people, while at the same time making specific efforts for including young people with fewer opportunities. A good example of this, at the project level, is "mixed ability" projects involving disabled and non-disabled young volunteers.

What has not helped the development of voluntary activities for young people with less opportunities is the simplistic evaluation of success for projects. It takes significantly more resources and extra support to involve disadvantaged young people and achieve successful outcomes. However but when policy success focuses on simple statistics, for example, the numbers of young people participating, it fails to push policy towards funding more expensive projects that work with the needs of the most disadvantaged. This problem is not fully reconciled in EVS, where these young people are targeted, as there are no European standards capable of measuring how many young people with less opportunities are reached. One solution is qualitative evaluation – similar to the proposal of Shalayeva who suggests the analysis of long-term biographies of people who participate in volunteering. A second solution proposed by Stanley might be to include indicators of the impact on young people's lives in terms of trust and involvement in political life and the reduction in crime that would give further political weight to the financing of such projects.

One barrier to participation has been the lack of financial resources for young people to participate in voluntary activities. It is often impossible for young people to take unpaid work when they need to support themselves and/or their families. One solution proposed throughout this book is to pay money for volunteering.[1] Paying money can be seen as contrary to the definition of volunteering but it depends on how the payment is defined; for example, "pocket money" is quite different to wages. Pocket money is given in many countries but the level of money and the consequences for taxation depend on the country that the volunteer is working in (Schröer). In some countries in Europe, taking up voluntary activities means that unemployment benefit and/or other forms of social protection such as paying for pensions and health care is stopped (Musiala). Family and/or child benefits are stopped in some European countries when young people volunteer abroad (Schröer). The EVS scheme gives compensation toward the loss of some social protection through a private scheme but not all voluntary activity programmes offer this possibility and, depending on the situation, this may not be enough (Musiala). Weekly income has been utilised with some success in the UK where it can be understood as "facilitating participation" for those who would not normally be able to afford it, rather than rewarding it with money (Stanley). Complications in providing financial help for voluntary activities include its legal status and whether it is then considered to be employment requiring taxation, social security, healthcare and pension schemes. Many countries do not have a standard legal status for volunteering and those countries that do have different arrangements for different countries (EC working paper on voluntary activities). Without a common legal framework across Europe for volunteers, it remains difficult to maintain minimum standards for transnational volunteers in terms of pocket money (Schröer), social protection, taxation and recognition by formal education or employers (Musiala). As Musiala highlighted, a minimum level of "social security, covering illness, accident, civil liability and repatriation", is required.

One solution proposed is that more European countries adopt and implement the Council of Europe convention or the recommendation created by the European Parliament and European Council on mobility 2001 (Chapter 1, Part 5) to achieve a basis for standards, but more effort is required politically to encourage states to ratify this convention.

The working group from the seminar recommended that removing obstacles to young people's participation in voluntary activities could be achieved through building a European volunteering infrastructure. The purpose of this infrastructure would be to remove inconsistent practices, provide minimum quality standards and work towards the elimination of obstacles to participation through addressing legal issues and providing information on all aspects of volunteering in all languages. The European volunteering infrastructure would provide the following services:

- offer tools to countries and organisations that do not meet quality standards;

- support networks of volunteers, voluntary organisations, and sending and hosting organisations;

- fund projects;

1. Paying money cannot be considered the whole solution to inclusion of young people with less opportunities, as EVS serves to highlight that participation for free does not lead by itself to an increased participation of young people with fewer opportunities and that numerous other issues and obstacles have to be tackled to encourage their participation (and that of organisations dealing with them).

- carry out and fund research to gain a greater understanding and a better knowledge of voluntary activities;
- facilitate the development of new forms of volunteering;
- help build partnerships between sending and hosting organisations;
- promote awareness of volunteering, in particular in the private sector;
- provide training on all aspects of volunteering, including mentoring, supervision, recruitment and monitoring.

The European volunteering infrastructure would have a particular focus on young people:
- it should provide tailor-made information to young people;
- it should ensure, in co-operation with national administrations, that laws are adopted on volunteering of young people;
- in co-operation with the national administrations, it should also work towards the removal of obstacles;
- it should fund projects involving young people;
- it should offer support to young people (e.g. on filling in applications, etc.).

Access to information and uptake of opportunities

The information available to young people on voluntary activities is an important part of opening up access to participation. Information is in general more available to groups from better off backgrounds and families with higher social capital. The infrastructure for disseminating information on volunteering is getting better through mechanisms such as the European Commission European Youth Portal, European Commission Eurodesk, Council of Europe Eryica and the partnership between the Council of Europe and European Commission European Knowledge Centre for Youth Policy. With the stereotypical image of the volunteer being older, white and female (Stanley), as Gran described, having the information available or receiving information is sometimes not enough. What is most important is who gives the information. Close by knit groups and communities may not be open to information passed in from outside groups (Gran). Information and encouragement to participate by family members (Machin, Severn and Potter), by peers (Gran) or by personal experience of volunteers helping them (Severn and Potter) is usually the most successful in terms of uptake. Thus it is interpersonal relationships, rather than a mass media approach, which were seen to be the motivator for taking up opportunities to volunteer (Severn and Potter).

What is useful in this section is Gran's distinction between explicit and implicit barriers to participation. Explicit barriers are, for example, financial and legal obstacles (such as visas) that have difficult but nevertheless clearer policy directions on the other hand, implicit barriers include family obligations, gender, religion and education and provide a more complex youth policy issue. As Gran states, leaving home to perform EVS in another country is not a possibility for all young people as many have obligations that prevent them leaving the home or the local community. Some young people across Europe hold religious beliefs. Those with strong beliefs, as Gran pointed out, may have an obligation to carry out religious activities which could be difficult to practice in the host country/family/organisation, such as dietary requirements, fasting, stopping work at particular days/times, and attending religious facilities. Gran also noted that young people may be under family obligations such as providing care for their own children or looking after siblings or elderly family members.

Those who are recruiting volunteers need to work with local minority communities in order to develop joint strategies for the dissemination and promotion of possibilities and work with the communities so that strategies can be developed to enable the participation of those with obligations to the communities. Information officers need to be from or have good relationships with these communities. Young people should be involved actively in recruitment, particularly those who have been involved in voluntary projects themselves.

Learning citizenship from volunteering

The third objective of the European Commission is common objectives is to promote voluntary activities with a view to reinforcing young people's solidarity and engagement as citizens. This section will focus on the extent to which the research reported in this book suggests a link between volunteering, and learning and implementing citizenship skills.

Throughout this publication, voluntary activities have been understood as a form of non-formal learning that provides learning opportunities through doing activities and participating in experiences. They differ from formal learning experiences through their "voluntary" nature and that learning in itself is not the explicit goal. Voluntary activities, as with other forms of non-formal learning, have been less documented, and the learning of citizenship skills has rested on "intuition" (Stanley) rather than hard evidence. This became a critical point in the seminar as participants argued that all voluntary activities *per se* do not teach citizenship or intercultural values. What were seen to be needed were clear and measurable criteria for the learning of citizenship. The general expectations for European youth policy relate to citizenship (preferably European) and building a sense of solidarity or social cohesion. Measuring the learning and then the implementation of the learning as active citizens is less well documented.

Citizenship and social cohesion are broad concepts which encapsulate many different aspects of learning, such as intercultural learning and human rights, which help young people live together in the global and diverse environment in Europe. The UK Government has set the criteria for the success of volunteering as community cohesion, active citizenship and cross – cultural work and is in the process of creating indicators for them (Severn and Potter). Stanley suggested that civil engagement could be seen from patterns of informal social engagements with family and friends, participation in voluntary and community organisations and engagement in the public realm.

One of the more developed projects in this field is Mutz, and Schwimmbeck's research in Germany, Netherlands, Denmark, Poland, Hungary, UK and Spain, which interestingly demonstrated a link between voluntary activities and the learning of social solidarity, social affiliation and social capital (another way to break down some of the aspects of citizenship). The requirements for this type of learning were: active participation, self-determination and responsibility given to the young people. These were affirmed by Moskwiak, who reported the wider findings of Kristensen (1999) about the benefits of "learning to leave". Kristensen (1999) has concluded that self-reliance and taking responsibility with support before, during and after the experience were quality criteria for the success of a mobility project. Machin supplied evidence that young people were not satisfied with their voluntary experience if they were given less opportunities than older volunteers to participate fully in the activities.

Another necessary criterion for learning citizenship was seen to be the "longer and more intense the engagement, the more sustainable the learning process", but experiences that were overwhelming with no pedagogical support and reflection were not effective (Mutz and Schwimmbeck). Despite the evidence that preparation, support during activities and reflection are criteria for learning citizenship skills, Germany and the Czech Republic were the only countries known to support the pedagogical training needed by volunteers on national voluntary schemes (Schröer). The difficulty also remains in transferring the new learning into the daily lives of young people. The requirements for the transfer of these skills into their everyday environment were said by Mutz and Schwimmbeck to need personal and societal recognition of achievements.

Most national voluntary programmes work on national agendas and in national borders, lessening the likelihood of learning European citizenship. International programmes such as the European Voluntary Service are therefore very much needed. The added value in performing voluntary activities abroad, such as in the European Voluntary Service, are claimed by Moskwiak to be the experience of living in another culture at a considerable geographical distance from home. These factors offer the opportunity for intercultural learning through "transformative" learning processes where everyday practices are performed differently, and subsequently challenge currently held cultural beliefs. The distance from home provides the open space to explore the differences and new identities. The emphasis was always placed on the need for reflection and pedagogical support, which is reaffirmed by recent research that reveals that travel, such as gap years before university, can reinforce stereotypes of other cultures rather than challenge them (Stanley).

Good practice

Certification of skills and competencies learned can be seen as the first step to providing evidence of learning citizenship. One example of certification given at this seminar was the Finnish study book where young people can demonstrate acquisition of skills such as communication and problem solving (Savisaari). The book is divided into subsections of different learning areas where young people can demonstrate, voluntary or leisure activities, their experience of "international activities" and "holding positions of trust and responsibility within NGOs" (Savisaari).

Since 2004 the EVS certificate has been an effective non-formal recognition tool. It has achieved this through its common European format, modalities and annexes, which contain a place for detailed description and evaluation of the skills gained through the voluntary work.

Further examples of good practice are the training courses run by the Council of Europe and European Commission partnership on youth training, which support the training of youth workers who will assist young people to achieve European citizenship skills through activities such as volunteering.

A non-European example is the AmeriCorps volunteer programme that has been considered a good model for national volunteer programmes to follow, as there is some evidence, although incomplete, to suggest that the young people who have participated in the year – long programme have developed a long – term ethic of civic responsibility (Stanley).

Policy implications

The need was highlighted for further research to take place to define clearly indicators for the learning of citizenship so that volunteering programmes can orient their programmes more precisely towards these outcomes. The recommendations from the working group at the seminar were that it was necessary at the level of policy to establish guidelines through research on voluntary activities in order to show what types of activities teach citizenship. These guidelines should contain examples such as "young people must participate in the design and administration of voluntary activities in order to reflect young people's viewpoints. This would help to safeguard young people's autonomy, responsibility and motivation in the context of volunteering". Volunteering as a methodology for learning citizenship should be promoted through formal and non-formal methods, such as citizenship education and peer training. And the working group felt that this entire framework should be located within a global perspective in order to consider what Europe can contribute at a global level.

Conclusion

There are, however, clearly still gaps in knowledge and consequently the first recommendation for policy is to develop the research projects to fill these gaps. The European Knowledge Centre for Youth Policy from 2005 onwards will collect data on youth voluntary activities and will serve as a database and resource for research and policy on this topic. What is needed is that European countries at a national level and comparative European research projects are initiated to add to the picture that this book has built in order to ensure that the database is fed with reliable data.

Volunteering certainly offers a powerful and positive opportunity for young people, from all backgrounds, though we remain less certain about its outcome. To maximise its full potential, there is clearly an urgent need for an effective and reflective infrastructure – for preparation, ongoing support, and follow-up. To consolidate the glimpses of that potential, as well as some of the pitfalls (both of which have been highlighted in this book), both quantitative (who and what) and qualitative (why and how) inquiry is required. It is commonplace to advocate for more research, but in this case, there are clearly pieces of the jigsaw that are missing if a full picture of voluntary activities is to be drawn. Equally, however, in the medium term, is the need for a robust policy commitment at all levels to enable voluntary activities to take place – for more young people with more purpose.

Reference

Kristensen, S. (1999) "Mobility as a Learning Process". *European Journal of Vocational Training,* 16, pp. 24-28.

Sales agents for publications of the Council of Europe
Agents de vente des publications du Conseil de l'Europe

BELGIUM/BELGIQUE
La Librairie européenne SA
Rue de l'Orme 1
B-1040 BRUXELLES
Tel.: (32) 2 231 04 35
Fax: (32) 2 735 08 60
E-mail:mail@libeurop.be
http://www.libeurop.be

Jean de Lannoy
202, avenue du Roi
B-1190 BRUXELLES
Tel.: (32) 2 538 4308
Fax: (32) 2 538 0841
E-mail: jean.de.lannoy@euronet.be
http://www.jean-de-lannoy.be

CANADA
Renouf Publishing Co. Ltd
I-5369 Canotek Road
CANADA OTTAWA, Ontario, K1J 9J3
Tel.: (1) 613 745 2665
Fax: (1) 613 745 7660
E-mail: order.dept@renoufbooks.com
http://www.renoufbooks.com

CZECH REPUBLIC/
RÉPUBLIQUE TCHÈQUE
Suweco Cz Dovoz Tisku Praha
Ceskomoravska 21
CZ-18021 PRAHA 9
Tel.: (420) 2 660 35 364
Fax: (420) 2 683 30 42
E-mail: import@suweco.cz

DENMARK/DANEMARK
GAD Direct
Fiolstaede 31-33
DK-1171 COPENHAGEN K
Tel.: (45) 33 13 72 33
Fax: (45) 33 12 54 94
E-mail: info@gaddirect.dk

FINLAND/FINLANDE
Akateeminen Kirjakauppa
Keskuskatu 1, PO Box 218
FIN-00381 HELSINKI
Tel.: (358) 9 121 41
Fax: (358) 9 121 4450
E-mail: akatilaus@stockmann.fi
http://www.akatilaus.akateeminen.com

FRANCE
La Documentation française
(Diffusion/Vente France entière)
124, rue H. Barbusse
F-93308 AUBERVILLIERS Cedex
Tel.: (33) 01 40 15 70 00
Fax: (33) 01 40 15 68 00
E-mail: commande@ladocumentationfrancaise.fr
http://www.ladocumentationfrancaise.fr/espace-client/

Librairie Kléber (Vente Strasbourg)
Palais de l'Europe
F-67075 STRASBOURG Cedex
Fax: (33) 03 88 52 91 21
E-mail: librairie.kleber@coe.int

GERMANY/ALLEMAGNE
AUSTRIA/AUTRICHE
August Bebel Allee 6
Am Hofgarten 10
D-53175 BONN
Tel.: (49) 2 28 94 90 20
Fax: (49) 2 28 94 90 222
E-mail: bestellung@uno-verlag.de
http://www.uno-verlag.de

GREECE/GRÈCE
Librairie Kauffmann
28, rue Stadiou
GR-ATHINAI 10564
Tel.: (30) 1 32 22 160
Fax: (30) 1 32 30 320
E-mail: ord@otenet.gr

HUNGARY/HONGRIE
Euro Info Service
Hungexpo Europa Kozpont ter 1
H-1101 BUDAPEST
Tel.: (361) 264 8270
Fax: (361) 264 8271
E-mail: euroinfo@euroinfo.hu
http://www.euroinfo.hu

ITALY/ITALIE
Libreria Commissionaria Sansoni
Via Duca di Calabria 1/1, CP 552
I-50125 FIRENZE
Tel.: (39) 556 4831
Fax: (39) 556 41257
E-mail: licosa@licosa.com
http://www.licosa.com

NETHERLANDS/PAYS-BAS
De Lindeboom Internationale Publicaties b.v.
M.A. de Ruyterstraat 20 A
NL-7482 BZ Haaksbergen
Tel.: (31) 53 574 0004
Fax: (31) 53 572 9296
E-mail: books@delindeboom.com
http://www.delindeboom.com

NORWAY/NORVÈGE
Akademika, A/S Universitetsbokhandel
PO Box 84, Blindern
N-0314 OSLO
Tel.: (47) 22 85 30 30
Fax: (47) 23 12 24 20

POLAND/POLOGNE
Głowna Księgarnia Naukowa
im. B. Prusa
Krakowskie Przedmiescie 7
PL-00-068 WARSZAWA
Tel.: (48) 29 22 66
Fax: (48) 22 26 64 49
E-mail: inter@internews.com.pl
http://www.internews.com.pl

PORTUGAL
Livraria Portugal
Rua do Carmo, 70
P-1200 LISBOA
Tel.: (351) 13 47 49 82
Fax: (351) 13 47 02 64
E-mail: liv.portugal@mail.telepac.pt

SPAIN/ESPAGNE
Mundi-Prensa Libros SA
Castelló 37
E-28001 MADRID
Tel.: (34) 914 36 37 00
Fax: (34) 915 75 39 98
E-mail: libreria@mundiprensa.es
http://www.mundiprensa.com

SWITZERLAND/SUISSE
Adeco – Van Diermen
Chemin du Lacuez 41
CH-1807 BLONAY
Tel.: (41) 21 943 26 73
Fax: (41) 21 943 36 05
E-mail: info@adeco.org

UNITED KINGDOM/ROYAUME-UNI
TSO (formerly HMSO)
51 Nine Elms Lane
GB-LONDON SW8 5DR
Tel.: (44) 207 873 8372
Fax: (44) 207 873 8200
E-mail: customer.services@theso.co.uk
http://www.the-stationery-office.co.uk
http://www.itsofficial.net

UNITED STATES and CANADA/
ÉTATS-UNIS et CANADA
Manhattan Publishing Company
2036 Albany Post Road
CROTON-ON-HUDSON,
NY 10520, USA
Tel.: (1) 914 271 5194
Fax: (1) 914 271 5856
E-mail: Info@manhattanpublishing.com
http://www.manhattanpublishing.com

Council of Europe Publishing/Editions du Conseil de l'Europe
F-67075 Strasbourg Cedex
Tel.: (33) 03 88 41 25 81 – Fax: (33) 03 88 41 39 10 – E-mail: publishing@coe.int – Website: http://book.coe.int